The Girl and the Ghosts

The True Story of a Haunted Little Girl and the
Foster Carer Who Rescued her from the Past

ANGELA HART

bluebird
books for life

First published 2017 by Bluebird
an imprint of Pan Macmillan
20 New Wharf Road, London N1 9RR
Associated companies throughout the world
www.panmacmillan.com

ISBN 978-1-5098-3904-9

3 5 7 9 8 6 4 2

A CIP catalogue record for this book is available from the British Library.

Typeset by Ellipsis, Glasgow
Printed and bound by CPI Group (UK)

Visit **www.panmacmillan.com** to read more about all our books
and to buy them. You will also find features, author interviews and
news of any author events, and you can sign up for e-newsletters
so that you're always first to hear about our new releases.

1

'Just a few days'

It was early on a Thursday afternoon when my support social worker phoned to ask us to take in a little girl called Maria. What sticks in my mind about that day was the amount of rain we'd had and the fact that flooding had been forecast for the outskirts of our town.

My husband, Jonathan, was loading up the delivery van in the pouring rain while I checked the list of orders for the afternoon's flower deliveries.

'Great weather for ducks,' he said, standing for a moment in the open doorway, dripping onto the doormat, before picking up another armful of flowers and heading back out into the deluge.

As soon as he had closed the door behind him the phone rang.

'Afternoon, Angela. How are you?'

It was the familiar voice of Jess, our support social worker.

'Great, apart from all the rain!' I said cheerfully.

'It's not great news for the festival, is it?' Jess said, as she knew I'd been involved in organising the annual event in the town and was preparing flowers for the parade floats.

'No, not good at all. If the weather's as bad as they say it's going to be, it will definitely have an effect on the number of people who attend. It's such a pity when so many people have put so much effort into organising it.'

I liked Jess. She was only in her mid-twenties but she was one of the best support social workers we'd ever had. She always made an effort to chat and find out what else was going on in my life outside fostering. The empathy and people skills she effortlessly displayed were priceless in her work, particularly when it came to dealing with the unique needs of each of the children she was responsible for.

'What she lacks in terms of years of practical experience she more than makes up for with her understanding personality,' Jonathan had commented one time, and he was spot on.

There was only one customer in our flower shop when Jess phoned, a woman I knew who was choosing some dried-flower arrangements to decorate the cake competition tent at the festival that Saturday.

I try never to be overheard when discussing fostering, which Jess understood, so as it was our part-time assistant Barbara's day off I carried on chatting to Jess about the weather and the festival until Jonathan came back in.

He appeared and realised immediately, from the neutral tone of my voice as I spoke to Jess, that the call was foster carer rather than florist related. So, when I nodded my head in the direction of the door that led into our house, where I could continue the conversation in private, he raised his thumb to indicate that he'd understood.

Closing the door to the shop behind me, I went into the kitchen and sat down. It had been a very busy morning and it was a relief to take the weight off my feet for the first time in the last three hours.

'OK, I can talk properly now,' I told Jess down the phone.

'Great, thanks Angela,' she said kindly.

I knew how busy she was too – I have never met a social worker who has enough hours in the day – and I was impressed by her patience. I can't imagine she had any real interest in the floral displays I described to her, but she knew me well enough to know I'm not the type to babble on about things unnecessarily, and that I was only making polite conversation because there was a customer in the shop.

'So, I have a little girl called Maria. She's only seven and I'd only need you to have her for a short while. Just a few days.'

'Well, we do have room,' I said. 'I'm sure it's fine. I'll just have to check with Jonathan. What else can you tell me?'

'Well,' Jess said, giving a little laugh. 'It's short notice – for a change! I'd need you to take her today.'

'Today?' I said with a question in my voice.

It wasn't unusual to take in a child at very short notice like this, because once a decision has been made that a child is going into foster care then immediate action often needs to be taken, particularly if the courts have intervened and made an order.

The question in my voice had more to do with Maria's circumstances. I wondered why the seven-year-old needed our help, and my immediate thought was, *Poor thing, I hope she's all right.* I knew Jonathan would feel the same way, but we had a rule that we took all fostering decisions together.

Though Jonathan and I had been working for many years as specialist carers for teenagers who needed a bit of extra support above and beyond mainstream foster care, we did take in younger children if the need arose, and if we had space. As it was we had two teenage boys living with us, which left us with one spare bedroom. At this point in time – the first half of the nineties – we were passed to take in up to three children at any one time, so I couldn't see any reason not to help Maria.

'What can you tell me about her?' I asked.

I heard the rustle of paperwork.

'In a nutshell, Maria's school contacted Social Services today because they were concerned about some quite severe bruising they noticed on her arms. It turns out there is bruising on her back too. She's been in foster care before, about eighteen months ago, but was returned to her mother. I've tried the same foster carer but unfortunately she doesn't have enough room at the moment for Maria.'

Jess mentioned the name of Maria's previous foster carer, who was a woman I knew well from the support groups for carers that Jonathan and I attended every couple of months. But before I had a chance to ask how Maria's placement went previously, Jess said, 'I have to be honest, there was a problem last time. Nothing major though.'

'What happened?'

'It was just that Maria wasn't getting on very well with the foster carer's daughter, who's about the same age as she is. It wasn't necessarily Maria's fault. The thing is, Maria can be a bit moody.'

Jess paused. While I said, 'I see . . .', and waited for her to tell me more, I thought about the two children who were already staying with us – Tom and Dillon – and about the possible impact Maria might have on their lives, even for a few days.

'When I say moody,' Jess went on, 'I mean she has a temper and a tendency to throw things when she doesn't get what she wants. But, as I say, it's nothing serious. The only reason I feel it was difficult during the previous placement was because the two girls were the same age and they fell out on a regular basis. And as the children you're already fostering are older, I really don't think that will be an issue.'

'Thanks for being honest,' I said. 'I trust your opinion, and I'm sure it'll be fine, though of course as I say I'll have to check with Jonathan.'

'Thank you, Angela! You're a star! The child protection team picked Maria up directly from her school earlier today and they've got an Emergency Protection Order. They have her sitting in their office at the moment, so I have to find somewhere for her to stay tonight.'

'Right. Give me a few minutes and I'll call you back.'

I could already feel the twinge of slightly nervous excitement I always get during that first phone conversation, when I'm asked if we can take on a new placement. I was already anticipating how Maria would fit in and was looking forward to meeting her and helping her settle.

When I went back into the shop, Jonathan was carefully wrapping up the flowers that had eventually been chosen by the customer who had been there when the phone rang.

'So, is it a girl or a boy, and how old?' Jonathan asked as soon as we were alone in the shop.

My husband knew from the animated look on my face, and the way I was itching to talk to him, that our social worker had been asking us to look after another child. I filled Jonathan in as quickly as I could and he gave a thin, sad smile.

5

'Bruises?' he said. 'And a moody temperament? Poor little girl. Of course we can manage a few days.'

I gave Jonathan a kiss on the cheek. 'I knew you'd say that. It's exactly what I thought.'

We were well aware that the few days could run into weeks or even longer, but we didn't need to discuss this. We'd looked after dozens of children who had arrived like Maria, emotionally or physically damaged, or both. We'd do whatever it took to make her feel loved and cared for while she was in our home.

'Tom and Dillon will be fine with it too, I'm sure,' Jonathan added. 'They've always been really good with the little ones we've had on respite care.'

Tom and Dillon – both aged fourteen – had emotional problems rooted in family break-ups and childhood traumas, so of course we had to consider the impact it would have on them to have a seven-year-old girl under the same roof. They were good lads though, well-natured and kind-hearted despite the bad hands they'd been dealt in life, and I agreed with Jonathan that both boys would be tolerant of a little girl of seven, even one with a tendency to be a bit 'moody' in the way Jess had described to me.

When I phoned Jess back and confirmed we would take Maria, she sounded relieved. 'Thank you so much, Angela,' she said. 'I'm really grateful. If you hadn't agreed, I don't know what I would have done, as there are no other vacancies in the area. I'll be with you as soon as I can.'

2

'I am not eating that'

Jonathan and I had just shut the shop when Jess arrived with Maria, who was a little waif of a girl with a mass of tangled mousy-blonde hair.

'Hello,' I smiled. 'Come on through to the house.'

I introduced myself and Jonathan, but Maria could barely look at us. Instead, she stared at the floor, and then fixed her gaze on a display of flowering plants in the shop.

'They're pretty, aren't they?' I said.

Maria nodded her head shyly. As she did so her hair fell forward over her face but she didn't push it back. This meant all I could see was one pale blue eye, nervously looking up at me.

Once we were in the kitchen Jonathan busied himself with making a pot of tea. He offered a cup to Jess and me and asked Maria what she would like.

She whispered, 'Nothing,' watching Jonathan with her one visible, unblinking eye.

Jonathan was still wearing the apron he'd had on in the shop, which he always wore to protect his clothes when he was loading the van or carrying tubs or boxes of flowers around.

'Sorry about this,' he smiled at Maria, pointing at his apron apologetically. 'You're probably thinking I look a bit silly. It's not a skirt though, I promise! It's just an old apron I wear in the shop.'

As Jonathan continued to do his best to distract Maria and engage with her in some way while he made the tea, I chatted to Jess on the other side of the kitchen, out of earshot of Maria.

I was hoping to get some more details about Maria's circumstances – ideally everything Jess knew that she was able to share – but I knew from experience that when an initial placement meeting comes at the end of a busy day like this, it doesn't always happen.

'I'm afraid we're going to have to rush through the initial placement meeting, as there's another emergency I have to deal with,' Jess said, which didn't surprise me. 'I've got my favourite job today – duty social worker! So I'll fill you in tomorrow with what information we have, if that's OK, Angela?'

It was more of a statement than a question so I nodded and agreed. In any case, I wanted to join Jonathan in his efforts to help Maria to settle in.

Jess hitched her large handbag onto her shoulder and passed me Maria's file to read later. She also completed some standard paperwork so that I had the contact details and emergency numbers for Maria's family and the social workers involved in her case. There was a backpack belonging to Maria, which Jess had placed in the hallway on her way in.

'Maria's grandmother helped me get some of her things together,' Jess explained, nodding towards the small denim bag. 'It should be enough for tonight. Then, hopefully, I'll collect some more tomorrow.'

'That's fine. Don't worry,' I told her. 'I know how busy you are.'

Raising my voice, I looked across at Maria and said cheerfully, 'We'll be OK, won't we, Maria? Do you think you'll be happy to stay here with us for a few days?'

Maria tilted her head to one side, which made her hair shift off her face so that I could see both her eyes looking at me quizzically. She studied me for a moment, as if she was very seriously considering the question. Then she nodded, took a couple of steps towards me and put one of her very small hands into mine.

Jess apologised for having to leave so quickly. She was good at interacting with children of all ages and had a way of putting them at ease, but when Jonathan saw her out Maria barely gave her a second glance when she said goodbye.

'Well, come on then, Maria,' I said after taking a slurp of my tea. 'I'll show you around the house, shall I?'

She nodded and very nearly smiled, and then Jonathan reappeared from the hallway.

'Are you sure you wouldn't like a drink first?' he asked kindly. 'We'll be having our evening meal soon. But maybe you'd like some orange juice or milk, or a glass of water?'

'I want Coke,' Maria said, suddenly fixing him with a steady, determined stare. 'And crisps.'

I gently explained to Maria that we didn't keep Coke in the house.

'We only have fizzy drinks on special occasions, like when we are on holiday or when we go out to eat,' I said.

She furrowed her brow and curled her lip, so I tried to lighten the atmosphere.

'If we did have bottles of Coke in the house, they wouldn't last five minutes!' I laughed.

I then explained to her that we had two teenage boys in the house, Tom and Dillon, who loved fizzy drink a little bit too much.

'Crisps,' she blurted. 'I want crisps.'

I told Maria that she could have a packet of crisps after dinner if she was still hungry.

'I want crisps now.'

'I'm sorry sweetheart, but you'll ruin your dinner. If you're really hungry you can have a piece of fruit to keep you going. Would you like that?'

'No, I want crisps!'

Maria now had an angry look in her eyes.

Jonathan leaned in to her just a little, being careful not to invade her personal space.

'Shall I let you into a secret?' he said. 'Angela loves crisps, maybe even more than you do. She would love to eat crisps before her dinner but she can't. It's not good for her diet, you see, and she's always on a diet!'

Maria eyed me up and down.

'It's true!' I laughed.

'Well *I'm* not on a diet,' she said.

'I know that, Maria,' replied Jonathan. 'I'm not either, but we all have to stay healthy, don't we? Eating crisps before dinner is not good for anybody.'

For a moment I thought Jonathan's little ploy had worked and I tried to chivvy Maria along to the kitchen door so we could go on a tour of the house.

'Come on then,' I said breezily. 'Let's go on up . . .'

'I *want* Coke.' Maria's eyes narrowed and the expression on her face was sullen as she repeated the words, very slowly this time.

'Well, sulks don't work with me,' I told her cheerfully but forcefully, heading to the hallway. 'So if you *don't* want juice, milk, water or any fruit, I'll show you where your bedroom is. Come on!'

If I'd had to guess what Maria's response would be, I think I'd probably have said she'd dig her heels in and refuse to be cajoled out of her sulk. However, to my surprise she followed me up the stairs, bringing her little bag with her.

Before opening her bedroom door, I showed Maria the storage box on the landing where I keep towels, spare clothing, extra bedding and so on, for boys and girls of different ages. As I handed Maria a clean, fluffy white towel to place in her room, she bent her head over it, inhaled deeply and said, 'It smells nice, like flowers.'

'I love the smell of freshly washed towels too,' I smiled. 'Now, which bedding would you like?'

I'd accumulated a very large collection of bedding over the years and Maria feasted her eyes on the array of sheets, duvet covers and pillowcases.

'These ones,' Maria answered, pointing to a pile of bright pink sheets and duvet covers with silver stars on that were, unsurprisingly, nearly always the first choice of little girls her age.

'Good choice,' I said. 'We can make the bed up later, after we've had something to eat. Now, this will be your room while you're with us.' I opened the door of one of the three bedrooms on the top floor of the house. 'If you want to leave your bag on the bed for now, you can put your things away later.'

I showed her where she could hang her clothes and how to switch on the bedside light.

'Will you help me put my things away?' she asked, suddenly sounding anxious and even younger than her years.

'Of course I'll help you,' I answered. 'We can do it together.' I walked across the room and opened the top drawer of the chest under the window. 'There's plenty of storage for your things, and I keep a few toys in here, which you can play with if you want.'

Maria was rooted to the spot, apparently admiring the bedroom, and for a moment she just looked at me quizzically. Then she suddenly began to balance on one leg while watching me expectantly, as if she was waiting for me to react in some way. When I smiled and nodded my head, she proceeded to cross the bedroom floor in a series of peculiar hopping movements, like someone crossing a river by jumping from one stepping-stone to another.

After placing her backpack carefully on the bed, she turned and hopped back to the door, then set off down the stairs ahead of me. I watched as she pressed herself against the wall and paused on each step to balance precariously on one foot before placing the other one on the exposed wood that bordered the carpet on either side of the step below. She descended the whole staircase in that fashion, avoiding placing any part of either of her feet on the carpet running down the centre of each stair.

If it hadn't been for the look of anxious concentration on her face I might have thought she was playing in some way, but something told me this was not just a quirky, childish little game. For this reason I didn't ask Maria what she was doing. Children who have had traumatic experiences often don't know why they do certain things, and asking them questions they aren't ready or able to answer can uncover buried memories that might be very upsetting or frightening for them. So, I just waited for Maria to reach the bottom of the stairs, then followed her into the kitchen, where we often ate our meals at the long, scrubbed pine table.

Tom and Dillon had been in their bedrooms when Maria arrived, and when I called them down for dinner a little bit later on they were as friendly and pleasant to her as Jonathan and I had thought they would be.

'Which school do you go to?' Tom asked politely.

Maria shrugged.

'Do you do any sport?' Dillon asked, giving Maria a little smile as he raised his eyebrows and looked genuinely interested in what she had to say.

My heart swelled with pride. We had been fostering both boys for a few years by now, and we had talked several times about their early days with us. Both had described feeling awkward, self-conscious and nervous when they first arrived. Tom had said he felt like he had landed 'on another planet' and Dillon had used the expression 'fish out of water' to try to explain how strange it was to suddenly find himself living in a house he had never been in before, with people he didn't know.

Other children we've fostered have told us that, looking back, they felt mistrustful of Jonathan and me. They couldn't understand why we would put ourselves to so much trouble for them. 'My family didn't care; why would you?' is how one girl, now in her twenties, put it.

13

Tom and Dillon had reassured me that they would always do their best to make other children welcome. They were being true to their word and I loved them for it, but Maria was having none of it. She didn't say a word, and instead just watched them silently, with her head tilted to one side and her hair once again covering one eye. Of course, I didn't put her under any more pressure; I understood she was already under quite enough for one day.

Jonathan has always been good at joking around with the children we foster, and he did eventually manage to make Maria laugh. He did this by singing a silly song he made up about a girl called Maria. The boys were used to Jonathan bursting into song like this. They started laughing and put their hands over their ears, and thankfully Maria copied and giggled. However, as soon as I put the first dish of food on the table Maria's laughter stopped abruptly. For a moment, she just looked at the meal I had prepared earlier with an expression of almost comically exaggerated disgust, and then announced, 'I am *not* eating *that*.'

'Do you know what it is?' Jonathan asked her in a casual but interested tone of voice.

Maria wrinkled her nose as if she could smell something very bad, then shook her head.

'That,' he announced dramatically, 'is a quite spectacular fish pie, home-made by Angela! And I don't mind telling you, she makes the best fish pie for miles around. Isn't that right, boys?'

Tom and Dillon readily agreed and held up their plates for me to serve them each a large, steaming portion of pie.

Maria put her hands on her plate so I couldn't serve her food.

'Do you know what?' I said. 'I think you might find you like it if you try it.'

I had been standing up to serve the pie and now I pulled out a chair and sat down at the table next to Tom, with my back to the kitchen sink. 'So what is your favourite meal, Maria? Perhaps we can make it one evening while you're . . .'

'I *want* sweets,' Maria shouted, jumping up from the table and stamping her foot.

'Here you are, Jonathan,' I said, ignoring Maria's outburst and handing my husband the garden peas.

Having lived for the first few years of his life in a house that echoed to the sound of angry, aggressive voices, Tom hated any kind of confrontation. As soon as Maria shouted I saw his shoulders hunch and he bent his head low over his plate, while Dillon shot me a glance of wry amusement before taking his cue from me and ignoring her too.

Having reached to take the bowl of peas out of my hands, Jonathan only just managed to tuck in his elbow a split-second before Maria kicked the back of the empty chair beside him, narrowly missing Jonathan's arm, and sending it crashing into the table. For a moment, her expression of sulky defiance turned into what appeared to be frozen fear. Then she took a step backwards, just out of arm's reach, and screeched, 'I want sweets! I want sweets!'

'Thanks, love,' Jonathan said, smiling at me across the table. 'Have you had the peas, Tom?'

I didn't look directly at Maria, but I could see her out of the corner of my eye, watching us, apprehensively at first and then with mounting anger and frustration as we continued to pass bowls of food around the table as if nothing had happened.

15

'I said I am not eating that,' she shouted eventually from the corner of the kitchen, where she stood with her arms folded across her chest and her chin jutted upwards. Still not one of us reacted, and so Maria stomped out of the kitchen and across the hallway, where we could hear her stamping her feet and ranting about how much she hated us and the 'shit food' we were trying to make her eat.

3

'I dont want it to be dark'

Jonathan and I didn't know as much then as we do now about the psychology of 'acting out' and there's still a great deal more for us to learn. But we did know that there's always a reason why a child has a temper tantrum, and we were also very well aware that any natural instinct to scoop the disgruntled child into your arms or cave in to their demands in an attempt to make them feel better is not helpful in situations like this. It's tough, because there have been countless times in my career as a foster carer when that is exactly what I've wanted to do, but I just can't, as it ultimately isn't fair on the child to reward bad behaviour.

Similarly, with children like Maria acting out in this way, 'time out' is not the solution to whatever problem they're venting, even though it's one of the suggestions some social workers still make. In my experience, it just makes the child more angry and frustrated and, because they are removed from the situation, they are less likely to learn from it. So, my response to Maria's behaviour was to allow her to get angry while I continued to talk in a calm, reassuring voice as I ate my meal - effectively setting a good example.

Dillon was sitting on the chair nearest the open door that led into the hallway, and he gave a gasp of surprise, then grinned when, a few moments after Maria complained about the 'shit food', a rolled-up scarf came sailing past his head and landed on the floor by the cooker.

I was just about to nod at Jonathan to indicate 'I'll go', in case Maria threw something that could break or hurt someone, when she suddenly reappeared in the kitchen doorway and said, in a quieter, although still grumpy voice, 'I'm hungry.'

'Well, it's a good thing we didn't eat your dinner then!' Jonathan grinned. He pulled out the chair beside his as he spoke, then smiled at me over the top of Maria's head when she accepted the plateful of food I dished up and then tucked in to her meal as though nothing had happened. If need be I would have provided a healthy alternative once we'd finished eating, perhaps a sandwich or something similar that didn't require cooking, but thankfully it didn't come to that.

After we'd eaten, Tom and Dillon went upstairs to do their homework and I cleared up in the kitchen, while Jonathan and Maria played a game of snap at the kitchen table, which she seemed to enjoy despite an initial reluctance to play. After that we watched a bit of TV and then Maria asked me if I had any books she could read before lights out.

'Of course,' I said, delighted at the request. It's often a struggle getting kids to read as much as they should, particularly if they come from dysfunctional homes where reading a book is not encouraged or even considered normal, as has been the case with a lot of children we've fostered.

'What do you like reading?'

'I like all kinds of books,' she said. 'I like stories about witches and wizards and magic things like that.'

'Then I've got just the books for you. Come on, I'll show you where I keep them and you can choose.'

We have books all over the house, so many that our bookshelves are overflowing. Fortunately, the collection of stories I had in mind was stored in a cupboard in Maria's bedroom, so I told her to say goodnight to Jonathan and led her up the stairs.

She sprang ahead of me, and I watched as she then climbed the stairs in the same peculiar way she'd done before, avoiding any contact with the carpet.

'I don't mind if you walk on the carpet. We all do, you know, sweetheart!' I said gently. I was worried she might trip and fall if she carried on like that, but she didn't respond.

Once in the bedroom I pulled out the box of books and Maria chose three from the series, which was about a witch and her cat. She turned each one over and read the back covers, devouring the words greedily as she made her selection.

'Can I read them all?'

'Well, let's see what time it is when you get into bed, ready to read, shall we?'

With that Maria began unpacking her bag as quickly as she could and, with my help, she was nearly ready for bed, with her belongings stored neatly away, in a matter of minutes. She even helped me make the bed, very willingly, even though it was a struggle for her to tuck in the sheets and put on the pillowcase with her little hands.

I was pleased to see that Maria had a pink nightdress and dressing gown, pink furry slippers, spare school clothing and a couple of soft toys. The clothes were not in good condition, but they were adequate, and better than many I'd seen other children arrive with. There were no toiletries but that is not unusual, and I always have a stock of new toothbrushes and flannels to give to children who come without.

As Maria got changed into her nightdress I slipped out and got her a new toothbrush from the bathroom cabinet, which I placed on her dressing table.

'Great! Just your teeth to do!' I said. 'There's a new toothbrush there for you.'

'What colour is it?' Maria asked as she looked towards the dressing table. She then started crossing the carpet to get it, using the same strange hopping motion she had on the stairs. It was as if she was trying to keep her feet off the carpet as much as she possibly could, which was intriguing. I didn't say anything, as she wasn't endangering herself and I didn't want to push her to talk about something that might potentially trigger an upsetting reaction.

'It's red,' I said. 'Is that OK?' Maria nodded, then hopped back to the bed as I added, 'We always keep our toiletries in our rooms, so they don't get mixed up in the bathroom.'

'That's good,' she said, and I showed her where everything was in the bathroom and left her to clean her teeth, which she seemed to do very well. I could hear her scrubbing them for a good two minutes as I busied myself with tidying some laundry on the landing.

Maria hopped from the bathroom to her bed and yawned as she pulled the duvet up to her chin.

'I'm not tired,' she said as she picked up one of the books from the bedside table. 'So can I have all three?'

'Let's see how we get on,' I said. 'You've done very well getting ready for bed so nicely. Let's start with this one, shall we?'

Maria eyed me suspiciously.

'Are *you* reading?'

'Well, I thought I might. Did you want to read?'

'I always read on my own.'

'Right then,' I said, thinking that was impressive for a seven-year-old. 'I'll come back in a few minutes and see how you are getting on.'

Less than five minutes later I returned to find Maria looking very sleepy, having finished the first book.

'I'm tired,' she said. 'I will save the others.'

'I think that's a good idea,' I said from the doorway. 'It's time to get some sleep now. Would you like me to tuck you in?'

'No, I'm fine thank you. But please don't turn out the big light,' she said quickly. 'I don't want it to be dark.'

In her haste to read, Maria hadn't bothered to switch on her bedside light and the main light was still on. Clearly, I couldn't leave that on all night.

'There's a night light,' I explained, walking over to the lamp on the chest of drawers and pressing the switch so it glowed. 'I'll leave this one on all night and just turn off the really bright one overhead.' I flicked the switch by the door. 'Is that all right?'

'Yes,' she said. 'It's pretty. I like it.'

The lamp was in the shape of a fairy mushroom and glowed with a soft red light. All the kids who used it loved it, even much older ones.

Maria turned on her side. 'But I want my mummy.'

'I'm sure you do, sweetheart,' I answered. 'Would you like a hug goodnight?'

'No, I'm OK,' she said, and I could tell from the sound of her voice that she was already almost asleep.

Later that evening, after Tom and Dillon had gone to bed too, I read through the notes in the file Jess had given me when she dropped Maria off at the house. As I always do when reading a child's notes for the first time, I felt a nervous knot form in my stomach, as you never know what you're about to read, and sometimes the detail is extremely disturbing and upsetting.

I settled in my favourite armchair and opened the file. It's never a simple case of reading a child's neatly explained history, laid out chronologically. We receive a synopsis, with comments made by social workers on relevant pieces of information they may have gathered from schools, doctors, the police and so on, but we don't get to see any of the original supporting documents from other sources or agencies outside Social Services.

It can sometimes be confusing to pick through the notes, but over the years I've got better at it and I know what to look for, which is anything that might help me understand the child and therefore be better placed to engage with them in a positive way.

Jess had made a hasty attempt to put Maria's file in some order, and it told me quite a lot. The first time Maria had come to the notice of Social Services had been about eighteen months earlier, as Jess had already told me that afternoon. Maria had been living at that time with her mother, Christine, stepfather, Gerry, and two older stepbrothers, Frank and Casey. This still appeared to be the case, from what I could gather.

Maria had been placed in foster care for about three weeks on that first occasion, apparently 'to give her mother a break'. It didn't state what Christine needed a break from. However, there were concerns raised by Social Services about the fact that Maria had suffered a broken arm in circumstances that were 'not entirely clear.' I sighed when I read that. Jonathan looked across and gave me an encouraging look.

'Not good?'

'No, but it rarely is. I'll fill you in when I get to the end.'

I read that when Christine was questioned about how Maria had broken the bone so badly – it was a very nasty break – she had stated it was the result of an 'accident' that happened when she was playing with her older stepbrothers. Maria had told the doctors and nurses who treated her at hospital that she 'couldn't remember' how it happened, which is what first rang alarm bells with Social Services back then. A quick look at the dates told me that this was when Maria was five years old.

The notes went on to state that throughout the weeks she was in foster care Maria had asked repeatedly to go home. I knew this was no indication Maria was happy at home with her mother and stepfather, because even children who have suffered terrible abuse, and even the most awful sexual abuse, usually want to be with their parents. This horrified me when I heard it for the first time, when I was a brand-new foster carer back in the late eighties, as it didn't seem to make any sense at all. Surely you would want to be a million miles away from your abuser, not begging to go back under their roof? Now I understand why children react like this. Their parents, however abusive, have provided them with the only life they've ever known. The abuse becomes their normality and, in spite of everything, offers a familiarity the children try to reclaim.

As Jess had told me on the phone earlier that day, it was

Maria's school that had alerted Social Services this time, when a teacher noticed bruising on her arms that didn't look as though it was the result of any kind of game. Then it was discovered she had bad bruising on her back too. This also looked too severe to be the result of an accidental bump.

I passed all the information I'd read to Jonathan. Neither of us stated the obvious, which was that it sounded as though she might be being harmed deliberately at home, by a member of the family. There was no point in saying that out loud, because we didn't know this for sure and it is wrong and potentially dangerous to speculate. As foster carers it is not our job to make judgements, and it is not helpful for us to form opinions that are not based on hard evidence or proven in a court of law. In the majority of cases we have contact with the child's parents, if they are on the scene and the child is with us for more than a short respite stay, and so having negative ideas about them or judging them simply isn't helpful to us or, most importantly, to the child whose care is paramount.

After I'd talked to Jonathan about what I'd read in Maria's notes, I mentioned the peculiar way she'd hopped across the bedroom floor and gone up and down the stairs.

'That does sound odd,' he said. 'But there's probably some explanation for it that makes perfect sense to Maria.'

He recalled a time when he was a little boy and stepped on a spider on the stairs, which scooted under the carpet. Then he wouldn't step on the same stair in case he trod on it and squashed it the next time.

'I did that for ages afterwards, even when I knew the spider couldn't possibly still be there. Maybe Maria's doing something similar?'

'Maybe,' I said, smiling at the thought of how typical it was of Jonathan not to want to risk hurting a spider, and to see an innocent explanation. 'Although the way Maria was going down the stairs seemed a bit more awkward – and risky – than if she was simply trying to avoid treading on a spider or something like that. What worries me is that she might fall and hurt herself. I don't like to question her about it, but if she keeps on doing it, I'm going to have to try to tackle it.'

'I think you're right,' Jonathan said. 'I wonder what the reason is?'

'I don't know, but there *will* be a reason of some kind. This isn't something a child does completely randomly and out of the blue, really, is it? You didn't see it, Jonathan, but I think it's repeated behaviour, and something must have triggered it.'

Jonathan sighed, and I knew what he was thinking before he said it.

'I sometimes dread finding out why children do things like this, don't you?'

I nodded. Some of the many children we'd fostered by this time had suffered horrific experiences in their past, which made them act out in all sorts of unusual and perplexing ways.

'Yes, I dread it too, but at least we might be able to help, if Maria feels able to talk to us.'

As usual, all we could do was be vigilant and create a safe and loving environment for Maria, as we did with all of our foster children. Then it was a case of waiting to see what happened next, and being ready to help in any way we could. Patience is something Jonathan and I both have, and I always say it's just as well, because sometimes we don't find out the truth about a child's past until years or even decades later.

4

'I don't like being hurt'

'Are you awake?' I whispered into the darkness.

'It's difficult not to be,' Jonathan answered.

'I don't want to go up again,' I said. 'I'm sure she'll settle; I'll give it another minute.'

Maria had been having nightmares and I'd already gone upstairs twice to check on her. Each time I'd crept up the short staircase leading from our bedroom on the first floor of our town house to Maria's bedroom on the top floor, she'd already calmed down. On both occasions I whispered her name softly and edged the bedroom door open ever so quietly, being sure to tell her it was me, Angela, and that I was just checking she was all right. Thankfully, both times I could see through the glow of the night light that Maria was already silent and sleeping again.

Now, suddenly, she was shouting out and thrashing around again. Jonathan and I couldn't make out what she was saying from our bedroom below. It sounded like a series of moans and eerie little screams, and I was very upset to think what might be going on in her head.

'Poor thing,' Jonathan said. 'But I agree. Don't go up again just yet. Let's hope she settles soon.'

We've fostered a lot of children over the years who have had good reasons to have nightmares. For some of them, waking up to find *any* adult standing in their bedroom would be a potentially traumatic experience, so I didn't want to go into her room unnecessarily. Moments later, silence fell again.

'Thank goodness,' Jonathan said. 'Let's hope we can all get some sleep now.'

Jonathan had had a very long and tiring day, going out at the crack of dawn to the wholesaler, restocking the shop and making deliveries all around the town. He fell back to sleep fairly quickly, but it took me a little longer. Every time I felt myself nodding off I'd snap open my eyes again at the faintest sound, fearing Maria might be awake again, disturbed by another nightmare.

As I lay in the darkness I found myself wondering what it was like for Maria at home, and what had really happened to her. I desperately hoped she hadn't been subjected to the physical abuse that it appeared she had.

Although Maria didn't shout out in her sleep again that night, she must have continued to toss and turn, because by morning her hair was so tangled it was almost impossible to get a brush through it.

'It's like this every day,' she told me as she sat, with remarkable patience, while I tried to restore some sort of order to the chaotic bird's nest it had become. 'I've asked Mum if I can get it cut, but she won't let me. So I try to brush it myself. But it hurts. And it still looks the same when I've done it.'

Having it cut did seem to be a sensible option, certainly if Maria continued to be so restless at night. It was something I thought Social Services might be able to ask her mother about, if Maria ended up staying a while, as she would need to give her permission. In the meantime, though, the leave-in conditioner I always kept in the bathroom cabinet came in very handy on that first day.

'That's good!' Maria smiled, looking at the bottle. 'But how did you know I would need it?'

'I didn't,' I replied. 'I always keep a bottle here in case anybody who stays needs it.'

Maria narrowed her eyes.

'So you are not . . . psychic?'

'Psychic! Heavens, no!' I laughed. 'I'm impressed you know that word, though, Maria. It's not one you hear every day, is it?'

She looked at me sideways and that was the end of that conversation.

Maria was very well behaved as she got ready for school and did everything I asked her to, including eating her breakfast of Weetabix and orange juice without complaint.

However, when it was time to leave the house she began to cry and say, 'I want my mum. When can I go home? Can I go home now?'

'I'm sure you're missing your mum, Maria,' I said, gently. 'But you still need to go to school. I'd have thought a clever girl like you wouldn't want to miss school. And you'll be able to see all your friends while you're there. So I'm sure you'll enjoy it.'

'I'm not a clever girl,' she said, eyeing me suspiciously as she used the back of her hand to wipe away the tears that had trickled down her nose.

'Aren't you?' I asked in a tone of exaggerated astonishment. 'Well, I *am* surprised to hear that, especially having seen how good you are at reading. Anyway, shall we get going now? We don't want to be late.'

I opened the front door as I spoke and, to my relief and surprise, Maria shuffled down the hallway towards me. However, she continued to repeat, 'I'm not a clever girl,' as she put her hand in mine, then stepped out onto the pavement beside me.

The route to Maria's school was a pleasant one, away from the main roads and most of it through a park. As we joined the other children and mothers with pushchairs who were hurrying along the path, Maria suddenly let go of my hand and darted off across the grass towards a little girl she had spotted walking up ahead. It didn't take me long to catch up with her, and for the next ten minutes she walked beside me again, chatting cheerfully to her friend as she did so.

I thought it must be distressing for Maria, having to walk to school with a stranger rather than with her mother, who she was obviously missing, but the animated conversation she was having with her friend seemed to distract her. When I pointed out a squirrel that was making a dash from the safety of one tree to another, and wondered aloud whether it might still be there when I walked back this way again to meet Maria in the school playground at three o'clock, they both looked at me and smiled.

'I hope so,' Maria said. 'I like animals like that.'

'Like what?'

'I mean little ones, that don't come and hurt you. I don't like being hurt.'

'Of course not. Nobody likes being hurt.'

When we arrived at the school we were in good time. I said goodbye to Maria and reassured her I would be in the playground at pick-up time. She smiled as she said goodbye, which was heartening to see. I then went to the reception to give the school secretary my details and let her know I was fostering Maria.

I had a busy day in the shop, but each time I had a break and time to catch my breath I thought about Maria's little face as I waved her off at school. It was great to have left her with a smile, and I thought how brave she was, as it can't have been easy for her to leave her mother and suddenly find herself staying with Jonathan and me. I know that when I was a little girl I absolutely hated it whenever I spent time away from my parents, even when the only place I ever stayed without them was with close family, who I'd known all my life.

I walked to the school in the afternoon, looking forward to seeing Maria and asking her all about her day, but as soon as she appeared I could tell she was in a completely different mood to the one I'd left her in.

'I'm hungry,' she snapped. 'Can I have crisps?'

'No, not before you've eaten your dinner. Like I explained yesterday . . .'

'Not *this* again!' she spat. 'I want crisps! I want crisps.'

'Maria, let's just get home and you can choose something healthy to eat.'

'Home! Your house, you mean? That's not home!'

By now some of the other mothers who were collecting children were giving me sideways glances. A lot of people in the town knew I was a foster carer as I'd done it for so long, and over the years I'd brought a succession of children to this school. Many didn't have a clue, though, and were looking on with everything from astonishment to suspicion in their eyes as Maria's temper tantrum got worse and worse.

'I'm hungry! I want to go home, to *my* house, to *my* mum!'

'I do understand what you are saying, Maria, and there is no need to shout. Now let's just start walking nicely . . .'

'No! I'm not going anywhere until I get crisps!'

'Right,' I sighed, parking myself on a bench. 'I think we might be here for a while then. I might as well take the weight off my feet.'

Maria looked at me quizzically as I calmly took a leaflet out of my handbag and started reading it. It gave details of all the stalls and raffle prizes on offer at the local festival that weekend.

'Oooh, that sounds good,' I said out loud.

'What does?' Maria demanded.

'First prize, four VIP tickets to the theme park.'

'What theme park?'

'Oh, that one that's just had lots of new rides added. What's the new theme they have? Something to do with wizards, I think . . .'

Maria was now standing in front of me with wide eyes, her temper tantrum suddenly forgotten.

'Can I try to win the prize? Can I, Angela?'

'I don't see why you can't have a few raffle tickets,' I said. 'I always buy raffle tickets for children who are well behaved.'

She thought about this for a moment and held out her hand.

I took it and stood up, and Maria walked home beautifully, chatting about her day and telling me how she had learned about Viking ships and had been chosen by the teacher to take the register to the reception, as she had done the best drawing in the class of a Viking warrior.

'That's wonderful,' I said. 'Well done.'

'Thanks!' she said, giving a little giggle.

My heart swelled. When she was in this frame of mind Maria was absolutely adorable and her sweet giggle was quite infectious. I hoped I could keep her in this mood for as much of her stay with us as possible.

When we got home Maria took off her shoes and said she was going upstairs to change out of her school uniform.

'That's a good idea!' I said brightly, but then my heart sank a little as I saw Maria edging her way awkwardly up the stairs, stepping only on the wooden edges of the staircase.

'What are you doing, sweetheart? I asked.

'I'm going up to my room, like I said,' she replied. 'Isn't that all right? Have I done something wrong?'

'No, not at all,' I answered hastily. 'I just wondered why you were walking on the wood again rather than on the carpet.'

Maria seemed bemused by what I'd said and replied, 'Because I'm not allowed to walk on the carpet.'

'You're not allowed to walk on the carpet?'

'No. Mum says I can't.'

'Your mum says you can't walk on the carpet?'

'Yes.'

'Oh, I see. Nobody can walk on the carpet at your home . . . ?' I tried to make it sound like a cross between a question and a statement.

'No, silly! I'm not allowed to, but everyone else can.'

The fact that it was something Maria obviously accepted without question made me feel very sad for her.

'Well, you can walk on the carpets here,' I told her. 'In fact, it would be better if you did. I think it's a safer way to go up and down the stairs.'

'Oh, OK.' Maria looked at me suspiciously for a moment, as though she thought it might be a trick. Then she shrugged and proceeded to climb the stairs in exactly the same way she'd been doing before I spoke to her.

Most children simply accept whatever happens in their family as being 'normal'. So, for Maria, 'normality' included being the only person who, apparently, wasn't allowed to walk on the stair carpet, and it was clearly a difficult habit for her to break as she continued to avoid the carpet for the duration of her stay.

While she was with us, Social Services was gathering information for an assessment, so that a decision could be made about whether or not Maria would be able to live at home again. I'd agreed that Maria could stay as long as this took. Maria was to have no direct contact with her mum, but she was allowed to talk to her on the phone, and she was also allowed to see her maternal grandmother, Babs, who lived close by.

'I love Nanny,' Maria told me cheerfully one day, on the walk to school. 'Sometimes I wish she was my mummy.'

'Do you?'

'Yes. She's kind and lets me do what I want.'

'She lets you do what you want?'

Maria scrunched up her face, as if deep in thought.

'Yes, like when I talk to her I can say what I want!'

'I see . . . you had a long chat with your mum on the phone though, Maria?'

'Suppose,' she said, then added with a critical tone in her voice, 'Veeerrry long.'

I had been in the kitchen while Maria chatted to her mum the previous evening. The call was arranged and agreed by Social Services and so I trusted that the social workers involved believed there was no problem with Maria talking to Christine, although they did ask me to always be present to supervise the calls. Obviously I could only hear half of the conversation, but it sounded to me as though it went well. Maria had a lot to say, and the call lasted at least fifteen minutes. In hindsight, however, I could see that Maria had given her mum long and detailed answers to all her questions, and afterwards she had told me she felt 'tired out'.

'Well, Maria, if you find it tiring talking to your mum for so long on the phone, perhaps you could let her know that? I'm sure she wouldn't want you to be on the phone so long that you feel tired?'

'Mmm,' she murmured, not looking convinced. 'I think she knows.'

'She knows?'

'Yes. She knows everything. They both do.'

'They both do?'

Maria shrugged and then repeated, 'I love Nanny,' before giving me a smile.

5

'So, what's Maria told you?'

During her first week with us Maria was invited to her nanny's for tea after school one night. As Babs lived close to our house, I volunteered to take Maria round there and collect her, which Babs agreed to. I'd been given her phone number by Maria's social worker and so was able to make this arrangement myself, and I was happy to find that Babs sounded very cheerful and accommodating and said she was looking forward to meeting me and seeing her granddaughter.

Maria was really looking forward to the visit, and when we walked there after school she seemed more animated than normal and started babbling away ten to the dozen, telling me all sorts of things about her family.

Maria talked about the fact she had two stepbrothers called Frank and Casey, who lived in the house with her mum and stepfather, Gerry, and she also had a half-brother, Colin, who lived with her nanny. Colin was a teenager and she told me, 'Mummy had Colin when she was young so he's always lived with Nanny and Granddad.'

Granddad Stanley was not Maria's 'real' grandfather – Babs had remarried – and he was 'on the sick', Maria informed me.

'I can't remember what's wrong with him, but he can go in a big deep sleep if he doesn't eat the right things,' she said.

I figured he was probably diabetic, and then Maria added, 'That's why I can't stay with Nanny. She has her hands full with Granddad! He is so poorly he can't even have a job!'

'Oh dear, I'm sorry to hear he's poorly.'

'Don't worry,' Maria added, 'he likes to watch telly in the daytime anyway. And he has to give himself injections, so he has to be at home in his chair all the time.'

Maria then went on to tell me in a very matter-of-fact way that she didn't know her real dad.

'He says I'm not his but Mum says that's a lie,' she divulged as she skipped along, holding my hand. She said it as flip-pantly as if she were talking about what she had done at break time at school, and I felt a pang in my chest. Not only was this sad to listen to, but it seemed this inappropriate and upsetting detail had been reported to Maria by her mother.

Poor love, I thought. *What a complicated family, and what a shame about Maria's father.*

Of course, I knew better than to take all of this information as read. I've found on many occasions over the years that children can embellish facts, bend the truth or choose to forget certain details when they take part in conversations like this. Given Maria's age I didn't think she would have set out to invent such a story – especially such an unfortunate one – but I did wonder whether the version of events she'd been brought up believing was accurate, and why her family would tell her such things.

Babs threw open her front door with a flourish when Maria knocked on the large brass door knocker.

'Babe! How are you!' she cried joyfully. 'Come and give Nanny a big cuddle!'

She scooped Maria into her arms and kissed the top of her head before she even looked at me. It was lovely to see.

'Sorry, love, you must be Angela. Where are my manners? Nice to meet you. Now come on in, the pair of you.'

Before I had time to politely suggest that there was no need to invite me in, I was being ushered into the lounge.

'Park yourself there, love. I'll put the kettle on. Stanley, we've got company. *Stanley!*'

Stanley was engrossed in a TV programme and was sitting engulfed in a cloud of smoke. An ashtray containing about ten cigarette butts was on the coffee table beside his large armchair, alongside a grubby plastic tub containing several different packets of prescription drugs.

Stanley reluctantly curled up the edges of his mouth to give me the most insincere and unwelcoming smile I had even been unfortunate enough to be on the receiving end of.

'Nice ta meet ya,' he said in a strong cockney accent, before immediately turning his attention back to the TV.

Babs had already put the kettle on, so I agreed to stay for a cup of tea. When I say 'agreed' I guess what I really mean is that I didn't have any choice but to accept. Babs was a characterful, curvaceous lady who wore her vibrant red hair in a fancy bun and had her lips painted with sugar-pink lipstick. She had a friendly, open face and was clearly an extrovert. My gut reaction was that I liked her. I felt she was a very warm person, but I was soon to find out that she was surprisingly blunt and plain-talking too.

'So, what's Maria told you?' she said to me.

She looked me in the eye and I could tell she was not a woman you could easily fob off with pleasantries. To make matters worse, before she settled herself beside me on the sofa she plonked down an extremely large, steaming mug of tea. My heart sank a little as I registered it was going to take me a while to drink.

'Oh, not much,' I said. 'Let me see now. Maria did tell me that Colin lives with you.'

'That's right,' Babs said. 'He's older than Maria, you see, nearly a man, looks after himself. It's a shame Maria's so much younger as I'd take her in too. Isn't that right, Stanley?'

She looked over to Stanley who grunted and nodded without taking his gaze off the TV screen.

'Anyway, love,' Babs went on, patting my arm, 'I'm grateful to you for taking care of her. It won't be for long, I'm sure, and Maria is welcome to visit us any time she likes.'

Maria was sitting in the corner stroking an elderly looking cat who was purring loudly.

Often the relatives of the children I foster are wary of me, and they certainly don't go out of their way to get to know me or become friendly. I was trying to work Babs out. Maria certainly seemed very at home here, which was a good sign. Then Babs suddenly leaned in to me and asked very loudly and indiscreetly, 'Did Maria tell you about her dad?'

'She did mention him,' I said, feeling anxious as Maria could hear every word that was being said. 'Anyhow, I'm very glad to have met you, Babs, and if you don't mind I'll finish my tea and get out of your way so you can enjoy your time with Maria.'

With that I took a large gulp of tea, even though it was still a bit too hot to swallow.

'Did Maria tell you her dad claims she's not his?' Babs responded. 'Well, let me put you in the picture, Angela. He is her real dad, and the only reason he says he's not is to hurt my daughter!'

I thought to myself that in fact it was Maria who was perhaps suffering the most hurt, particularly at this moment in time. 'Well, it's been nice to meet you and I think I'll get going now . . .'

'No need to rush off. Like I say, Maria's welcome any time, and so are you, Ange. I'm grateful you're looking after her. My daughter's done nothing wrong, of course. It's these men. Can't rely on any of them to look after kids the way we women do, eh, Angela? That Gerry, I blame him.'

She rolled her eyes and nudged me conspiratorially, as if we'd been friends for years and were gently ribbing the men in our lives because they couldn't do an everyday task, like making a child's packed lunch, as well as we could. It seemed wholly inappropriate for Babs to be talking this way about a father supposedly disowning his daughter.

Realising I was not going to be able to escape as quickly as I wanted to, I encouraged Maria to tell Babs about some of the things we'd done in her short time with us. We'd gone to the festival and Maria explained that though she didn't win the theme park tickets in the raffle she wanted, she did win a toy in the tombola.

'I could choose,' she said proudly.

'So what did you choose?'

'A fairy doll!' Maria beamed.

Babs rolled her eyes once more.

'It's all fairies and witches and magic with you, isn't it, Maria?'

She nodded and smiled, but when Babs added, 'No wonder, I blame your parents,' the smile slid off Maria's face.

I looked at Babs and raised my eyebrows, not knowing quite what to say.

'She's psychic, my girl,' Babs explained. 'My mother had the gift and so has Christine.'

'Oh, I see,' I said.

I didn't want to get caught up in a conversation like this. While I'm open-minded and I appreciate that some people do appear to have more 'intuition' than others, I didn't feel comfortable discussing this in front of Maria. I thought any talk of psychic powers might be a little unsettling for a seven-year-old girl, although given the way Babs was I figured Maria had probably heard plenty of things like this before.

'Right,' I said, rising to my feet. 'I really must be going now and I'll be back at the agreed time. See you later, Maria. Thanks for the tea, Babs.'

Maria nodded and smiled at me and carried on stroking the cat. She seemed very relaxed and happy to be there, despite Babs's inappropriate chatter, and as I left Babs told me she was cooking Maria's favourite dinner of chicken nuggets and potato waffles with spaghetti hoops.

'I like to spoil her, don't I, Maria?'

Maria nodded again. 'You're the only one who treats me nice,' she said.

Babs completely ignored this, but I made a mental note of

this comment. I would have to pass this on to Social Services, as well as Babs's cryptic remark about blaming Gerry, as I was obliged to do whenever I heard something that might require further investigation.

When I picked Maria up later she was in a good mood and asked me enthusiastically if we could bake some cakes together.

'Me and Nanny watched a cookery show on TV. Can we make fairy cakes?'

'Of course,' I said. 'I love baking.'

'Good. Nanny said she was not much good at baking and I'd better ask you! She said she expected you'd be good.'

I smiled, but I also felt slightly uncomfortable. It didn't take a genius to work out that though Babs was happy to see Maria and include her in her life, she didn't appear to be particularly willing to put herself out for her granddaughter, over and above having her to visit.

The following evening, Maria helped me bake some biscuits and cakes. At one point she was sitting at the kitchen table, singing loudly while rolling out some raw biscuit dough, when she suddenly jumped up, stood on the chair and started waving her arms above her head, doing a little dance.

'I'm glad to see you're feeling so cheerful,' I told her, putting one hand on the back of the chair and getting ready to steady her with the other if the need arose, as it looked as though it probably would. 'But maybe it would be better to do that with both feet on the ground!'

'I'm sorry,' Maria said, jumping down off the chair and taking a few steps away from me. 'I didn't mean to. I'm sorry.'

'It's all right, Maria,' I said, taken aback by her reaction. 'I'm not cross. I just don't want you to fall off and hurt yourself. Do carry on with the song though. I was enjoying it.'

Unfortunately Maria didn't sing again, and I was sorry to have broken her happy mood.

In fact, she didn't speak again either, until we were putting cut-out biscuits shapes on a baking tray. I spilled a bit of flour on the floor, which landed by Maria's feet, and this made her shriek and go very still and quiet for a moment.

Then she suddenly exclaimed, 'I jumped on the sofa.'

You can sometimes tell when a child is trying to say something more than the words suggest, and that was certainly the case now. For this reason I was very careful to keep my tone as neutral as possible as I repeated, 'You jumped on the sofa?'

'Yes.'

Maria paused.

'When?' I asked her eventually, thinking she meant she had done it at our house.

'At my house,' she said. 'They were cross with me. So he made me jump off other things. The table first, and that bit of wood at the end of the bed.'

'I see.'

There was another pause. Maria looked at her hands and started picking at the skin around her nails, as if this was suddenly a very urgent task that took all her attention and meant she couldn't look at me. Then she breathed in, as if she was about to dive off a big diving board and needed to inhale as much breath as she possibly could.

'Then he said I had to jump off the drawer thing in Mum's room, which is quite high and . . .'

'And?'

'And I was scared. It wobbled a bit when I stood on it and I said I didn't want to jump. I don't know who . . .'

'You don't know who?'

'I don't know who pushed me. Mum and him were standing right beside me, laughing. But I hurt my foot when I fell on the floor. And I banged my head.'

'So *someone* pushed you?' I asked her, my voice still flat and as matter-of-fact as I could keep it in the circumstances.

'I think so. Mum said I was a crybaby and it was my own fault.'

'I think that I would have probably cried if I'd hurt myself.'

'You would?'

'Yes, I would, definitely.'

'Are you cross with me, Angela?'

'No! Not at all. I'm sorry if you thought I was cross when I asked you to get down off the chair,' I told her. 'I just didn't want you to get hurt.'

Maria was now staring at the flour on the floor. 'You could see where I walked,' she said, somewhat mysteriously.

'Yes, I expect I would,' I said, guessing that she meant she would make footsteps in the flour if she walked in it.

'I wish we could eat them now,' Maria then said, changing the subject abruptly and dropping a duck-shaped piece of biscuit dough on to the baking tray. 'How long will they take to cook?'

The next half an hour or so passed pleasantly as the biscuits baked and Maria waited eagerly to taste one once they had cooled. Unfortunately, before bed, her mood suddenly changed again, for no obvious reason.

'Why do you nag, nag, nag,' she snapped when I asked her to go upstairs and get into her nightie.

'It's bedtime, Maria,' I said calmly. 'I'm only asking you to do what you need to do before bed.'

She huffed and puffed up the stairs as she criss-crossed between the wooden edges; then when she got into the bathroom to clean her teeth she kicked over the waste bin and told me she hated my house.

'I'm sorry you're feeling like this,' I said. 'Maybe I could read with you tonight. Would you like that?'

'No, all your books are rubbish!'

'Well, then, perhaps we could visit the library after school tomorrow and you could choose some books for yourself. How about that?'

'Why are you being nice? I bet you want to make me jump off the bookcase, don't you? You're just pretending to be nice.'

'Maria, I would certainly not want you to jump off the bookcase. You might hurt yourself, and that is the last thing I want. My job is to keep you safe and comfortable and to look after you as best I can, and that's all I want, Maria.'

She scowled at me and then suddenly blurted out, 'I don't like the games Mum and my stepdad make me play.'

'I see,' I said, not flinching or showing alarm. 'You don't like the games, Maria?'

She picked up a book and thrust it towards me. 'Read me this,' she said rudely.

I took the book from her hand and stayed quiet for a few moments, to give her space to expand on what she'd said about the games, but she didn't.

'I think it would be more polite if you said to me, "Angela, please can you read me this?"' I said as kindly as I could. 'Right, let's get started . . .'

As I've said before, it's very important not to put words into the mouth of a child when they make a disclosure of any kind. For example, if a child makes a statement such as 'Daddy took me upstairs', you have to be extremely careful simply to repeat what they've said so that they know you're listening, but you don't ask them any questions. There are two reasons for this. First, you might cause the child further upset by probing, and, second, you might say something that could later be construed, if a case goes to court, as having prompted them to say something they didn't really mean.

Later that evening I made notes in my diary about everything Maria had told me that day, which I would pass on to Jess the social worker when I saw her next. As I did this, Jonathan praised me for keeping calm and sticking meticulously to the rules we'd been taught at the numerous training sessions we had attended over the years.

'It's second nature now after all this time,' I responded, even though I was pleased by Jonathan's praise. Fostering can be very tough at times, and having a partner like Jonathan there by my side, encouraging me every step of the way, has been invaluable and has helped keep my spirits up on many an occasion.

We both recalled a good example we'd been given on one particular course, which illustrates very well how easy it is to introduce a thought into a child's mind. The story we were told was this. A nursery teacher said to a group of children, 'When we walk down this road, we're going to pass a house with a blue door.' Then, later that same day, she asked them, 'Do you remember when we walked down the road and saw a house with a blue door?' And the children said that they did. A few days later, she asked the children, 'Do you remember when we walked down the road last week and we passed a house with a red door?' This time, the children looked a bit confused, and while some of them said that the door was blue, others weren't sure. But after the teacher told them the same thing repeatedly over a period of weeks and then asked the children what colour the door was, they all said it was red. Inevitably, if you apply the same principle to emotional feelings and reactions, it can have a similar effect.

For example, when you ask a child, 'Are you upset because Tommy hit you?' it's possible the child doesn't really know why he's upset. However, when you suggest a reason, he or she may latch on to it and then, in his or her mind, that *is* what caused the upset.

I sincerely hoped, despite all I'd heard so far from Maria and Social Services, that there was an innocent explanation for her bruises. I also hoped the 'games' and the jumping off the furniture business were not as sinister or peculiar as they seemed. In hindsight this sounds like a naive wish, but I always live in hope. I think I have to be like that in order to do my job, because if I didn't try to focus on the positive and wish for the best-case scenario, I think I could end up in a very dark and depressing place, which would be no good for anybody.

'I know we can't, but I really wish I could just ask her what she meant by the "games",' I said to Jonathan when we went to bed.

'I know,' he admitted. 'I can't stop thinking about it. Poor

Maria, I'm afraid she's been through more than we might ever know. No wonder she has nightmares.'

Right on cue we heard Maria calling out in her sleep. Fortunately, she soon settled that night and I didn't need to go to her, but this didn't mean I slept soundly myself – far from it. I couldn't bear to think that such a sweet little girl had been subjected to any kind of abuse, and the increasingly likely possibility that this had happened made my heart heavy.

6

'Can I still see you?'

After Maria had been with us for almost three weeks we had news about her case. Christine had admitted to Social Services that she had 'accidentally' caused the bruising on Maria's back. Christine claimed her actions were out of character, but that she had been suffering from depression. She insisted to Social Services that she hadn't intended to cause Maria any harm, but had given her daughter a 'gentle shove' during an argument and this had caused Maria to slip down the stairs, which is how she also hurt her back.

As a result of Christine's admission, it was subsequently decided that Maria was being moved to another foster home, where she would be looked after for as long as it would take Social Services to decide if there were any grounds to bring a case against her mother. I found out about this when Maria had a meeting with her social worker in the lounge of our house. Maria excitedly ran into the kitchen afterwards, where I was making jam, to tell me the news. 'Guess what, Angela? I'm not going home! I'm going to stay with some other people like you!'

I was pleased at her reaction because Maria's happiness was

paramount. However, I found it upsetting that a child of her age was even in this situation, and that she seemed to have accepted it quite readily. I'd have been utterly devastated if I were in her shoes as a seven-year-old, and so what did that say about how Maria was treated at home, or about her general state of mind? After all, she had told me more than once that she wanted to go back to her mummy, so how come she was suddenly so pleased about this?

I also felt a pang of sadness on a personal level. In the short time she'd been with us I'd bonded with Maria. We'd got into a routine with me detangling her hair and chatting on the way to school. I enjoyed reading to her and helping her choose books to read herself, and we'd had some really happy times together playing board games and baking. Despite the fact she was not always the best-behaved child, I would miss Maria.

Jonathan and I did say that we were happy to keep Maria with us for longer, but Social Services said they would prefer to move her to another foster home. The reason for this was that Jonathan and I were trained to look after teenagers with specialist problems, which many foster carers weren't. It therefore made practical sense for us to be available for another teenager, while Maria could be looked after by any mainstream carer in the area who had the space available for her.

'The main thing is that Maria seems happy to be going to another foster home,' Jonathan said.

'Always the voice of reason!' I smiled. 'But you are right. And thank God Social Services is investigating this thoroughly.'

On the day she left us I helped Maria pack up her things and I gave her a couple of books to keep, which she was delighted about. 'I don't think Gerry will mind,' she commented absent-mindedly, which seemed a rather odd thing to say, but I let it go.

Maria gave me a big hug before she was collected by her social worker.

'Can I still see you?' she asked. 'Can you come to Nanny's for a cup of tea one day?'

'I'm sure I could arrange that,' I smiled. 'I have your nanny's number and she has mine, so leave it with me, Maria. Good luck!'

The prospect of potentially seeing Maria at Babs's house made it a little easier to say goodbye to her. Jonathan and I have kept in touch with many of the children who have come to us as teenagers over the years, but more often than not we never hear again from young children like Maria who come to us on a short respite visit, as there is not usually a grandparent like Babs acting as an intermediary.

I made a point of calling Babs the following week, to ask how Maria was and to see if perhaps we could arrange to have a cup of tea together.

'Course you can, love. Maria's here tomorrow. Pop in. I might have something stronger than tea, to tell the truth!'

'Oh, why is that?'

'Celebrations, Angela. Christine has seen the light.'

'What d'you mean?'

'Her and Gerry split up. I always said he was a wrong 'un. I used to tease Christine, what with her psychic powers and all. "Couldn't you see him coming?" I'd say. Good riddance to him!'

A feeling of relief washed over me. Maria's future was still uncertain as the Social Services investigation and possible criminal case against Christine dragged on, but at least if Maria did end up back home one day, she wouldn't have to live with Gerry. Apparently his two grown-up sons, Frank and Casey, had gone with him.

'Well, let's hope this is the fresh start Maria needs,' I said.

Unfortunately, when I visited Babs, any celebrations she may have planned were forgotten. As a result of the Social Services investigation, Christine had been charged with a Schedule 1 offence. I knew that such offences – now known as Risk to Children offences – are listed in Schedule 1 of the Children and Young Persons Act 1933, which was intended to protect children against 'cruelty and exposure to moral and physical danger'. They're serious offences, and Babs was extremely defensive of her daughter.

'It's him,' she trilled. 'That Gerry. It was all his fault. As if my Christine would hurt a hair on Maria's head.'

Maria was engrossed in playing with the cat while this conversation took place. I was pleased to see she looked well and she told me she liked her new foster home. Babs had clearly told her about Gerry and Christine splitting up, as Maria added, 'But I want to go back to Mummy now Gerry has gone.'

She went on, 'I like the foster carer; she's like you, Angela. She's kind and she doesn't shout, and she reads with me.'

'That's great to hear,' I said.

'Yes, but Nanny said I'll go home soon, because Gerry's gone, and I want to go home to Mummy.'

I was irritated by the fact Babs seemed to have no filter when it came to discussing sensitive issues with Maria. She talked freely in front of her, and I was on edge the whole time as I felt this was inappropriate. As a result I only stayed for half an hour.

When I left I promised Babs and Maria I'd keep in touch, as I wanted to know how Maria got on.

'I'll tell you all the gossip,' Babs smiled, again inappropriately, I felt. 'Don't you worry. I'll pop over to you next time, shall I?'

'Yes, you're very welcome to,' I found myself saying to Babs. 'Just give me a ring or call into the shop.'

This is how, over the course of the next few months, Babs became a regular visitor to our home. She would arrive in the shop or knock on our front door and sail into our kitchen as if she'd done so all her life and was a close member of the family. I didn't really mind, as long as I wasn't busy doing other things, and I always put the kettle on and had a catch-up with her whenever I could, to find out what was happening to Maria.

Through Babs I learned that Christine was subsequently prosecuted and found guilty of the Schedule 1 offence she was charged with. She was not given a custodial sentence, but the court ordered Christine to attend some parenting classes. I imagined that she would never be allowed to have Maria live with her again after her conviction, but to my astonishment Babs eventually informed me that Maria was being allowed to go home, provided Gerry didn't return.

'Quite right,' Babs said, helping herself to a biscuit from the tin on my kitchen worktop. 'It was all his fault. Christine would never hurt Maria, not on purpose. As if she would!'

This remark about Gerry didn't really seem to make any sense, as Christine had admitted to accidentally causing the bruising on Maria's body. I never did hear the details that emerged in court but I had to respect the law, trust that Social

Services had made the correct decision and accept that Christine did not pose a threat to Maria and would be helped by the parenting classes.

One day, not long afterwards, Babs called into the shop to announce proudly that, 'Maria is back home with her mum, where she belongs.' She also told me that Maria had asked after me, and that she'd like to see me. 'Here's Christine's number,' Babs said. 'Give her a call. She said she'd like to meet you.'

I felt slightly sceptical about this as I'd never met Christine before and didn't know how she would receive me, but I did want to see Maria and so I did give Christine a ring, the following week, after first checking with Social Services that it was OK with them.

'Oh, Angela, it's great to hear from you!' Christine said, sounding genuinely enthusiastic. 'Why don't you come over? Maria was only saying the other day how much she missed you!'

I felt comforted by Christine's manner. Perhaps she'd turned over a new leaf, having come so close to losing Maria? I truly hoped so.

I arranged to call in to see Maria and Christine one day after school, at their house. I was pleasantly surprised. It was neat and tidy, Christine had clearly made an effort with her appearance and was wearing make-up and a nice top and jeans, and Maria looked well. She was wearing new socks, her hair was neatly tied back in a small ponytail and she told me all about some new books she was reading.

'I'll show you!' she said. 'They're in my bedroom.' With that Maria got up and went out of the front door rather than climbing the stairs as I expected her to.

I looked at Christine and saw that her cheeks had flushed a

little. 'She's daft, my daughter!' she said, trying to sound breezy but actually sounding slightly nervous.

'What do you mean, Christine? Why has Maria gone out the front door?'

'I don't know, it's something she always does. You watch, she'll be back in a minute!'

I heard Maria enter the back door, run up the stairs, go back out of the back door and reappear at the front.

'Look,' Maria said proudly, showing me her books.

'Well, aren't you lucky?' I said, admiring the books. 'But tell me Maria, why . . .'

'It's a game she plays,' Christine interrupted. 'Isn't that right, Maria? She doesn't like walking on the carpet in the hallway so she runs round the back. Kids, hey! Mad, isn't it?'

Of course I remembered what Maria had said about not being allowed to walk on the carpet, but I didn't say anything. I was here as a visitor, and this experience made me want to continue being invited to Maria's home. Not only did I want to see her, but I wanted to make sure she was all right.

For her part, I soon discovered that Christine had an ulterior motive for inviting me into her life. Before I left she asked if I'd have Maria for a day at the weekend to give her a break.

'It's hard being on my own,' Christine said. 'I think I'm a better mum when I have a bit of time to myself.

I discussed this with Social Services and it was soon decided that it would be written into Maria's care plan that she could come on regular days out with Jonathan and me, and any other children we were looking after. The idea was that this would help support Christine and hopefully increase the chances of Maria settling happily at home long term.

As a result, over the course of the next few months, Jonathan and I took Maria on all kinds of trips and days out with Tom or Dillon or both, plus any child we had with us for a brief respite stay. We went swimming and ice skating, visited a local wildlife park and saw several films at the cinema. Sometimes we treated Maria to a McDonald's, which was by far her favourite treat of all, and she'd devour her Coke and fries in record time and always ask for more, even though she knew we would never let her have seconds.

After one such day trip, Maria said she was very tired and wanted to cuddle up in her duvet and watch a DVD as soon as she got home to Christine's. I was tired too, to be honest, and I willingly accepted a cup of tea when Christine offered it to me. She didn't always bother, and I thought it would be good to have a chat while Maria was otherwise engaged.

'So how are you managing, Christine?' I asked.

'Well, it's a struggle on my own, but you're a godsend, Angela. I actually got some decorating done today, which I really wanted to finish.'

'That's great to hear! Which room did you do?'

'My bedroom,' she said. 'Come on, I'll show you if you like.'

With that Christine led me to the hallway saying, 'Come on up!'

'I'd love to see it, but I mustn't stay long,' I told her, as I followed her up the stairs. 'I've left Jonathan finishing off a couple of jobs.'

'It won't take a minute – come and see!' Christine said, pausing at the top of the stairs for a moment before opening a door that led into a room directly above the living room and adding, 'It took me ages to decide what colour paint to choose. What do you think?'

'Oh, it's lovely!' I exclaimed, peering in with one foot on the landing and one in the bedroom, as I didn't want to intrude too much. 'That's a really nice colour. You've obviously got a flair for decorating, Christine. Well done! You should be very proud of yourself.'

'Oh, I am,' she said.

As she spoke I heard the toilet flush, and I turned around to see the bathroom door opening, revealing a very startled look-ing man in his underpants.

'Christ alive!' he said, immediately jumping back into the bathroom and closing the door behind him.

'Gerry?' I said, horrified.

I had never met Gerry, but I had seen a photograph of him once, in an old album Babs showed me and Maria at her house. He had a hooked nose, scruffy hair and beady eyes, and this was definitely the same man.

I glanced quickly at Christine, who shrugged and tried to act as though nothing had happened as she led the way back down the stairs.

'Glad you like it,' she said loudly and cheerfully. 'I did put a lot of hard work in, and like I say it's helpful for you to take Maria out as I can get so much more done . . .'

'Christine,' I said, as we reached the bottom of the stairs, 'what is Gerry doing here?'

'What? Oh, don't bother about that. He, er, just called round to get some stuff he left ages ago. I forgot he was here. He'll be gone in a minute.'

'But he's not meant to be here at all, is he?' I said, wanting to add, 'And it doesn't look like he's just popped in if he's in his underpants,' but I held my tongue.

'Anyhow, like I was saying, what do you think of the decorating, Angela? Do you *really* like it?'

'Yes, like I said, it's lovely, Christine, but right now I'm a bit distracted by seeing Gerry here.'

Christine rounded on me.

'Leave it, please, Angela,' she said. 'I don't want to talk about it, and quite frankly it's none of your business, is it? You're not Maria's foster carer any more, so why are you interfering?'

Maria had appeared in the doorway.

'Maria, babe, you tell her!' Christine said.

'Tell her what?'

'Tell her that Gerry doesn't live here any more. He just popped in for some bits, didn't he? Remember I told you he'd do that? Silly me! I thought he'd have been and gone by the time you came home!'

Maria stretched her lips into the shape of a wide smile and said robotically, 'Yes, Mummy. Gerry doesn't live here now.'

I'll have to let Social Services know, I thought. It was not going to do any good for me to make a scene here at the house, but I would put in the call as soon as I could. I said my goodbyes and left with a racing heart.

Jonathan was in the shop when I got back, and as soon as I walked in the door he sensed that something was wrong and immediately asked me what the matter was. When I explained what had happened he was gobsmacked.

'I don't understand,' he said. 'If Gerry really had popped

back for some belongings surely Christine would have made sure he did so when nobody was likely to bump into him . . .'

'Indeed. But I don't believe for one moment he'd popped back, do you?'

Jonathan's eyes widened. He is such an honest and truthful man, he had naturally tried to make some sense of the scenario, rather than suspecting serious lies were being told.

'I'm afraid you are right, Angela. He might be a very odd character, but even Gerry wouldn't be in his underpants unless he was living there, or doing more than simply calling in to pick up some things.'

Jonathan paused and then said something that took me by surprise, as it was something I hadn't thought of. 'Do you think there is a possibility Christine *wanted* you to see him?'

'No,' I replied. 'I mean, she fell over herself trying to cover it up.'

'But could that have been a double bluff? I wouldn't normally think along those lines, but this is just so odd. You don't suppose Christine is scared of Gerry?'

'You mean she deliberately made me see him, pretended to him it was an accident, and all along wanted me to call Social Services?'

Jonathan shrugged and looked perplexed.

'Ouch!' he suddenly exclaimed, as our thoughts floated in the air between us. Jonathan had been so engrossed in trying to work out what had happened at Christine's that he'd accidentally pricked himself with a pin he was attaching to a corsage. A large drop of blood appeared on the tip of his thumb and he reached for a tissue.

'What a mess!' he complained, but I knew he was talking about Maria's home, not the blood.

'I know,' I said. 'I'll go and call Social Services now. I'm sure it will mean Maria is taken away again, but what choice do we have? She can't stay there if Gerry is on the scene again.'

'Exactly, Angela. Maybe Gerry was never even off the scene?'

We looked at each other aghast. Maybe we'd been hood-winked for months? Maybe Christine wanted Maria taken off her again? We had no idea of the truth. All we could do was the correct and moral thing, and alert Social Services that the rules they had set down to protect Maria were being broken.

7

'There are heads in the clouds'

'Oh dear. Thank you for letting me know,' Jess said when I broke the news about Gerry being at Christine's house. 'Unfortunately, this is something that happens all too often.'

'I imagine it does,' I replied, feeling glad Maria's care plan had incorporated her days out with Jonathan and me, or this may not have come to light.

Jess thanked me for telling her what I'd witnessed and told me she would report back as soon as she had any news.

I heard nothing more for days and days. I was anxious the whole time about how Maria was getting on, and in the end I left a couple of messages for Jess asking for an update. When she eventually got back to me she apologised for not replying to my calls more quickly and said there was no news yet.

'It's busier than ever,' she said, sounding flustered. 'I do apologise. But I know Maria's case is being dealt with. It's a complicated one. You'll have to bear with us.'

Another week went by, and another, and by the time Jess contacted me again about Maria almost a month had passed.

'Is everything all right?' I asked, because Jess sounded hesitant on the phone, which wasn't her usual style.

'Well, the fact is, it has been decided that Maria is allowed to stay at home with her mother Christine. Gerry is not allowed to live with them, but he is allowed to visit.'

'What? But that's ridiculous! Surely he's either safe around Maria or he isn't?'

I didn't normally speak so frankly, but I was incensed. I struggled to understand how this decision had been made.

'I'm sorry, Angela, but that is what Social Services has decided. It's out of my hands now. Unfortunately, the powers that be have to focus on the facts, not gut reactions. He has clearly passed their investigations and Social Services do not think Maria is at risk from having him visit.'

I knew that Social Services would have information we weren't privy to, as this was nearly always the case with any child. As foster carers we were only given information Social Services deemed useful and relevant to our role. I understood this completely, because why should private details about families be shared unnecessarily? Jonathan and I really wanted to believe Social Services had made the right decision and we had to assume that Gerry had been thoroughly investigated and that he posed no threat. Once again, we had no choice but to trust the system, but nevertheless we worried non-stop for Maria.

Christine became distant after this incident. She was hard to get hold of and only ever rang me when she was 'absolutely desperate for a break' and wanted me to take Maria out for the day. I obliged every time, even if Jonathan and I just took Maria for a walk into town or to the country park for a picnic. She was always well dressed and on good behaviour on these occasions, although she did act in a way that was a little unnerving sometimes.

'Would you like an ice cream?' I asked her one day.

'Yes please! You're kind, Angela!' Maria said spontaneously, and then she quickly looked behind her, as if she was worried someone had overheard her saying the wrong thing.

'Are you all right, Maria?' Jonathan asked.

'Yes. My mum is kind too, and so is Gerry! So, so kind! And lovely!'

Jonathan and I looked at each other, feeling bemused. It was as if Maria was saying something she felt she ought to say or had been taught to repeat, but as neither Christine nor Gerry were here we couldn't understand why she felt compelled to say this now.

On another occasion, Maria stood on top of a climbing frame, peering into the sky.

'What are you looking at?' I asked.

Maria seemed very worried and was standing statue-still.

'Nothing, just looking,' she said very quietly.

Jonathan tried to lighten the situation by saying, 'Come down Maria, you've got your head in the clouds!' to which she replied wistfully, 'There are heads in the clouds.'

'Heads in the clouds?'

'Yes.'

Jonathan and I then started trying to look for shapes in the clouds, to try to make a game of it.

'That cloud looks like an elephant with big ears!' Jonathan said.

'I can only see the eyes,' Maria said, narrowing her own eyes.

*

I continued to phone Babs from time to time and she called into the shop or came for a cup of tea occasionally, always unannounced, which I'd got used to.

One day she told me very matter-of-factly that Christine and Maria had moved out of the area the previous week, to live with Gerry and his two sons, Frank and Casey. On top of this, Colin had decided to leave Babs and Stanley's house and move in with the rest of the family too.

'Who'd have thought it?' Babs said. 'One minute it's just Christine and Maria and now there's six of them all under one roof. I ask you. I hope my daughter knows what she's doing.'

Babs was putting on a brave face but she seemed quite put out, which was hardly surprising. She loved her grandchildren dearly and it must have been awful for not just Maria to move many miles away, but Colin too. And all so suddenly, it seemed.

I was struggling to take all this information in, and I was especially concerned about the fact Maria was living in the same house as Gerry, which as far as I was aware was not permitted by Social Services.

'Are you concerned about Maria?' I asked.

'Of course I am! But what can you do? My Christine won't be told anything, will she? It'll probably all end in tears, but good luck to them.'

'But how do you feel about Colin going? He's lived with you all his life.'

'To be honest, Angela, it was time he moved out. I miss him, of course, but he's old enough to make his own mind up. It can't have been much fun living with me and Stanley, if the truth be told. Poor Stan's in a bad way at the minute . . .'

Babs then proceeded to tell me the ins and outs of Stanley's various medical conditions, the schedule for his hospital appointments and a procedure he was having performed, and how their benefits were being increased because he was now not just 'on the sick' but registered disabled.

I listened politely and nodded in all the right places, but really all I could think about was Maria. She was now living with her big brother and two grown-up stepbrothers, plus Gerry and her mum. Would she be all right? How would she adjust to this new set-up? And what about school? The area they had moved to was miles away – too far for Maria to attend the same school, where as far as I knew she was doing well. *What an upheaval for her*, I thought.

I made a call to Social Services after seeing Babs, as I had no idea if they were aware of Maria's new circumstances. A duty social worker said she'd pass this information on to the correct people but gave no indication of whether Maria's social worker already knew all about these changes.

'I'd like to say something positive to put your mind at rest,' Jonathan said when I voiced all my concerns that evening. 'But I'm afraid I can't think of anything. I can't imagine why Colin would want to move in with Gerry and his boys after living his whole life with his grandparents. And I can't imagine how Gerry will cope, having two children who aren't his own living in his house. It's all very worrying. It's almost as though Christine is quite deliberately stacking the odds against her being able to manage.'

Being a foster carer is hugely rewarding in many ways, but there are negatives and frustrations too. One issue we've faced many times over the years is the fact that, however long a child might have lived with you – and, admittedly, Maria had only been with us for a matter of weeks – you have no right to interfere in their life. All you can do when you see something going wrong or have concerns is alert Social Services. Then you have to take a step back and let the local authority and legal system deal with things in whatever way they consider to be best.

As I've said before, you have to trust that the system works. Inevitably, however, because social workers are only human, and because they almost invariably have workloads that no one could possibly hope to get on top of, they sometimes get things wrong. Therefore, I can never relax and think the problem is over when I've put a call in to Social Services, because unfortunately this isn't always the case.

With Maria I was very concerned that Christine and Gerry were somehow getting away with playing the system to their own advantage. Of course, I had no evidence that would make Social Services act differently, so all Jonathan and I could do was hope for the best and try to maintain contact. Christine still had our phone number, but now that she had a few extra pairs of hands at home, and lived quite a distance away from us, I didn't expect to hear from her. And I didn't.

'I don't need help from anyone,' she told Social Services eventually, and the stipulation in Maria's care plan that I would be on hand to support Christine became redundant.

I kept up the contact with Babs, however, and was grateful that she seemed to want to stay in touch. She was very good at keeping me posted with developments, thanks to her naturally gossipy nature and the fact she liked to be the one who passed on news first.

'I've got something to tell you!' Babs announced loudly and

importantly one day, blustering into the shop as Jonathan was serving a mother and daughter and several other customers were browsing.

'Come into the back, Babs,' I said swiftly, giving Jonathan a nod.

Babs installed herself at the kitchen table and said, 'Have you got sweeteners?' as I put the kettle on. 'Only I'm trying to lose weight.'

'Yes, I'm the same. Never have sugar. Now what is it, Babs?'

She announced flatly that Colin and a bin liner full of his belongings had arrived back on her doorstep.

'How come?' I asked, startled. 'He hasn't been gone very long. What has gone wrong?'

'Money. Gerry said Colin wasn't paying enough towards his keep, but how can he pay more when he's on a low wage at the warehouse?'

'I see. When did this happen?'

'Yesterday. Colin's glad to be back. He's been telling me some terrible things about that man Gerry. He's very spiteful to Maria, apparently. And my Christine's not much better, by the sound of it. I can't believe it, but I trust Colin's word. He's a truthful boy.'

I felt sick to my stomach.

'I know you'll probably report all this to Social Services, Angela, but I don't care. I've told them things myself, actually. I have the social worker's number. Christine would hit the roof if she knew, but I want Maria to be safe.'

'What exactly has Colin said about Gerry and his mum?'

'Basically, everything has to be done according to Gerry's rules, most of which sound as though they're petty to the point

66

of obsessive – folding your clothes in a certain way, for example, and putting your toothbrush in exactly the right place, at exactly the right angle, in the bathroom cabinet.'

Babs paused for a moment to blow her nose. He cheeks were flushed and even though she sounded indignant and was trying to be strong, I could tell she was very upset.

'And when Maria gets something wrong or doesn't do something she's supposed to do, Colin says that man goes berserk. Apparently, a couple of days ago, he hit her so hard he sent her flying down the hallway, just because she didn't fold her towel the right way.'

A sob caught in her throat, but Babs continued, 'When Colin said something about it, and tried to stand up for her, Gerry scooped up all his stuff, put it in a bin liner and brought him back here. At first Colin only told me about the row over his keep. He said he never wanted to leave his granddad and me in the first place, but Christine and Gerry put pressure on him to move in with them. They wanted the extra keep, you see. They told Colin that quite openly, it seems. Gerry threatened to beat him up if he told anyone else, so Colin was too frightened to say anything, until now.'

I did indeed call Social Services and it later emerged that teachers at Maria's new school, as well as at least one of her new neighbours, had already raised concerns with their local Social Services. The teachers had reported seeing bruising on Maria's body, and the neighbour had reported hearing violent rows and what sounded like a person falling down the stairs. Very frustratingly, Maria's files from our local Social Services had not followed her to her new home, so there had been no monitoring of the family at all, despite Christine's previous conviction. It was just good fortune that Maria's teachers and the neighbour were vigilant, because their concerns meant a new investigation had already started before I phoned up and passed on what Babs had reported to me.

Some time afterwards I was told by Social Services that Christine had been given a choice. The first option was that she could agree to a voluntary care order, which would mean putting Maria into care voluntarily. In this case, Christine would still have to be consulted before any decisions could be made about Maria's care, and Christine would effectively maintain her parental rights. Alternatively, if Christine did not agree to a voluntary care order, Social Services would go to court and obtain an order to remove Maria from the family home.

In the end, Christine agreed to a voluntary care order, which was the most sensible decision in the circumstances, as Maria was going to have to leave the family home one way or another. The question was, where would Maria live?

Jonathan and I were asked if we were potentially willing to take her in again, just for a short time while a permanent mainstream foster carer was found. Of course we agreed, as at this time we still only had Tom and Dillon living with us permanently. However, as Maria was living in a different area now, this was not a simple fix. Each authority has its own budget and its own set of foster carers, so there was a lot of red tape to deal with.

'I hope she comes back to us,' I said to Jonathan.

'Me too,' he replied. 'I think it would be the right thing, even for a short time. Let's hope it works out.'

'Yes, let's hope. I don't expect things will happen quickly though. These things never do, not when there are two local authorities involved.'

8

'They're making it all up'

Eventually it was decided that Maria was coming back to stay with us. As I predicted, there had been lengthy delays because the two separate local authorities were involved, but ultimately it was decided that Maria would be better off with us, at least in the short term, as we knew her and we lived close to her nanny.

Social Services ultimately wanted to match Maria to a carer or carers she could potentially stay with long term. With Jonathan and I continuing to be specialist carers for teenagers, we understood we would only be used to help out with Maria in the short term. However, we also knew that a so-called 'short term' placement for a child of Maria's age could easily be extended. Technically, 'short term' can mean anything up to two years, but we'd had experience of this being extended further still, so in reality Jonathan and I had no idea how long Maria might stay with us this second time.

I didn't mind the uncertainty one bit. Jonathan and I were delighted Maria was coming back. Tom and Dillon agreed that it would be nice to see her again too. Before her return I was informed by Social Services that since the last time we'd seen

Maria she had started attending church. Gerry had converted to a particular faith, and he insisted Maria did the same and practised the religion regularly. This entailed weekly visits to a specific church, plus Bible classes and some home study. The social worker who gave me this information didn't hold back in sharing her forthright views about Gerry's demands.

'To be absolutely honest, Angela, I think the stepfather's insistence that Maria sticks to these rules is more a case of him exerting control than anything. I am reliably informed that he does not practise the religion regularly himself, and nor do his two sons, even though he insists Maria does. However, we have to comply with the family's wishes.'

I understood completely. Social Services have to be scrupulous about ensuring that the religious wishes of a family are met, and Gerry's choices had to be respected, even if he *was* motivated by his desire to control Maria, which I had to admit did seem likely given what I knew of him.

Before she moved back in I made sure I did some research into the religion Maria followed. It was not what I considered a 'mainstream' religion and I knew next to nothing about it, except for the fact that Christmas is not celebrated in that particular church at all. I remembered this from a boy I had gone to school with, decades earlier. He had always attracted curiosity and pity from the other children when he said he wasn't getting any presents from Father Christmas, and I had felt sorry for him.

I got a couple of books from the library and learned that followers of the religion observe the Sabbath on a Saturday. They also have a strict code of ethics, which includes not drinking alcohol or smoking, plus they have a preference for a vegetarian diet, although they can eat meat that is 'biblically clean'. McDonald's sprang to mind, as I remembered how much of a treat it was for Maria to have a burger, fries and a Coke on special occasions. I had no idea if their meat was 'biblically clean', and I bristled as I imagined myself asking this question of one of the staff at the McDonald's in town. The thought made me hope Maria had given up meat completely, as at least this could be easier to stick to correctly.

Once I felt a little better informed I went to a Saturday service at the nearest church, where I sat at the back of the small, sparsely decorated building and just listened to what was going on. Everyone seemed pleasant and friendly, and after the service I made arrangements for Maria to attend the church after she moved back to live with us. I found everybody extremely helpful and understanding when I explained the situation. I wouldn't normally tell strangers that I'm a foster carer, as often the children prefer to keep this information private and I don't think it is anybody else's business. However, on this occasion it seemed sensible, as otherwise I imagined questions would be asked about why I didn't follow the same religion as Maria, or why she had no family members going to church with her.

'Oh, I think I know who Maria's family is,' one of the church elders said, looking downhearted. 'She has a stepfather called Gerry, if I'm not mistaken?'

'That's correct.'

'That man!' she lamented. 'He shouldn't be allowed to be a member of our church!'

'Shouldn't he?'

'No! He's so *rude*!' she stuttered, then checked herself. 'In any case, we will all welcome Maria. Her stepfather will not affect things there; please be assured of that.'

It was decided that Jonathan and I would hand Maria over to an appointed person who would be waiting at the door to collect her at church each Saturday. I was told we were very welcome to stay, or that if we left the church and came back we could step inside at the end of the service and wait for Maria to be brought to us. Bible classes took place on a Thursday after school, and similar arrangements were made for these too.

It was a lot of preparation, especially as we didn't know how long it would be needed for, but it was very necessary, to meet Gerry's wishes. I wanted to have everything in place and make sure the plans would run smoothly, and after visiting the church I felt I'd done my best and was ready to fully support Maria.

The day arrived for Maria's return, and I found myself feeling anxious and nervous. She had just turned nine by this time – it was hard to believe that so much time had passed since her first stay with us, when she was seven. I'd made up the bedroom using the same set of bedding she'd chosen on her previous stay, as I felt it might be nice for her to have something familiar and to know I'd remembered which duvet cover she had picked out. I'd also checked there were plenty of books in the bedroom that suited her age group, as I expected she'd still be an avid reader. Foodwise, I'd learned that Jonathan and I didn't actually eat any of the meat that was classed as 'unclean' in any case, so that was one less thing to worry about.

I couldn't really work out why I felt as worried as I did when everything was organised, and I was really looking forward to seeing Maria and welcoming her into our home again. Then a question from my mother made me realise why I had these feelings.

'How lovely!' my mum had exclaimed when I told her Maria was coming back. Mum had only met Maria briefly last time, but she remembered her name and knew I'd kept in touch with her grandmother, Babs, on and off.

'What sort of a girl is Maria? What's she like?'

'Well,' I started, and then I didn't know what to say next. In that moment I realised I could give my mum one of any number of answers here. I thought of how sweet Maria could be, when she was baking or reading, for example. Then I thought of the tantrums she had when she wanted the crisps and fizzy drinks that I wouldn't give her. I also remembered how she avoided the stair carpet, and how she seemed to put on a bit of an act sometimes, when I imagined she thought Gerry or her mum wanted her to behave in a certain way.

'That's a very good question, Mum,' I finally said. 'She's a lovely little girl, but one whose character is complicated to explain. You never really know which Maria you'll get. She could be stroppy and difficult, and she could be absolutely lovely. Charming but challenging is perhaps another way of describing her. It'll be interesting to see how, or if, she's changed.'

I hoped and prayed that, despite her experiences, Maria's positive characteristics were winning through as she got older.

When I heard a car pull up outside I looked out of the window and saw Maria, Christine and Gerry. My heart sank at the sight of Gerry behind the wheel, but to my relief he stayed in the car while Christine brought Maria to the house. Jess was in her own car behind them, as she had to accompany them and have an initial placement meeting with Jonathan and me.

'Angela!' Maria smiled when I opened the front door.

She looked as if she was going to hug me, but then she stopped herself and stood back.

'Come on in. Jonathan and I have been really looking forward to seeing you. How are you?'

'Good,' she smiled.

Christine marched into the kitchen without being asked, in the same way Babs had done many times. She seemed in good spirits though, and when I suggested that Maria might like to go upstairs and take her bags to her room Christine said, 'I'll give you a hand, if that's OK. I'd like to see your room, babe.'

By now Jonathan had come through from the shop, said his hellos and put the kettle on.

'You're not going to sing that Maria song again are you?' she said in an exaggerated groan.

'I might!' Jonathan said. 'If the mood takes me!'

Maria giggled, and I was pleased to see that the ice seemed to have been broken very easily. In fact, it felt as though Maria had barely been away. She didn't even look much different, apart from the fact her hair was a bit longer and she'd grown an inch or so.

Christine and I made polite conversation as we climbed the stairs with Maria while Jess stayed in the kitchen with Jonathan. Maria, I was pleased to see, stepped normally on the stair carpet and chatted about a book she was reading.

'Don't know where I got her from!' Christine quipped. 'I've never read a book in my life!'

I smiled as politely as I could, even though I was not impressed by this remark as it wasn't encouraging to Maria. When we reached the bedroom Maria busied herself with taking things out of her bags and looking around to see what had changed. We'd had quite a few children staying with us for short respite stays since Maria was last with us, and she spotted immediately that a few things were different, like the bedside table, which we'd replaced as it had become a bit tatty, and there was a new blind on the window as the old one had been broken by a rather heavy-handed boy.

When she spotted the duvet cover she grinned. 'You know I like that one!' she said. 'That's clever!'

Again I gave a rather subdued smile. I wanted to make much more of a fuss of Maria than I was, but I felt restricted with Christine there, and I didn't want to do anything that she might take exception to.

Christine, however, clearly felt able to speak her mind and say exactly what she wanted, as she suddenly blurted out, 'They're making it all up, you know.'

'Pardon?'

'Social Services. None of it's true, what they're saying we did to Maria. Those social workers are just trying to make me look bad. They don't like me because I tell them what I think and refuse to play their stupid games. I hate them all. Anyway, Maria will tell you that what they're saying about us is all lies, won't you?'

She poked her daughter's arm with her index finger and Maria nodded and looked at the floor.

'Well, you don't need to worry about Maria, at least,' I said. 'We'll look after her.'

My heart really went out to Maria when Christine went to leave shortly afterwards. She'd accepted a cup of tea but didn't seem interested in chatting with her daughter or enjoying the time with her. Instead she made small talk about a programme she'd seen on television. The worst thing of all was that, as she said goodbye, leaving Jess, Jonathan and me to finish the initial placement meeting without her, Maria took a step towards her mum, apparently hoping for a hug, but Christine just pulled a face and raised her elbow, as if to shake her daughter off. It was heartbreaking seeing the expression on Maria's face change from nervous expectation to hurt, then to sadness and acceptance of her mother's irritable rejection.

Later, when I went upstairs again with Maria to help her finish her unpacking, she seemed to have a sudden thought. She pounced on one of the bags, almost ripping it open before pulling things out and scattering the floor with sweatpants, T-shirts and all the other items of worn and torn clothing it contained.

'It might be better to put things away as you get them out,' I said, tentatively. 'Is there something I can do to help? Or would you prefer to do it yourself?'

'I'm looking for something,' she said, distractedly, tipping the contents of a small black plastic bag onto the floor next to where she was crouching, then sitting back on her heels and adding, with a sigh, 'But it's not here.'

I would have asked what the 'something' was, but I didn't have time to say anything in response before Maria leapt to her feet and started throwing the contents of the bag around the room, shouting, 'It's not fair. I hate them.'

'Is there something I can do to help?' I asked again, catching a sock as it flew past my head.

'I'm looking for Benji,' she snapped, kicking the already cracked casing of a computer game and sending it skidding across the floor. 'He's like a . . . what do you call those things? A soft toy. He's my favourite one. Nanny bought him for me. I was going to call him Patch, because he's got a patch over one eye. Then Granddad said he was like a dog called Benji, in a film. Mum knows I don't like going anywhere without him. But he's not here!'

'Well, that explains why you're upset,' I said. 'I think I'd be upset if I had a favourite soft toy and couldn't find him. Maybe you could phone your mum? I expect she just forgot to put him in the bag. But don't worry, I'm sure she'll drop him round for you. Maybe put your things away first though. It would be a shame if anything got accidentally damaged.'

As I said this I felt a pang. The clothes and belongings Maria had brought with her were not in good condition, and everything looked shabby, old or damaged in some way.

'Will you help me?' Maria said sweetly. 'Then we can do it quickly and I can phone Mum?'

In one of the training courses Jonathan and I had been on, it was mentioned how important a child's personal possessions can be, especially the things they bring from home. It doesn't matter if the clothes that are packed up for them are too threadbare or too small to be worn, as was the case with several of the items of clothing in Maria's bag. What might look to anyone else like a bag full of rubbish could actually be a bag full of memories of home for a child. So, we leave it to them to sort through the contents and decide what they want to do with everything, and only ever help if they ask us to. I would always wait for a child to ask me to wash an item of clothing too, as even the smell of their clothes might remind them of home.

For some children, of course, all their memories of home are horrible ones, and sometimes a bag of clothes gets dumped in the large store cupboard in the hallway and is never looked at again. When that happens, we might eventually ask the child if there's anything in the bag they want to keep, but not until they've been with us for a substantial amount of time – possibly as much as a few years. Sometimes they say, 'No. Just throw it all away.' But sometimes a pebble from a beach, a toy car with no wheels or a doll with one arm can have special significance and be very important to a child.

For Maria, however, it seemed that the only thing she really wanted was Benji.

I helped her unpack and we made the room neat and tidy. Then she phoned Christine, who assured Maria she would drop the toy round 'soon'.

'That's good,' I said. 'Would you like to choose another soft toy from the basket to have in bed with you?'

'No thanks,' she said. 'I only like Benji.'

Maria went to bed without a fuss after reading for a while. She didn't seem to have progressed very far with her reading but was nevertheless enjoying a book about a magic kingdom, which seemed to have really captured her imagination.

'Do you believe in magic?' she asked me.

'Now there's a question. I believe magical things can happen, yes, I do.'

'Do you believe in ghosts?'

'No, Maria, I don't think I do. I like ghost stories though!'

'Do you know my mum can talk to ghosts?'

I remembered Maria had said something about psychics before, and that Babs had told me Christine was psychic.

'Your mum can talk to ghosts?'

'Yes, she has special powers. She spoke to Great-Grandma once. She told me all about it.'

'Did she?'

'Yes. Night night, Angela. I'm tired.'

Maria turned on to her side and snuggled under the duvet. I set the night light for her and said goodnight.

Bless her, I thought. It seemed so inappropriate to involve such a young girl in talk like that. As a girl myself I remember being quite scared of any mention of the supernatural or claims that you could communicate with the 'other side'. There was a medium called Doris Stokes who was quite famous many years ago, and I remember being fascinated but also quite alarmed by her. I heard her on the radio one time and it made me wonder if I was going to suddenly hear from an ancient relative who had died many years earlier. I couldn't get the thought out of my head, and I avoided hearing Doris Stokes speak after that.

When I told Jonathan about the conversation I'd had with Maria he sighed. 'And to think Christine has been telling you that Social Services is "making it all up". I think it's so irresponsible to put these ideas in a young child's head. I don't believe a word of it, but even if I did I would never discuss such things with a child. It makes you wonder what else Christine and Gerry have been saying to poor Maria.'

9

'I don't want to see him*'*

Christine didn't drop Benji round as she'd promised and although Maria phoned her mum several times over the next few days and Christine always said, 'Yeah, yeah, I'll drop him round next time I'm in town,' she never did. So eventually, when it became apparent that, despite knowing how precious and comforting Benji was to her daughter, Christine wasn't actually going to bother, I told Maria, 'Don't worry, we can ask your nanny to get him for you next time she sees your mum. Shall I give her a call later?'

'Yes,' Maria said. 'But you speak to her. I don't want to.'

It was a comment I found very strange in view of how close she had been to Babs in the past.

'You don't want to?'

'I said, I don't want to.'

Maria fixed me with a cold stare which told me not to pursue this, but I made a mental note to find out more about what had gone wrong between Babs and her granddaughter too.

At the weekend, Jonathan and I drove Maria to church as planned, which seemed to go well, and as a treat afterwards we took her to McDonald's. We had just parked the car in the busy car park when Maria said, 'There's something wrong with my door. It won't open.'

A few years earlier, when I was looking after an autistic girl, I had forgotten to put on the child lock and she opened the door of the car when it was moving. Fortunately, she was strapped into her seat, but it gave everyone a terrible shock and Jonathan had to do an emergency stop. I put it down to experience and considered it a lesson well learned. I had never repeated the hold mistake, which is why Maria could not unlock the car door herself.

'There's a child lock on the door so that it can't be opened by mistake,' I explained to Maria. But her confusion had already turned to anger and she wound down the window, leaned out and opened the door from the outside.

'Please don't open the door like that,' I said, undoing my seatbelt. 'It's much safer if you let us do it. We wouldn't want you to—'

But before I could finish what I was about to say Maria jumped out of the car and ran at full pelt across the car park. As she did so another car that had just turned into the car park had to slam on its brakes.

'Maria!' I screamed.

It was a horrible moment. She froze on the spot and the colour drained from her face as the car, driven by a young lad who had music blasting from his speakers, stopped inches away from her. I was at her side moments later, apologising to the driver who had also turned white, and taking hold firmly of Maria's hand.

'Honestly, sweetheart, the door was locked for a reason, to

keep you safe. I will always let you out; there was no need to do that. Please don't do that again, and please never run in a car park or anywhere near cars. It's our job to keep you safe, so please help us.'

'I was perfectly safe with my mum,' she snapped back at me, fixing me with an angry, sulky stare. 'I didn't have to come and live with you again. It's all Social Services' fault, making up stories and telling lies about Mum.'

Something Jonathan and I have often noticed, with other children too, is that sulks that occur on the way *in* to McDonald's tend not to last very long, and Maria's subsided completely when I asked her to choose which meal she would like. It was a decision that took her ages to make, mainly because she wanted the toy that came with the child's meal but with an extra-large adult's meal to accompany it! In the end, she had the child's meal with a Coke, followed by a McFlurry, by which time child locks on cars and sulking about being told off were distant memories.

The following day we chose as a family to go to a water park. Maria couldn't swim so she was a bit sulky again when she thought that was all we were going to be doing. But her face lit up when she saw all the different water slides, and she had a great time sliding down them and plopping like an excited porpoise into the shallow water at the bottom. She got on well with Tom and Dillon too, which was a pleasure to see.

'What a great day we've had,' I said to Jonathan when we got home quite late that afternoon. 'There were only a few sulks, which thankfully didn't last long. Things are looking up!' I obviously spoke too soon, and that evening the sulking returned for what seemed to be no reason, or at least no reason we could put our finger on.

The first thing we knew about it was when Maria stripped her bed, threw all the bedding into the hall and began to scream, 'I want to go home and live with my mum.'

'Social Services have to do what's best for you,' I told her when she stopped screaming long enough to draw breath. 'But you may well be able to go home once all their checks have been completed. In the meantime, try not to worry about it. You'll see your mum soon, and the rest of the family.'

'I don't want to see *him*,' she shouted. 'Just Mum!'

It may seem harsh to talk to such a young child about Social Services and 'checks', but I knew from the social workers and from my past experience with Maria herself that she understood and was used to this language. I was trained to be honest and open about such things when the child was already aware what was happening.

I eventually managed to soothe her by talking to her calmly and changing the subject to books and stories she was interested in, although it took quite a while.

The next day she woke up in a good mood and seemed to be in really high spirits when she came home from school by taxi. This was now the arrangement, for the time being, as Maria's school was some distance from our house, in a neighbouring county.

'I got a star for my story,' she said, showing me one of her English books. 'Miss said I used good adjectives.'

I read the story and praised her, as it really was a very imaginative and well-written story about a missing puppy. After that she waited excitedly by the phone in the kitchen for a call from her mum, as arranged and agreed by the social workers. The fact her mum had still failed to bring Benji round had not been mentioned for a day or two, but I hoped that after this phone conversation Christine might finally sort this out. The fact Maria had written about a missing puppy hadn't been lost on me, and I knew she was still pining for her soft toy. There had been no more mention of her nanny and why Maria had said she didn't want to speak to her. I had not forgotten this and was hoping Maria might open up about it, when she felt comfortable.

I prepared dinner while Maria was on the phone, and after about ten minutes she put the receiver down triumphantly, looking like the cat who'd got the cream.

'Guess what! Mum says she's seeing her solicitor and that she's going to get me back soon. I mustn't tell my stepbrothers though, because they don't know. It's just our secret, Mum said.'

Jonathan and I swapped glances.

'It's a secret?' I said.

'What's for dinner?' she said.

'Toad in the hole,' I replied.

'What?' she said, wrinkling her nose. 'It sounds disgusting! I'm not eating that! My mum wouldn't make me eat that.'

'Shall I tell you how I make it? I think you might be surprised, because the mixture has the same ingredients you put in to make pancakes . . .'

'Yuck! Can't we go to McDonald's?'

'No, we can't. I've made this and I think you'll like it. Tom and Dillon say it's one of their favourites.'

'Where are they?'

'They'll both be home very soon; they've had clubs after school.'

85

'I can hear them!'

With that Maria ran to the front door, flung it open and darted off down the side passage, heading in the direction of the playing fields at the back of the house.

Fortunately, Jonathan still had his shoes on after coming through from the shop and he gave chase as soon as he realised what she'd done. I watched from the kitchen window as Jonathan sprinted up to Maria and caught up with her as she approached one of the climbing frames. He was swift on his feet, thank goodness, and she had no chance of getting too far away before her reached her.

I could see Maria standing with her hands on her hips, evidently shouting at Jonathan, but at least she'd stopped running away when he reached her. This could have been a much more tricky situation, because as foster carers we try not to touch the children in any way at all, in case it stresses them out or is misconstrued in any way. I knew Jonathan would not be able to grab hold of Maria to stop her running off, as you might your own child, and that he would need to rely on talking her round. Happily, moments later I watched as the two of them walked back to the house, Maria stomping two paces in front of Jonathan, head bowed and her face set in an angry grimace.

Incidentally, I have recently been told by a new foster carer that a child she was looking after falsely accused her husband of hurting him. Her husband had taken the boy down off a wall he was climbing dangerously while trying to run away. Subsequently the boy was removed and the couple placed under investigation. After that they decided to give up fostering as they had not realised how it would affect the other jobs they did, which required them to have a clean police check. In the end, nothing was proven and her husband was cleared, and the carer was later informed that the boy had a history of making unsubstantiated accusations about carers, which was something they were not told before the child moved to live with them.

At least we were not in a situation like that with Maria, but I can't pretend things weren't difficult. Maria seemed to be a much angrier and more aggressive child than the seven-year-old girl we'd first met, and I woke up every morning wondering what the day would hold, and hoping she would not create trouble for herself, or for others.

10

'Break things in the house'

At this point in time, Jonathan and I were preparing to take Tom and Dillon abroad on holiday in the near future. We had no idea if Maria would still be with us by the time the trip took place, but when we agreed to take Maria on again I'd mentioned this to Social Services, just to be on the safe side.

'If it comes to it and you can amend the booking we will pay for you to take Maria too,' a social worker called Claire told me after speaking to several bosses. Claire was Maria's social worker now, and she was very young and inexperienced but very willing to please.

'Gosh, that's great news,' I'd said at the time, as this was unheard of to my knowledge. I was grateful to have this peace of mind, as of course I wouldn't have wanted to cancel our holiday, and nor would I have wanted to leave Maria out.

Now, however, I had an awful thought. What if we did take Maria on holiday and she ran off on us, like she did with Jonathan on the playing field? Imagine losing her in a foreign country. It didn't bear thinking about, but it was something that started to prey on my mind. If she could escape from a locked car and dart out of the house – two places where I thought she was safe and secure – what might she do in a busy public place? Jonathan and I would need eyes in the back of our heads.

Unfortunately, over the course of the next couple of weeks Maria ran off at least half a dozen times. One morning when her taxi arrived for school, she got into the cab, slid across the back seat and then got straight out of the other side, exiting onto the busy high street. Jonathan had to abandon the shop to chase Maria all the way down the high street and bring her back to the taxi. She pulled a similar trick when we took her to church on Saturday, running off down a back passage that fortunately led to a dead end. And when I took her to buy new underwear and some school shirts one afternoon she gave me the slip and hid in a changing room when I wasn't looking. Thankfully, a sharp-eyed store detective had seen what had happened and came to my aid as soon as he realised what Maria had done.

'I wondered what her game was!' he laughed. 'You're meant to be buying clothes in here, not playing hide and seek, young lady!' he said kindly.

Maria rolled her eyes and I thanked the guard profusely. My pulse had risen when I turned and saw Maria had gone, and I still felt in shock for some time afterwards and was very grateful the situation had been defused so quickly.

'Maria, you are too old for me to have to keep hold of you, so I need you to stay with me and stop this running away.'

'I can't help it.'

'You can't help it?'

'No. I ran off all the time from Gerry. He thought it was funny. He made me do it.'

89

'How could it be funny? It's dangerous for you to run off, wherever you are. It really is not funny, Maria. Your safety is my priority and I want you to please stop running off. It is not a game.'

That evening after school, the boys were watching a film that was rated fifteen and over. Jonathan and I never falter when it comes to following the guidelines on films, computer games and even music CDs. When you are dealing with children who have been through tough times and bad experiences, you have to be extremely careful not to trigger any memories that might cause them unnecessary upset. We trust the ratings given by experts and adhere to the guidelines very rigidly, as it is the best way of protecting the children in our care.

'Can I watch the film?' Maria asked.

I explained that she couldn't, as it was a fifteen, to which she replied, 'Gerry let me watch eighteens.'

'Gerry let you watch eighteens?'

'Yes, but I didn't always want to. He likes horror movies and I don't. He thinks it's funny to be scared. He tried to make me *really* scared one night.'

'He did?'

'Mmm.'

Maria went very quiet and appeared to suddenly freeze. She looked deep in thought and then she began to recite a story, very quietly, as she stared into space, her eyes glazed and beady-looking.

'*Psycho*. That was the name. I didn't like it. I hid behind the sofa and Gerry said I was a wimp. I pretended to watch but I didn't really. I put paper in my ears, so I couldn't hear.'

'Oh Maria, so you only pretended to watch, you didn't really see it, or hear it?'

'I tried, but it was hard not to. Then Gerry made me go in the bathroom.'

I'd seen *Psycho* once, many years earlier, and of course the famous shower scene immediately popped into my head. I think I almost knew what Maria was going to say before she said it, but I prayed I was wrong.

'Gerry came into the bathroom. He knew how to open the lock from the other side. I was scared 'cos he crept in and I could hear Frank and Casey laughing. Then Gerry started hitting the shower curtain with something. I screamed and saw it was a knife.'

'A knife?'

I felt sick and had a too-vivid image of this scene in my head.

'A plastic knife. Frank had it for Halloween. It had blood painted on it. It still scared me.'

'I'm sure it did.'

'They all thought it was funny, and when I cried Frank called me a crybaby. I hate him!'

The phone rang in the kitchen, interrupting us. I'd lost track of time, but it was Christine on the line, ready for one of her scheduled talks with Maria. I recognised her number as it appeared on the digital display below the handset.

Maria picked up the phone robotically, and then she began reciting a detailed list of everything she had done over the past few days, giving minute details, such as, 'The pen I used to write my story was one that belonged to the school. All the children use the same ones. Angela has lots of pens, but I don't need to take them to school. I showed Angela my story and she said it was very good. I like writing stories. I like school. I like English. We went to a water park at the weekend. Angela's mum played cards with me. We went shopping for new clothes. I got new socks.'

She sounded robotic again, and not at ease or even genuine. The truth was, even though Maria was still keen on reading and she did like to write, her schoolwork had gone rapidly downhill in the time she'd been living back home with her mum. She was frequently in detention or on report, and she had been in trouble for fighting with other children and swearing at a teacher.

During Maria's phone conversation with her mum, Jonathan came in and began to quietly put away some shopping he'd picked up on the way back from making an evening delivery. As he did so, all of a sudden, I noticed that Maria went very quiet and had an anxious expression on her face. She listened intently to her mum for a few minutes, saying nothing. Then, as if repeating something she'd just been told, Maria said in an expressionless way, 'Break things in the house.'

We were always careful not to ask Maria direct questions about anything that was said during the phone calls she had with her mother. Our role was to protect her and make sure she wasn't upset during these calls, not pry into private conversations between mother and daughter. But when this particular call came to an end I did gently ask what she meant when she said 'break things in the house'.

Maria looked startled when I spoke to her. I think she must have been so focused on what her mother was saying – and on relating her detailed list of events – that she had forgotten

Jonathan and I could hear what she was saying. And, after staring at me for a moment with a look of shocked apprehension on her face, she suddenly bolted for the door and ran off at breakneck speed, again heading down the side passage that led to the field at the back of our house.

'Not again!' Jonathan said, abandoning the shopping he was still putting away, grabbing his shoes from the hall cupboard and chasing after Maria once more.

'I'll stay here,' I said, partly because Jonathan was much faster on his feet than me, but also because Tom and Dillon were upstairs in the living room.

I fully expected Jonathan to return with Maria minutes later, as he had on the previous occasion when she shot over the field. I looked out of the window to see what was happening, but to my dismay there was no sign of Maria, and Jonathan was fast disappearing from view, right at the far end of the large playing fields, which were bordered by trees and bushes and had various paths and passageways leading in several different directions. I saw Jonathan stop and put his hand to his mouth, and realised he must be calling Maria's name. Then he looked all around him, clearly not knowing which way to turn.

'Boys!' I called up the stairs. 'Can you both come down please! I need your help.'

Tom and Dillon came down straight away and began putting their shoes on even before I'd finished telling them what had happened.

'We'll take one side each,' Tom said, as they darted down the passageway.

'I'll stay here in case she comes back!' I called. 'Don't go too far – come back soon if you can't find her! First of all, go and tell Jonathan you're helping!'

I stood at the window fretting as I watched the boys run up to Jonathan and then all three of them scatter in different directions. I wanted to chase with them but I dared not leave the house.

Fortunately, it was still light and I told myself Maria really could not have gone far and would soon be spotted and returned home safe and sound. A sudden memory of the time she nearly got run over in the McDonald's car park flashed in my head and I tried to push it away. *Surely she won't run across a road? Please don't come to any harm, Maria!*

It was a full fifteen minutes before Tom finally reappeared, from behind a hedgerow at the edge of the play area. Maria was by his side. I honestly could have cried when I saw the two of them walking back, and I ran out in my slippers to greet them as they neared the passage leading to our house.

Maria looked at the ground as Tom explained that he had found her hiding in old Mrs Moore's garden.

'I just had this feeling that that was where she was,' Tom said. 'We were talking about Mrs Moore the other day.'

He gave Maria a kind smile and I was pleased to see that he had taken on something of a big brother role, which he'd slipped into almost without me noticing over the past few weeks. Mrs Moore had died recently and it seemed that a few of the local kids had been playing in her overgrown garden, where she had an old shed with lots of interesting tools and gadgets inside that fascinated the kids.

'Good inside knowledge!' I said to Tom, as we all looked up

and saw Jonathan and Dillon running towards us. 'Come on,' I said, 'let's all get back inside. Thank you for your help, boys.'

Dillon wanted to know every detail of Maria's 'rescue' while Jonathan kept quiet and just gave me the nod that meant, 'Thank God. We'll talk about this later.'

Back in the kitchen I asked Maria if she'd like a cuddle, then wrapped my arms around her and told her that I wasn't angry with her and that she was safe with us.

Maria clearly had problems in her life and had issues with her mother and stepfather. Experience had taught me that I had not even heard the half of what went on in their family home. If Gerry thought it was funny to frighten a small girl by making her watch an adult horror movie and then scaring her with a plastic knife, what else was he capable of? And if Christine was capable of urging Maria to break things in our house, as I suspected she had, then what sort of a woman was she? Maria needed love and understanding. It must have been so confusing for her to grow up with role models like Gerry and Christine, not to mention Frank and Casey, who seemed to be complicit in their dad's mistreatment of Maria.

I made a note in my daily diary of what I'd heard Maria say on the phone to her mother, and I reported it later to our support social worker, as well as telling her about Maria running off again. When I was a younger and less experienced foster carer, I know I would have worried about admitting to Social Services that a child in my care had run away like that, in case I was judged unfairly or even investigated for failing in my duty. Now, though, I had the experience and self-belief to trust that the authorities would see that Jonathan and I had done nothing wrong. Thankfully they did. Both Jess and Claire offered nothing but support, and in fact Jess told me, 'Angela, you are doing a sterling job. You can't make your home a prison; please do not doubt yourself. We're extremely grateful you are persevering with this placement.'

The investigation into Christine and Gerry was still no closer to reaching its conclusion, it seemed, and so Social Services were grateful for all the help they could get in keeping Maria in foster care.

Very shortly after this incident, Jonathan and I were asked to listen on speakerphone to all the phone calls Maria had with her mother, so that we could monitor what was being said on both sides. We never did hear any more about whether Christine was confronted about the 'break things in the house' comment.

'Do you really think she was telling Maria to break things in *our* house?' I asked Jonathan when we talked about it one evening. 'To get back at us for some reason?'

'I don't know,' he said. 'I've been trying to make sense of it myself. Perhaps Christine thought that if Maria did break our things, we wouldn't want to look after her any more and then she'd be sent back to live at home.'

'Or maybe she just resents us,' I suggested, 'because Christine sees us as part of the establishment, lumped together with the social workers?'

Jonathan nodded sagely. 'Or it could just be that Christine wants Maria back so that she'll get the money that was cut from her family allowance when she was taken into care.'

Jonathan pulled a rueful face and added, 'I know that sounds like a harsh thing to say, but from what we heard about why she wanted Colin back, for his keep, it's not beyond the realms of possibility, is it?'

'No,' I said. 'Sadly, I've learned that when it comes to fostering, nothing is beyond the realms of possibility.'

11

'It's unusual for a girl so young . . .'

One day, when Maria and the boys were at school and we were in the flower shop, Jonathan laid an armful of dahlias on the counter and said, 'We can't take her with us, can we?'

I had been filling the tall, conical vases that ran the length of one wall of the shop with the flowers Jonathan was bringing in from the van, after a trip to one of our suppliers. I sighed and wiped the back of my hand across my forehead as I said, 'I've been thinking the same thing. It breaks my heart to have to admit it, but we just can't take the risk. I'm afraid of losing her every time we go out *here*. But what if it happened in another country?'

Maria's stay had extended into its second month and the holiday we had planned with the boys, to Portugal, was imminent. Unfortunately, Maria had continued to dart off from us, seemingly at any opportunity. Often it happened when we said no to a demand for Coke, crisps, sweets or whatever it was she'd decided she couldn't live without at that particular moment. We could be anywhere – out shopping, walking to town or just relaxing in the house – when Maria would suddenly turn on her heel and run off. I was constantly on my guard and, if I read the signs correctly, I'd grab hold of the back of her T-shirt just as she was about to bolt. I think some of my neighbours and customers must have wondered what on earth was going on, because whenever Maria was with me I was on high alert, only half listening to what other people were saying. Most of my attention was on Maria and what she might be planning, because the consequences of her running away and getting lost or injured didn't bear thinking about.

'Having Maria run away in Portugal is simply not a risk we can take, Angela,' Jonathan said regretfully. 'I didn't want to say anything to you until I'd examined the possibilities from every angle, to see if there was some way round it. But I haven't come up with anything yet. Will you speak to Claire and try to work something out?'

'I'll call her later,' I told him. 'Let's hope she can find somewhere for Maria to stay while we're away.'

This was an awful dilemma. We could not let the boys down and cancel the holiday, but we desperately didn't want to upset Maria either. I found myself wondering if there was any way Babs could have her granddaughter for the fortnight, but then again she had told me time and time again that she already had enough to cope with as Stanley needed so much care.

Claire was very understanding when I explained the situation to her on the phone later that morning. 'Don't worry, Angela,' she told me. 'I'm sure I can find somewhere for Maria to stay while you're away. I'll let you know as soon as I do.'

'Thanks. Will the promise Social Services made to pay for a holiday for her still stand if she does end up staying with us, so we can arrange to take her somewhere else in the future?'

I asked. 'Only I'd really like to be able to explain this to Maria, to soften the blow.'

'It sounds like a reasonable request,' Claire replied. 'I'll check and let you know about that too.'

'OK. Just one more thing. I don't want to interfere, but have you ever considered asking Maria's grandmother to provide respite care? I think that could be less disruptive for her, and of course we know it is definitely only for the fortnight we're away, so Babs would not have to worry about it being extended.'

There was a sharp intake of breath.

'No,' Claire said. 'There is a good reason for this, Angela, but it is not possible for Maria to live at her grandmother's house. We have looked into it and, well, the requirements aren't there, shall we say.'

My heart sank. What other secrets did Maria's family hold? And did this have something to do with Maria's puzzling refusal to speak to her nanny? I didn't quiz Claire as there was no point and it was not my place, and besides I had already mentioned to my social worker that Maria was refusing to speak to Babs. However, I found it infuriating not to be given more informa-tion, particularly as Maria was freely allowed to visit Babs, Stanley and her brother Colin, if she wanted to. Surely if there was an 'issue' with any member of the family, Maria should not be allowed to visit at all? I also thought about Babs's explanation about why she could not look after Maria, and I inevitably ques-tioned her honesty. If she had not been entirely truthful with me about this, what else had she lied about? It seemed that Babs and Christine thought little of telling untruths and keeping secrets, and I thought it was no wonder Maria had the behavi-our problems she did. In order to thrive, children need to be brought up with a strong moral code; they need to be taught the difference between right and wrong and they need to know the importance of behaving with honesty and integrity. Maria's family didn't seem to provide any of those things, which was such a pity, and so very difficult to put right.

As it turned out, Maria's previous foster carers agreed to have her while we were away. I was relieved that at least she wouldn't be going somewhere completely new, with people she didn't know at all. And once that had been agreed, it was just a case of telling Maria herself, which I did one evening just before we ate our meal.

I was not looking forward to this. I didn't want to disappoint Maria, but nor did I want to take any risks with her safety. Similarly, I didn't want to compromise the enjoyment of the holiday for the boys, and so I took the bull by the horns and told myself it was for the best, and I really did not have a choice.

Maria listened quietly. The words stuck in my throat, if I'm honest. Maria had never been on a holiday or seen the sea or a beach. In fact, before the family moved out of the area, she had never travelled more than a few miles from the town we lived in, which is where she was born. As I was explaining the situation I wanted to pull the words back into my mouth. I wished I could stay with her and Jonathan could take the boys to Portugal, but that wasn't the solution we wanted. It wouldn't be the same. Jonathan and I always worked in partnership and we didn't want to change that.

'It's OK, I didn't think it would happen anyhow,' Maria said with a shrug. 'I'm not bothered. If I stay with you longer, can I go on another holiday one day?'

Maria knew that Social Services had offered to pay for her trip because Christine had been cock-a-hoop about this, and so it was a reasonable question.

'Yes, of course you can,' I replied. 'As long as Jonathan and I are happy that you're going to be safe.'

'Do you promise?' she asked, looking at me intently, with her head on one side.

'Yes, I promise,' I said.

A couple of days later, Claire phoned to tell me that Social Services would keep their promise too, and that they would pay for Maria to go on holiday with us if the opportunity arose again, and of course if Maria's habit of running off had stopped.

We enjoyed a good holiday with the boys and Maria went off to the other foster carer's without a hitch. During this period, however, Maria's mother had been busy making complaints about us to Social Services over all sorts of things. She went mad about us not taking Maria on holiday, accusing us of being selfish and uncaring and making Maria feel unwanted, which was very unkind and hurtful. It seemed that Christine was not consulted about Maria going into respite care while we were away, but unfortunately it was not down to Jonathan and me to consult her. This was the job of Social Services, and we had no influence over how they chose to operate, but that didn't stop Christine blaming us for the situation. She didn't seem to care how she hurt us or made us feel, because she would openly criticise us when she was on the phone to Maria and knew we had it on loudspeaker and could hear every word.

Christine also complained about us dropping Maria at church and not staying for the service, despite the fact it had been agreed that we would take her to the door, make sure she was handed over to a vetted church official and collect her each time. Christine had accepted this in the beginning, but again this didn't stop her criticising us and trying to undermine us. When these complaints didn't make Social Services dance to Christine's tune, she fished around for anything she could find and she variously accused us of not giving Maria drinks when she asked (this meant we didn't give her the Coke and other fizzy drinks she wanted), not getting her to school on time (her taxi was occasionally late or held up in traffic), not taking care of her hair properly (even though Christine refused to let Maria have it cut shorter as she wished and had requested) and – incredibly – 'not allowing her to watch TV like the others'. When I questioned this last complaint, it emerged that Maria had mentioned to her grandmother the fact she was not allowed to watch the fifteen certificate film the boys had watched.

Not long after the holiday we had a placement meeting with Maria's social worker, plus Christine, Gerry, our support social worker and the head teacher from Maria's school, Mr Benson. Normally, that sort of meeting would have been held at the Social Services' office – the previous one had taken place there, minus Gerry – but for some reason this one took place at Maria's house. Jonathan and I had to travel there while Maria was at school. We weren't looking forward to it and I had no desire to meet Gerry properly in person, but of course we agreed to do as we were asked.

When I mentioned the meeting to Maria she gave me a wide grin, but I can't say her face lit up.

'That's good!' she said, somewhat unconvincingly, holding

her fixed smile. 'It's good that you are seeing Mummy and Gerry!'

I felt a pang of pain when I saw Maria go through what appeared to be an act. What exactly had happened to her at home, and why did she feel the need to pretend everything was fine when she really didn't need to in front of me?

'It's unusual for a girl so young to behave like Maria,' I commented to Jonathan.

'What do you mean?'

'Well, children of her age are normally easier to read. Remember little Kim? She hated her stepdad with a passion and, because she was only eight years old, her feelings were very obvious.'

'Yes, I see what you mean. Maria's not such an open book, is she? It's hard to tell what she really thinks and feels. That's a bit of a worry, isn't it?'

Maria maintained her apparently happy act when she got ready for school the next day.

'It'll be great for you to see Mummy,' she repeated, 'and Gerry! I wonder if Frank and Casey will be in. I *hope* so!'

Her supposed enthusiasm just didn't seem to ring true, and I must admit I was becoming increasingly nervous about how this meeting would go. Clearly, with an investigation taking place, her whole family could very well be on the defensive, and we already knew how Christine felt about Social Services and the 'lies' they supposedly told.

Unfortunately, when Social Services have intervened and removed a child from their parents, foster carers like us are often viewed as the 'enemy', colluding with the authorities. Of course, we have nothing to do with the decision to put a child in care, and we are only here to provide the care a child needs, but many parents can't or won't view it that way and, as I'd already started to work out, it seemed that Christine viewed Jonathan and I as part of the 'establishment' she despised.

12

'He made my skin crawl'

When we pulled up at Christine and Gerry's house I was pleased to see it was in a smart part of town and looked fairly well kept. It was a hot day, and the small front lawn was neatly cut and pansies and marigolds were blooming in hanging baskets either side of the front door.

Christine appeared, wearing a short sundress and large mirrored sunglasses so you couldn't see her eyes at all. She seemed friendly enough at first though, nodding and saying hello to us and telling us to come into the house, before unexpectedly making a pointed remark about Maria's hair.

'Have you been brushing it?' she asked me accusingly.

'Of course,' I said. 'Although it isn't easy to brush through as she does have a lot of tangles. We're coping though!'

Maria still had trouble sleeping and often tossed and turned in her bed, but I didn't mention this as I was sure it would only have antagonised Christine. Instead I tried to be as bright and breezy as possible, but Christine seemed hell-bent on scoring points against me.

'*I'm* the only one who's ever been able to do her hair properly,' she said.

I shared a discreet look with Jonathan. We'd seen this kind of behaviour many times before, with parents trying to prove their competence and reclaim their authority over their child. We never rose to it, of course, and in fact I always felt some sympathy for a parent in Christine's position. It must be very difficult to have your child taken into care, and in many cases the parents have been dealt a bad hand in life themselves and are not always to blame for their circumstances or their behaviour, which is very sad.

Christine led us through the house to the garden, where there was a table, some chairs and a small striped parasol, which she sat underneath. Sweltering in the sun were the two social workers and Mr Benson, the head teacher. Christine indicated that we should sit down on the chairs beside them.

Once the pleasantries and introductions were over, Christine called through to the house, asking Gerry to come outside. It was hard to read Christine on this particular day because of her sunglasses, but we had no such problem with Gerry as he made his feelings towards us very clear.

'Waste of time,' he muttered as he stalked out of the house in a dirty vest and tracksuit bottoms. 'Interfering busybodies.'

One of the social workers invited Gerry to sit down with us, but he said he'd prefer to stand and positioned himself on the other end of the patio, arms folded and staring at us.

Maria's social worker, Claire, led the meeting, spelling out that Social Services were still looking into Maria's case and that therefore they wanted her to stay with us for a little longer than originally anticipated. Jonathan and I readily agreed to this, and

I told the group, 'Maria seems to have settled in well, and we're very happy to have her stay with us a little longer.'

As I finished talking I heard Gerry snort. 'Settled in well,' he said, mimicking my voice. 'Oh we're *so* happy to have her!'

It was embarrassing to be mocked like this, but I bit my tongue and shook my head gently, indicating to Claire that I didn't want to confront it.

Mr Benson offered his support and ran through the problems Maria was having at school.

'We're accommodating her as much as we possibly can,' he said at one point.

'How very accommodating!' Gerry muttered, tut-tutting and shaking his head. 'We're all so happy and accommodating, we all want to do the best for Maria. My arse!'

'All right, Gerry,' Christine said, but he completely ignored her and continued to stare at us, which was making me feel increasingly uncomfortable.

Eventually, he strode across the garden and started pacing up and down beside us. You didn't have to have a degree in body language to be able to tell that he was incredibly hostile towards us, but just to make sure no one missed the point he continued to interject very rudely. At one point he fired a belligerent question at Jess, which she attempted to answer quietly and politely, despite Gerry's increasingly aggressive tone. He wasn't happy with the response and he then proceeded to ask Mr Benson, 'Which interfering cow of a teacher told you about Maria's bruises in the first place, anyhow? If it weren't for her, none of this would have happened. Some people need to learn when to keep their nose out. It was an accident. Read my lips – ac-ci-dent.'

The head teacher tried to contain the situation by explaining that the teacher in question was following guidelines and doing their job properly, to which Gerry replied, 'Only doing their job, only doing their job, only doing their job.' Even when we resumed our conversation and tried to move on, Gerry continued to repeat this phrase, like a stuck record.

Then he began to circle our chairs, repeating in an angry imitation of the head teacher's voice, 'Only doing their job, only doing their job.'

Claire asked Gerry if he would like to sit down and take part in the conversation we were trying to have, but instead of answering her he walked back across the grass to the other end of the garden, raised one arm in an imitation of a Nazi salute and shouted, '*Jawohl mein Führer,*' which he kept repeating over and over again, becoming more agitated each time he said it. Finally he spat, 'Only following orders – yes my leader! Yes sir, no sir, three bags full sir!'

Christine lit a cigarette and took a long drag, and then she started examining her deep pink nail polish, as if that were far more important than anything that was happening in her garden.

It was a frightening and deeply unpleasant experience. My heart was pounding and I could sense Jonathan tensing in his chair beside me. I was relieved when one of the social workers finally took the initiative and suggested we should continue the meeting at the nearest Social Services offices. Christine and Gerry both refused to come with us so we left without them, much to everyone's relief, I think.

The meeting at Social Services – held in a tiny waiting room as that was the only space available – concluded quickly. Both social workers, the head teacher, Jonathan and I were in agreement that we would maintain the current status quo as investigations continued. It was made clear to us, without going into details, that Maria's case may take a little longer to be dealt with than first anticipated, but Jonathan and I readily agreed that we would carry on as we were in the meantime, and that Maria was welcome to stay with us for as long as necessary.

When we were alone later Jonathan sighed deeply and unloaded about how he had felt in the company of Gerry.

'I can't imagine how Maria was able to live in that environment,' he said, shuddering. 'We were in Gerry's company for less than half an hour and it completely unnerved me.'

'And me. I felt scared, actually. I mean, when he was stalking around it felt like he might erupt at any minute.'

Jonathan nodded. 'I hate to say it because I prefer to look for the good in people, but I get the sense that he's someone who hasn't any boundaries, and that there's nothing he wouldn't do if he felt like it. I can't see any good in him at all I'm afraid – in fact he made my skin crawl like nobody ever has before.'

Hearing this made the hairs on the back of my neck stand up because Jonathan is not given to making statements like that. He has a naturally generous nature and being critical of a person is not something he does easily or lightly.

'Poor Maria,' I said, and I also gave a shudder. 'I can't imagine how she lived with Gerry. It must have been awful. I know it's not up to us, but I really hope she doesn't go back there.'

13

'I don't need to tell her'

Christine failed to turn up for Maria's next placement meeting – held approximately six weeks later – despite all the complaints she continued to make about how her daughter was being cared for by Jonathan and me, the school and Social Services in general. Christine's excuse was that she couldn't get into town, which was where the next meeting was being held because of how the first meeting had gone at her house.

'That wasn't true,' Babs revealed to me afterwards, in her usual gossipy fashion. Despite the fact Maria was still adamant she didn't want to see her nanny, I continued to see Babs, as she would often call round when Maria was at school. On this occasion Babs had popped into the flower shop, supposedly shopping for a gift for a friend, although she didn't actually buy anything.

'Christine was actually *in* town at the time when the meeting was taking place,' Babs informed me. 'She told me there wasn't any reason why she couldn't attend. I'm afraid she was just being her usual awkward self!'

This was not a good situation and I felt a pang of worry in the pit of my stomach. Maria's life was already complicated, and she didn't need her mother being disruptive and uncooperative like this. What was she trying to achieve? It didn't make sense to me, because what good was this behaviour to Maria?

I tactfully mentioned the fact Babs had not seen Maria for a while, as I'd done several times, but Babs gave the same response she always gave. 'Kids!' she said, shrugging her shoulders and raising her eyebrows. 'I don't know what goes on in Maria's head, but she'll come round, all in her own good time!'

Most children of Maria's age would not have been aware the placement meetings were even happening, let alone who attended, but she always asked me and wanted to know exactly what was going on.

'Did Mummy go to the placement meeting?' she asked me directly. 'Claire said there was another meeting. I asked her, last time she came to see me.'

'Did you? Well, your mum couldn't make the meeting I'm afraid.'

'Oh,' she said. 'And I'm reading my Bible.'

'I know you've been reading your Bible, sweetheart,' I said. 'I'm sure your mum and Gerry would be pleased. Perhaps you could tell your mum all about it next time you talk on the phone?'

Unfortunately, her mum's phone calls had dwindled and she hadn't heard from her for weeks, but I was hopeful there would be another call soon.

'She already knows I read it every single night, it's OK. I don't need to tell her.'

This seemed a slightly odd thing to say, but I didn't press Maria. I left it, and that night I found Maria poring over her

Bible. She seemed to have got more and more engrossed in it as each week passed, and most nights she read it in favour of her fiction.

She told me she loved her Bible classes too, and I believed her, because of the way she behaved when she attended them. Sometimes she was in a temper about something on the way to her classes, but as soon as she entered the room where they were held she became extremely calm and behaved impeccably. It was as if a switch had been flicked, which was then sometimes flicked back again as soon as the class was over. It was unnerving to witness. Maria would emerge from the class looking the image of sweetness and light, and as soon as she was alone with Jonathan and me again she would usually kick off and have a tantrum, often picking up from exactly the same point where she had left off an hour earlier.

'Do you think she's scared of the people at church?' I asked Jonathan after the same thing had happened a couple of times. 'They all *seem* very nice and they've gone out of their way to fit in with what suits us best, but Maria seems to be afraid of letting them see her behaving badly.'

'I was wondering the same thing,' Jonathan said. 'They are really good with her though, and they do genuinely seem to want to do whatever is in her best interests. Maybe some gentle questioning would be in order.'

The following Saturday, when I picked her up after church, I asked Maria if she'd enjoyed the service.

'It was OK,' she said. 'I like it when we sing the songs. The piano's a bit rubbish though, and the lady who plays it has really short fingers. She crashes down on the keys as if she's trying to break them!'

'Well, at least your Bible study seems to be going very well and I'm glad you seem interested. It's funny, isn't it, how much easier it is to do something we find interesting than something like . . .'

'Maths,' Maria interrupted, and we both laughed. Then her expression became serious again as she added, 'But I have to do the Bible study whether I like it or not, you know. He sees everything I do.'

I assumed Maria was talking about God, and I allowed her the space to say something else if she wanted to, but she then changed the subject and asked if we were doing anything later on in the day.

'Actually, yes! We're having a barbecue. My mum's coming over. Would you like that?'

'Yes!' she said. 'Can we do toasted marshmallows?'

'I don't see why not. Come on, let's get to the shops.'

Maria helped me prepare for the barbecue, and when my mum arrived she ran up to her and started chatting away. They'd got to know each other by now and seemed to get along well, even though my mum always did that typical thing of saying how she was growing so quickly, and asking how she was getting on at school.

'I don't like maths or PE, but I like reading and writing,' Maria said this time.

'I know all about your reading!' Mum said, as she'd babysat once or twice when Jonathan and I had to go to training evenings. Mum had been passed by Social Services to do this many years earlier and it was a great help to us. She generally enjoyed herself too, playing cards and board games as well as reading with the younger children. She was particularly impressed by Maria's reading skills, and she had also started to teach Maria to crochet, as one night Mum had brought a pattern and some wool with her and Maria was really interested to learn.

'But tell me, Maria, why don't you like PE? I used to *love* it when I was girl.'

Maria giggled. 'I bet you did those funny old-fashioned things, like hockey.'

'I did, actually! Don't you play hockey?'

'No. We do netball. But mostly we have to do gymnastics, and I hate it. I think it's stupid the way the girls have to prance around the gym "doing gymnastics".'

She said the last two words with exaggerated sarcasm, in what I assumed was supposed to sound like her PE teacher's voice. 'And while we "*do* gymnastics" in one gym, the boys are in another gym using the trampoline. Why can't we do that too? It's racism, and it's not fair. I *hate* PE.'

'Discrimination, I think you mean, dear.'

'Dis-crim-in-ation,' Maria copied. 'That's it. We should all be in the same nest!'

'I agree, you should all be in the same boat,' Mum said sensitively, not wanting to correct Maria's language twice in such a short space of time.

Jonathan was listening to all this, and he could see that Maria was getting a little hot under the collar, so he tried to do something about it.

'I used to love PE when I was a young boy,' he said. 'I was quite good at it too. In fact, I could stand on my hands for at least five minutes.'

'Can you do it now?' Maria asked him excitedly, having just learned to do a handstand herself for a second or two before toppling over. 'Go on, Jonathan, do it! Do it!'

'OK. Stand back and I'll show you.' Jonathan put the barbecue fork down on the table beside him and rubbed his hands together. Then, with a look of intense concentration on his face, he ran across the grass for a few steps, crouched down, put his hands under his toes and said, 'See. I'm standing on my hands.'

'I don't get it.' Maria looked puzzled for a moment, and then the penny dropped. 'Jonathan, you're silly!' she said, before getting to her feet and showing him how to do a *proper* handstand.

I thought Jonathan had managed to prevent Maria getting herself into a bad mood about school and all the things she didn't like, but unfortunately it wasn't that easy. After she'd performed her handstand, and a cartwheel just for good measure, she plonked herself down and started to complain once more about PE.

'I don't like PE or *any* of the subjects. I don't like school at all,' Maria said.

Mum raised an eyebrow and I knew she was itching to remind Maria that she liked English, but over the years Mum had learned not to intervene with the children as much as she felt naturally inclined to. Mum was never party to the problems and issues any of the children had and we never discussed anything about their backgrounds or their private lives, but she understood very well that the children we fostered often needed careful and sensitive handling.

The truth was things hadn't been going well at school for Maria, and I'd been called up to the school several times by the extremely patient head teacher. The problems usually centred around what the teachers described as 'temper tantrums', but on several occasions Maria had climbed out of windows or bolted out of the main doors, causing panic and prompting teachers or classroom assistants to give chase.

One of the issues I discussed with the head teacher was tiredness. Maria often complained to me that she had trouble sleeping, although fortunately the nightmares she'd had at the age of seven seemed to have stopped. I explained to the head teacher that the journey to school by taxi took forty-five minutes, which meant Maria had to get up earlier than most children, and so it was perhaps no wonder she was tired.

'And unfortunately, children who have suffered trauma in their life often experience sleep problems,' I added, 'as I'm sure you are aware.'

The head nodded. 'As well as being prone to hyperactivity, mood swings, disruptive behaviour, temper tantrums and perhaps even depression.'

It was my turn to nod. 'Indeed,' I said, feeling very glad he understood. Not all teachers I have encountered are so well informed, and in the past I've had to fight against primary-school children being excluded because of their poor behaviour, arguing that it is not their fault and the very last thing they need is to have their routine and education taken away.

In view of all the trouble Maria had been getting into at school, we feared the worst when Maria's form teacher phoned one day.

'How are you?' I said anxiously.

'Fine,' the teacher replied breezily, which came as a pleasant surprise. 'It's nothing to worry about, Mrs Hart. I'm ringing because an outing has been arranged for the class that involves a walk through a country park.'

'Oh, I see.'

'And the thing is, because Maria has been doing a lot of running off, bolting out of the classroom and so on, we wondered if either you or Mr Hart would be able to come on the trip with her, as an extra pair of hands?'

I said we could certainly arrange that, and Jonathan and I decided that he was the best person for the job, as he was faster on his feet.

When the day came, Maria was actually quite excited to have Jonathan with her, and her behaviour was impeccable.

'Funny, isn't it?' the teacher mused. 'You never know which Maria is going to turn up, do you?'

Jonathan smiled. 'Angela and I have said the same ourselves. I'm pleased you seem to know her so well.'

From that point on, whenever there was any extra-curricular activity or a sports day, Jonathan or I attended as a 'class helper', although in reality Maria was our sole focus. One of the teachers had let slip that had we not been willing to assist, Maria would not have been allowed to take part in some activities. I accepted that the school had to put Maria's safety first, just as we did, but it was still quite upsetting to think that such a young girl might be left out because of her behaviour, which was largely no fault of her own.

14

'It doesn't make any sense'

Another issue soon arose, and this one involved Babs. I still hadn't got to the bottom of why Maria wouldn't talk to her nanny or visit her like she used to. This was bothering me, particularly as it had gone on for months and reached the point where Maria was refusing to even speak about her grandmother. For instance, if I mentioned that Babs had called in for a cup of tea or that I'd bumped into her in town, Maria would blank me and pretend she hadn't heard what I was saying. I knew Babs had been ill with flu for several weeks and when she was finally better I thought it might be a good time to try to nudge Maria into seeing her grandmother again.

One afternoon, after the taxi had brought Maria home from school and we were sitting together in the kitchen while she drank a glass of milk, I discussed the fact Babs had been poorly and I asked Maria if she'd like me to call her nanny and arrange a visit. Of course, I hadn't forgotten what the social worker had said to me about there being a good reason Maria could not live with her grandparents and brother Colin, but I had to trust Social Services' decision that visits to the home were safe, and I felt Maria's relationship with Babs in particular was an important one to maintain.

'Would you like me to give your nanny a call and fix up a time for a visit?' I asked.

At first Maria ignored me, but I carried on. 'I know she'd love to see you, and I'm sure it would cheer her up, after she's been ill. Or you can phone her yourself if you'd rather.'

'No thanks,' Maria said, staring straight ahead and wiping the white moustache off her top lip with the back of her hand.

I was disappointed by her answer, but didn't say anything more about it until the next day, when I said, casually, 'Just let me know if you want to phone your grandparents at any time, won't you, sweetheart? I'm sure they'd be glad to hear from you.'

'I'm fine thanks,' she said, almost irritably this time and in a tone of voice that indicated quite clearly that she didn't want to talk about it.

I hadn't ever seen Maria interact much with her grandfather, but her relationship with her nanny had always been close. I simply couldn't understand her apparent indifference to my suggestion that she might like to contact her. What was even more difficult to understand was Maria's reaction when we saw her grandmother in town one day.

It was a Saturday morning and, after picking her up from church, Jonathan and I had taken Maria into town to buy her some new shoes. I was just about to push open the door of the small, family-run department store Jonathan and I have been going to for years, when I saw Babs and Colin walking along the high street towards us. Colin spotted us at almost the same moment, and I was struck by the delighted expression on his face when he saw his little sister. He smiled and said hello, but instead of answering him and without even acknowledging her grandmother, let alone giving her a hug as she used to do when she greeted her, Maria suddenly darted into the store as fast as her legs would take her.

Babs looked surprised, and then hurt, and I was completely bemused. Jonathan immediately dashed after Maria, and when I got through the door, followed by Babs and Colin, I could see that Maria was crouching down behind a counter. She was clearly trying to hide, but you could see the top of her head.

'I'm sorry,' I said to Babs and Colin. 'I don't know what she's doing. Do you want to wait while I . . . ?'

'No, it's all right, Angela, love,' Babs replied. 'Kids, hey! Maybe I could drop by your house tomorrow to see her?'

'Of course,' I answered. 'We're going out in the afternoon. But come and have a cup of coffee late morning, if you can.'

Maria was still crouching behind the counter, pretending to be reattaching the Velcro strap on her trainers, when I caught up with her. She seemed upset, and she kept looking around her, almost as though she was holding her breath waiting for something really bad to happen.

'Didn't you see your grandmother and Colin?' I asked gently.

'Yes.' She sighed as she said it, the way she often did when she was annoyed or uncomfortable.

'Didn't you want to talk to them?'

'No. I don't have to if I don't want to. It's my choice.'

Baffled by her response, but not wanting to force her into a confrontation, I answered, simply, 'Yes, I suppose it is. Well, I think the department we want is on the first floor. Come on, let's go . . .'

Maria stood up cautiously, looking over her shoulder and staying very quiet as we made our way to the escalator.

'It doesn't make any sense,' Jonathan said later. 'I mean, it wasn't a game, was it? She was serious.'

'No. No, it definitely wasn't a game,' I answered. 'Maria was clearly upset, and actually seemed quite scared.'

Unfortunately, Maria shut herself in her bedroom when her grandmother came to the house to see her the next day.

'Never mind,' Babs said. 'I'll stay for a coffee anyhow.'

She installed herself at the kitchen table and chatted about the weather, the state of the pavement outside the local super-market, the price of petrol and goodness knows what else. The only topic she avoided was the rather important one of the family, and Christine. She made no reference whatsoever to her daughter, or to Stanley or Colin for that matter. If you didn't know better you'd have thought she'd come to visit me simply as a friend, and that we didn't have Maria in common.

When Babs eventually left, after drinking a second cup of coffee and sampling one of my home-made scones, she made no attempt to call up to Maria or try to make her change her mind about seeing her. I thought that was a bit odd, as I think I would have done that if I were in Babs's shoes, but then again Babs was a very different person to me. She seemed to live in quite a superficial world and didn't tend to analyse situations, or dwell on the emotional impact of scenarios like this.

'Give me a call when Maria gets over it,' Babs said as she left. 'Whatever "it" is!'

She chuckled and tottered off, as if she didn't have a care in the world.

However much Jonathan and I racked our brains, we couldn't think of any reason why Maria would start avoiding someone she had always loved and trusted. In fact, as far as we were aware, Babs had been the only constant source of kindness and affection throughout the many tumultuous, traumatic events of Maria's young life. It was heartbreaking to have Maria avoid her grandmother like this, but there was nothing we could do except make it clear to Maria that she could talk to us about it, and we were here to help if she needed to discuss anything at all. She said she didn't want to, so all we could do was hope that whatever it was that was making Maria react that way would eventually come to light, so that it could be talked through and dealt with.

15

'I've got the gift'

One day, Maria's social worker, Claire, rang to tell me that Christine had put in a complaint to Social Services because she said we weren't allowing Maria to phone her.

'But *she's* supposed to phone Maria,' I said, baffled and irritated, 'and she doesn't always call when she has arranged to!' The truth was that Maria had called her mum on numerous occasions, but Christine hadn't answered the phone, or responded to the messages Maria left for her.

I imagined Christine might be causing trouble about the phone calls because she had to be on speakerphone with either Jonathan or I listening in, which clearly wasn't ideal for her.

'It seems like the same old story,' I lamented to Jonathan. 'Christine is twisting the truth and trying to blame other people for the problems in her life, but the fact is she caused this situation in the first place!'

After the 'break things in the house' remark that Maria had seemed to repeat when she was on the phone to her mum, there actually were a few unexplained breakages in the house. For instance, the toilet-roll holder became unhinged, as if someone had tried to pull it off, so it was hanging down at an angle. I found the handle of a mug that I'd had for years, bought by one of my former foster children for Mother's Day, chipped so badly I could no longer use it. And one morning I came down to make breakfast and discovered the freezer door had been left open all night with a drawer pulled out, so I had to throw quite a lot of food away.

We had no proof that Maria was responsible for any of those three things, and it could have been a complete coincidence that they happened in the wake of that phone call, but of course it did cross our minds whether Maria was deliberately causing damage. I was cross with Christine for making me suspicious of Maria like this, because it's important to see a child in a positive light and to look for the good in them above all else.

After I explained to Claire about the fact Christine didn't call when she was supposed to, we then heard that Christine had claimed she couldn't afford to phone her daughter.

'I see,' I said patiently. 'Well, we don't mind paying for the calls at all. In fact, as I've said, we've always made it plain to Maria that she can use the phone to call her mum.'

After that it was agreed that Maria would phone her mum at 6.30 every Thursday evening after Bible classes, but that didn't really work either. Despite the fact Christine had chosen the time herself, she rarely picked up the phone when Maria called. I found it very upsetting to see Maria standing there, clutching the receiver, listening to it ring and ring and then trying not to sound as disappointed as she clearly was when she left a mumbled message for her mum.

On the occasions when she did manage to speak to her mother, it was even more heartbreaking. Maria did not look at ease at all, and she would sit there with her shoulders hunched as she reeled off a list of every single thing she'd done – every meal she'd eaten, what time she'd eaten it, every television programme she'd watched, every card or board game we'd played with her and who had won, who she had played with in the park behind the house – literally, everything. Her eyes would be closed and she looked to be in deep concentration as she tried to remember every detail. Whenever Christine made a snide remark, as she often did, Maria would shut her eyes really tightly, as if she was trying to block it out.

'You did crochet with Angela's mum? Well that doesn't sound much fun!' was a typical Christine comment. 'Board games on a Friday night? Aren't you bored living there, babe?'

Maria would choose her words carefully. I could tell she wanted to please her mother and agree with her point of view, but Maria didn't want to offend Jonathan and me, and the truth was she usually thoroughly enjoyed doing crochet and playing board games.

'It's OK,' she'd say. 'I'm fine, Mum, don't worry.'

The calls would always last for a minimum of twenty minutes and Maria seemed drained at the end of them as she did most of the talking, until she had completely run out of things to say.

It was impossible not to notice that Christine didn't ever say anything during the phone calls she had with Maria to suggest that she felt any real affection for her. It was horrible seeing the anxiety on the little girl's face as she tried to answer her mother's questions about what she'd been doing. They weren't the friendly, interested sort of questions you would normally ask a child, and it was clear that Maria found it very stressful having to recite her carefully memorised list of events, which only ever seemed to gain any approval from her mother if they could be interpreted in some way as being negative, or could be twisted in a way that reflected badly on Jonathan and me, our home or Social Services.

Unbelievably, Christine then went on to make yet another complaint to Social Services, this time because she claimed that the calls Maria made to her weren't lasting long enough.

It was a claim that was easily refuted by our phone bills, which showed quite clearly that all the calls Maria made to her mother's number either lasted a few seconds, when she left a message as the phone was not picked up, or for between twenty and forty minutes when the calls were answered. So then Christine complained once more about the fact that either Jonathan or I listened in, but again this was an accusation I shouldn't have needed to defend, as Social Services had made this rule.

During the period when all this was taking place, Maria's social worker, Claire, moved to another town. Unfortunately, the new social worker who took over from her, Rebekah, seemed to take Christine's side and came across as being critical of Jonathan and me whenever she presented us with Christine's latest complaint.

'But we were *told* to listen in to the phone calls,' I said, trying not to sound as affronted by her tone of voice as I really felt. 'I don't have a *personal* interest in hearing what Christine's saying. In fact, there are plenty of other things I could be doing to occupy my time, as I'm sure you can imagine. However, it was a stipulation imposed by Social Services, which I expect you already know, as you'll have read the records and reports in Maria's case file.'

'Yes, well ... I'm sure you can understand the way the mother feels,' she said.

'And I'm sure *you* can understand why listening to the phone calls was thought to be necessary, for the child's sake,' I retorted.

It wasn't the fact that the social worker seemed to be entirely on Christine's side, without knowing the details of the case, that incensed me so much as her apparent criticism or even condemnation of *our* behaviour, which was guided by what we had been told to do. Even though Jonathan and I had our reservations about Christine because of what we'd seen and heard about her, we did everything we could to support her so that she retained a relationship with her daughter, for Maria's sake.

However, despite my irritation with whatever the social worker said, I always bit my tongue as best I could, though it was not always easy.

It turned out that Christine had also complained to Rebekah that I was 'confrontational', which was definitely not the case when it came to interacting with Maria's mother. I take my role as a foster carer very seriously indeed, and so does Jonathan. It doesn't matter how difficult, obstructive or downright rude a parent may be; I never lose sight of the fact that being difficult, obstructive or rude in return will not only have absolutely no effect on the parent, but might create a pull in the child's mind between the mother or father they love, however badly they've been treated at home, and the foster carer they ought to be able to feel safe with.

Most of the social workers we've dealt with over the years have been professional, reliable, reasonable, experienced and extremely hard working. Sometimes, though, you come across one who is easily manipulated by people like Maria's mother, who've had a whole lifetime of practice. Rebekah was certainly like that, and I know that some other foster carers found her attitude unhelpful too. In fact, she didn't last in the job for very long, which was perhaps for the best. Foster carers need to feel supported by the system, not under unnecessary scrutiny from it.

Through Babs, I started to gradually have more of an insight into Christine's world and personality. Babs loved a good 'chinwag', as she called it, and if you caught her in the right mood – or perhaps I should say 'wrong' mood – she could talk until the cows came home, and didn't seem to have much of a filter on what she was saying.

Considering I was Maria's foster carer, and that there was an ongoing investigation into Christine and Gerry, you'd have thought Babs would have been cautious in what she said about her daughter, but that wasn't the case at all. Mind you, I knew that Babs herself was not averse to calling Social Services if the mood took her, so I suppose this was not surprising.

'Christine only seemed to care about Maria until she reached the toddler phase,' she told me as she dunked a succession of chocolate fingers into her tea one afternoon when Maria was at school. 'She was very good with her when she was a baby – and she was like that with Colin too. Far more interested in babies. But as soon as they got to the age of four or five, when they started going to school and developing their own personalities, she lost interest.'

'What a shame,' I said. 'I wonder why.'

'I wish I knew. Maria was always hungry when she came to visit us,' Babs went on.

My heart sank.

'The first thing she'd do when she came through the front door was go into the kitchen and start raiding the cupboards, looking for something to eat. One time she tried to eat dried noodles from a pot, not realising you had to add hot water!'

The more I heard, the more I had my doubts about whether Maria should be allowed to ever live back with her mum and stepdad. Of course, my opinion would not sway the decision Social Services and the courts would ultimately come to, and all I could do was keep my eyes and ears open, and record anything I felt the social workers ought to know about, including things Babs said.

One incident I told Social Services about was a strange phone call Maria had with her mother one Thursday evening. The conversation started off as usual, with Maria reciting everything she'd done, in fine detail.

'. . . then Angela combed my hair because it was all tangly. She used the tangle spray and it didn't take long. I had a purple clip today, my favourite!'

'Oh, that old thing? I know Angela got it for you, love, but I've got a nicer one I'll give you, one you'll like much better.'

'OK. Then the taxi came and it was long.'

'Long?'

'I mean, the journey to school is always long, but the taxi was a bit late so it was really long today.'

'Couldn't Angela take you if the taxi is late?'

Maria stared intently at the floor. She was clearly embarrassed by her mum's question, as it was said in a rude tone of voice, and the intention was obviously to try to undermine me and the way I was caring for Maria.

'Er, I had PE today but I hated it.'

'I knew you were going to say that. It was gymnastics, wasn't it?'

'Yes, how did you know?'

'It's my gift, Maria, don't you remember? I've got the gift. Never forget that. Maybe you will have it too, when you are older.'

Maria appeared to freeze for a moment and then she quickly said, 'Oh, just a minute, Mum. I think Angela wants to use the phone.'

I was sitting quietly in the kitchen with a magazine open on the table and hadn't said anything. But without turning to look at me, Maria said out loud, 'You need the phone, don't you Angela?' Then she said into the receiver, 'Yup, sorry Mum. I'll speak to you next week,' and abruptly ended the call before Christine had a chance to object.

Maria obviously felt embarrassed by what she'd done and avoided catching my eye. I didn't want to make her feel any worse, so I just gently told her that she could talk to me about her mum, or anything that might be troubling her.

'OK,' she said, but then changed the subject.

Inevitably, though, Christine made yet another a complaint to Social Services, this time claiming – with some justification under the circumstances – that I was cutting short her phone calls with Maria.

Despite her various complaints and apparent resentment when Maria was excited about something she'd done with us, we did manage to remain on reasonably good terms with Christine. It was difficult sometimes, particularly on the many occasions when she seemed to be intent on being as obstruct-ive as possible. But it was important to keep the peace and remain on civil terms, for Maria's sake, which as far as Jonathan and I were concerned was the only thing that really mattered.

As we were to discover in the months that followed, how-ever, it sometimes seemed as though everything was con-spiring to make it as difficult as possible for us to do what we believed to be the right thing for Maria.

16

'Are you looking forward to coming home?'

There was a message on our answerphone one day, from Gerry's mother Cherie.

Jonathan and I had met her just the once, very briefly, when she spotted Maria in town, as we were doing a bit of shopping, and came over to say hello.

'We're coming to see Maria when she gets home from school,' Cherie said on the message after reminding me abruptly who she was.

After I'd listened to the message, I went into the flower shop to talk to Jonathan.

'I assume "we" means her and her husband,' he said, when I told him about the message. 'I know we don't have any reason to expect the stepfather's parents to cause any problems, but I think I'd better be there when they come, just in case his mother's uncompromising tone is an indication that the son is a chip off the parental block! Barbara will look after things here, I'm sure. First, though, I think you should call Social Services to ask their advice.'

'Good idea,' I agreed. But I had only just walked back into the house when the doorbell rang. As soon as I opened the front door, Maria's step-grandmother Cherie, followed closely by her husband Clive, pushed past me and walked into the hallway.

'Oh, hello!' I said. 'I didn't expect you to be here so soon.'

'You got the message though?'

'Yes, but only just. Do you want to come through? Maria's in the kitchen. Shall I make some tea?'

'Thanks,' they said, making no attempt or offer to take their shoes off, even though I was removing mine and putting my slippers on. We had a rule in the house that nobody wore shoes, to help keep it clean.

Cherie and Clive were fairly polite in their manner but I still felt uneasy, not having run this past Social Services. I hadn't even been aware that Cherie had my phone number, and I had no idea what her relationship with Maria was like. Despite this, instinct told me that it would be foolish now, and possibly counterproductive, to risk alienating them and giving them a reason to create a scene that might upset Maria or ultimately antagonise Christine and Gerry.

Fortunately, Jonathan had followed me into the house, so we all gathered in the kitchen together, where Maria and Tom were playing a game on his laptop. As soon as I could be certain that no one else would see me doing it, I smiled gratefully at Jonathan to let him know how glad I was that he was with me. He nodded discreetly and I knew he had the same uneasy feelings about this visit, but also shared my view that it would have been wrong to be anything but polite and welcoming.

Unfortunately, Maria's face was a picture when she saw them.

'Hello Maria, my babba!' Cherie gushed, throwing her arms around the startled little girl.

'Hi!' Maria managed. The colour had drained from her cheeks and written all over her face was the question, 'What are *you* doing here?'

Tom excused himself and left the room, and I didn't blame him. The atmosphere was suddenly tense. In fact, it was as if a cloud had descended over our kitchen, casting a dark, ominous shadow above our heads.

'I've come to tell you not to worry, Maria. We'll get you back. Don't you worry about it. They won't keep you in care. There's no reason for it. You'll be going home soon, don't you worry.'

Maria looked very uncomfortable, and as soon as Cherie had said her piece Maria looked back at the game she'd been playing and didn't say anything.

'Do you understand, Maria?'

Maria continued to look at her computer game and clearly had no intention of engaging in this conversation. I could see that, but Cherie seemed convinced that Maria simply hadn't understood, and so she became even more determined to get her message across.

'You'll be out of here soon,' Cherie said, raising her voice. Glancing at Jonathan and me, she went on, 'No disrespect, but you don't belong here, Maria. You should be at home, there's no reason to keep you away. We're fixing it. It'll all be better soon. Don't worry!'

I'd walked over to the kettle but decided not to make a pot of tea after all, despite having offered. This was unacceptable behaviour in my book, and I had to do my best to get Cherie and her husband out of our house as quickly and diplomatically as possible.

'Goodness me, I hadn't realised the time, Cherie. I hope you don't mind but I'll have to get on with the dinner now, we've a lot to do this evening and I need to help Maria with her homework.'

Cherie barely acknowledged me, but then made another, rather bizarre, attempt at getting through to Maria. Even Clive looked a bit nonplussed, as Cherie appeared to have a lightbulb moment and announced triumphantly, 'Just think of yourself as being like the boy in that film . . . Oh, what's the name of that film?' She turned to her husband as she asked the question, but he just shrugged, and a moment later she answered it herself. '*Goodnight Mister Tom*, that was it!' She sounded jubilant. 'Do you remember, Maria? He gets sent away from London during the war and then he goes back to live with his mum.'

'Well, maybe that's not the best . . .' I interjected, my memory of the film being that the child had some very traumatic experiences, which I didn't want Maria to think might have some bearing on *her* situation. Now that she had warmed to her theme, however, Maria's step-grandmother wasn't about to let the subject drop.

'That's it!' she said again. 'You're just like one of those refugees. So you don't need to be scared, because we'll definitely get you back.'

Fortunately, however, Maria was no longer paying any attention at all to what Cherie was saying and was completely engrossed in catching characters in her computer game. At least that was the impression she gave.

I decided to tentatively ask Cherie if Social Services had agreed to this visit, as I suspected they hadn't and I thought that might be a subtle way of getting Cherie to leave sooner rather than later.

In a tone of voice that conveyed very clearly the fact that she didn't care what might or might not be 'allowed', she replied, 'We are Maria's grandparents. We have a right to see our grandchild.'

Fortunately, after then begrudgingly making a little bit of small talk with us, Cherie took the hint and left, with Clive following behind. I was very relieved when they had gone. I got the sense that Cherie's behaviour might be almost as erratic and unpredictable as her son's, and although Jonathan was incredibly polite to them, I knew without asking that he had the same feeling.

I left Maria and Jonathan busy together in the kitchen while I went upstairs to the living room to phone Social Services and report what had happened, as we were bound to do. It turned out that Cherie and her husband should not have had any contact with Maria while her case was being investigated, which I had suspected. I reassured the duty social worker that the visit had been brief, we did not leave Maria alone with her step-grandparents and that we had felt, in the circumstances, it was best not to cause a scene that might have upset Maria.

Social Services offered us complete support, thank goodness, although I was not told specifically why the step-grandparents were denied access. Following this visit Cherie and her husband were reminded that one of the conditions of the voluntary care order was that *all* contact with Maria had to be prearranged and supervised and that any visits that were agreed upon were not, under any circumstances, to take place at our house.

The most important thing in any situation like that is always the safety of the child. We would have asked the step-grandparents to leave if Maria had been at all upset, and we also would have phoned the police if they hadn't done so without arguing. Fortunately, as things turned out, Maria didn't seem unduly bothered by the visit, and I'm very glad to say the incident wasn't ever repeated.

Learning to deal with the families of children has been an ongoing learning curve for us, ever since we started fostering. Jonathan and I sometimes talk about our early days almost thirty years ago, when I first decided I wanted to do fostering and he agreed to give it a try.

One of the things we look back on with amazement now is how naive we both were and how straightforward we thought it would be. What we assumed would happen would be that we would take a child into our loving home and they would be as happy to live with us as we were to have them. Then, when whatever problem had precipitated their stay in care was solved, they'd go home again, and we'd repeat the process with another child. It didn't ever work like that, of course, for a whole multitude of reasons, which seem so obvious to us now, but which we hadn't taken into account at all when we started fostering all those years ago.

Something else we hadn't even considered was the fact that children's families can sometimes cause far more problems than the children themselves. In those early days, we didn't think about the parents and grandparents who don't want to look after their children, the ones who aren't allowed to, or the ones who don't know how to and consequently feel bad about themselves if someone else succeeds where they believe they've failed.

It didn't even cross our minds that when some parents see their children's lives being turned around by someone else, their instinct might be to manipulate everyone involved – telling the social worker one thing, the child another and the foster carers something else – in the hope that the placement will break down, thereby proving that whatever problems the child was experiencing weren't the parents' fault after all. It's an aspect of fostering that's often very relevant, however.

'At least Cherie wasn't as bad as some of the family members we've encountered,' Jonathan reflected afterwards.

'Quite,' I said, immediately thinking about one of the most upsetting scenes we'd ever had with a parent.

Jonathan knew precisely what I was thinking about.

'That awful father,' he said. 'Now *that* was a bad situation.'

The incident we were both thinking about happened a few years before Maria first stayed with us. Jonathan and I were at a meeting with a social worker, a young lad called Jimmy and his highly volatile father.

'Are you happy living with Angela and Jonathan?' the social worker asked.

'Yes,' Jimmy replied with some trepidation.

With that his father leapt up and almost flew across the table before punching his young son in the chest. The poor boy didn't know what to do. He was embarrassed and hurt and completely confused. I wanted to wrap my arms around him, tell him it was all right and give him a big cuddle, but of course that would have enraged the father even more. Instead, Jonathan and I had to sit there silently while the social worker dealt with the situation, and we were both so shaken up it took us some time to regain our composure. That is why we say that, although we've fostered some children whose behaviour has been extremely challenging, unfortunately some of the most difficult people we've had to deal with over the years have probably been some of the parents.

It's important as a foster carer to believe in yourself, trust that what you are doing is for the benefit of the child and try to ignore, as best you can, any unjustified negative reaction and input from families. It's not always easy to do this because even though we are highly trained, and are taught how to deal with the most difficult situations, at the end of the day we are human beings too. Our feelings get hurt, we sometimes doubt ourselves and at times it is incredibly difficult for Jonathan and me not to follow our gut reactions when we witness inappropriate contact or communication from a parent or a member of the child's extended family.

Happily, as I said earlier, the many professionals we deal with are, on the whole, very supportive of our role, and this helps to counterbalance the bad press we sometimes get from families. For instance, not long after the visit from Cherie, I had to take Maria for one of her regular medical check-ups. She was required to have a medical assessment prior to the impending court hearing that would decide whether she could return to her family, and it was my job to take her to the GP.

'Hello Maria and hello Mrs Hart!' the doctor exclaimed chirpily. He was the same GP we'd seen when Maria first arrived several months earlier, when I took her for a routine check-up required by Social Services, and he was clearly pleased to see us.

'You're looking very well, Maria,' he smiled, before running through all he needed to do, such as checking her weight and height and asking some questions about medication, diet, possible allergies and so on.

When he'd finished the GP remarked, 'Well, I must say Mrs Hart, I'm astounded by the progress Maria has made since I last saw her. Her eyes are clearer, her skin's a better colour, and she's obviously far less anxious than she was even just a couple of months ago. Whatever it is you're doing, it's working!'

It's nice, on a personal level, to feel that someone like that understands what you're trying to do and is aware of at least some of what's involved in trying to do it. What's even more important for Jonathan and me, though, is knowing that we've made a difference to a child's health and wellbeing. I was thrilled Maria was making such good physical progress, and that helped me stay positive whenever I heard another barbed comment down the phone from Christine.

'We'll get you away from there, don't you worry,' Christine said during a subsequent phone call to Maria.

During another call, Gerry came on the line.

'Are you looking forward to coming home?' he asked.

'Yes,' Maria said uncertainly.

'Are you telling the truth?'

'Yes.'

'That's good, because you know that I know when you are lying, don't you?'

'Yes, Gerry. I would never lie to you!'

I indicated to Maria that she needed to ask for her mum to come back on the phone, as she was only meant to speak to Christine, not Gerry, but Maria seemed very eager to please Gerry and tell him what he wanted to hear. I could sense she was afraid to rush him off the phone. Afterwards, I gently asked her how she was feeling.

'Brilliant!' she said, giving me one of her false-looking smiles. 'I can't wait to go home!'

I found it painful to watch her and listen to her when she behaved like that. It was as if she was scared Gerry was going to appear at any second and would catch her out if she said the wrong thing, but he lived miles away, so how come he had such a hold on her like this? Needless to say, I was also cross that Christine and Gerry, like Cherie, were making statements and promises they had no right to, as Maria's fate was out of their hands.

The imminent court hearing was taking far longer than anticipated, but I was in no rush for it to happen. As well as being healthier than when she first came back to stay with us, Maria was doing better with her schoolwork and her behaviour in school had improved too. Jonathan and I were happy to have her for as long as it took, and it made us quite sad to think that, whatever the courts and Social Services decided next, Maria would be leaving us – either to go home or to go and live with a permanent mainstream foster carer.

'I'll miss her,' I told Jonathan.

'Don't think about that yet,' he said, wisely. 'Just focus on how you are helping her. Think what the doctor said: Maria's making good progress. You should give yourself a pat on the back, because this is not an easy scenario at all.'

I knew Jonathan was right, and I told him so, adding that it was also a good thing that Maria was making progress at school. Still, I couldn't help worrying about Maria's future. The fact I would miss her was a minor concern compared to the much more important issue. Would Maria continue to thrive when she entered the next chapter of her life?

17

'He can see me'

Over the next few weeks, Maria continued to go to church every Saturday and to do her Bible-reading sessions. Everyone at the church did what he or she could to ensure that it all fitted seamlessly into her life, and ours, and Maria never once complained.

'Are you looking forward to going to church this morning?' I asked her one Saturday as we were driving there.

'Yes, of course!' she gushed, somewhat unnaturally.

'That's good. But you know, Maria, you are allowed to say if there is anything you don't enjoy, and I don't just mean with church.'

I said this because Maria's tendency to pull a fake smile had been more noticeable lately. When my mum asked her about school she said it was 'brilliant' even though I knew this wasn't entirely true. Despite the fact Maria's academic work had improved, I continued to get the odd call from the head teacher about temper tantrums and reports that Maria had run out of a classroom. Plus, if I asked Maria how she felt her phone call with her mum had gone, for instance, she'd say it was 'fantastic'.

One time she even added, very unconvincingly, 'And it was even better than normal because I got to say hello to Gerry!'

Maria's eyes narrowed when I told her she was allowed to say if there was anything she wasn't enjoying.

'I won't be cross with you,' I smiled. 'You can tell me if there is anything at all you want to say about church, or school, or anything else.'

'He can see me,' she said very seriously, gazing at the church, which had just come into view as I turned a corner.

'God? Do you mean the presence of God is all around?'

Maria blanked me as I parked the car, and she went into the church without saying another word.

Christmas was coming and I received a phone call from Babs.

'Christine and Gerry don't want Maria to have any presents,' she said. 'But I'm just going to get her something, Angela. I'll just tell Maria to keep it a secret. I mean, I ask you – how can you refuse a child presents at Christmas?'

'I see, thanks, Babs,' I said, thinking that I was going to have to run this past Social Services. I didn't want to have this conversation with Babs, as she was talking in the conspiratorial way she often did, and I could tell she wanted to recruit me to her way of thinking. I didn't want to get caught up in a situation that could cause trouble in the family, and I didn't want to ask Maria to keep secrets from her family, so I tried to change the subject. However, Babs would not drop it.

'Between you and me, Angela, Gerry *does* celebrate Christmas. He gets presents for his lads and he and Christine have all the trimmings and the tinsel. I saw it for myself last year. I don't think it's fair that only Maria has to stick to the rules.'

I was horrified to hear this, but not entirely surprised. It seemed that Maria always got the raw end of the deal within her family, with Gerry being the person laying down the unfair rules. Why Christine didn't challenge him I could not imagine.

Before I spoke to my social worker I decided to ask at the church about Christmas celebrations, or the lack of them, and one of the ladies who did the Bible classes explained to me that there was nothing in the Bible to suggest 25 December was a special day. 'But now that it has become so commercialised,' she went on, 'some people prefer to focus only on God on that day, so that they don't get involved in the materialism of it all.'

'In other words, it's a choice, not a rule that is set in stone?'

'Exactly, Angela. Some members of our church do celebrate Christmas in some way, but others don't. Everybody is individual.'

I imagined most families supported each other in this choice and didn't set different rules for different people, as Gerry had. I didn't mention this, of course, because I knew there was already hostility towards Gerry within the church, and what was the point in creating more? I felt very cross, though, on behalf of Maria.

I called Social Services and discussed this issue with our support social worker, Jess. I explained that one of the problems was that Tom and Dillon, and indeed Jonathan and I, and my mother, would all be celebrating Christmas together, complete with presents and all the usual treats and festivities. As Jess considered this, Christine put in a request to Social Services for Maria to spend the day with different foster carers, who wouldn't be celebrating in any way.

'I'm sorry, Angela,' Jess told me. 'I'm going to have to try to fix this up; there is no way round it. Maria is on a voluntary care order and Christine's views have to be catered for as best we can.'

I understood, though I wasn't happy with the situation. It wasn't the fact Maria wouldn't get presents, but the thought that she would be spending Christmas Day with strangers while the rest of us – including Gerry, Christine and her stepbrothers, not to mention her brother, Colin, Babs and Stanley – all enjoyed the festivities that made my heart bleed.

Thankfully, when it came to the crunch, Jess failed to find a suitable foster family who shared the same religious beliefs and could take Maria in. Several of the families from the church offered to have her, as I think Maria must have told them what had happened, but that wasn't possible either because none of them were approved foster carers.

Anyone looking after a child, whether as a parent, guardian, foster carer, teacher or childminder, constantly has to make decisions. For people who are employed in some capacity as child carers, there are innumerable laws and regulations that govern what they can and can't do. However, there are still some decisions that have to be made on the basis of common sense and life experience, and it seemed to me that this was a case where common sense needed to prevail.

There was an article in the national newspapers a couple of years ago about two children who were moved to a different foster home after the foster parents were accused of holding their hands too tightly as they crossed the road. It's because of absurdities like that, which do occur from time to time, that Jonathan and I don't always agree with every edict and decision made by Social Services. But we do always stick to the rules, because whatever our own personal feelings might be, they *are* the rules and we are professionals doing a job.

However, that doesn't mean that we don't sometimes find a way around doing something we know would be unfair for a particular child, which, in Maria's case, meant giving her presents *at* Christmas that weren't *for* Christmas. Jonathan and I discussed this at great length, and worked out exactly how to handle it.

'What we've decided,' I told Maria, 'is that we are giving you some presents to congratulate you for all your achievements while you have been staying with us.'

'What achievements?'

'Doing well at reading. Learning to bake biscuits. Learning to crochet with my mum.'

'Gerry won't like it,' she said flatly.

She had a point, of course. I wished I could say, 'he'll never know' or 'don't tell him', but of course that would have been wholly inappropriate. Maria already held lots of secrets – her mum and Gerry made sure of that, from what I could gather. The last thing I would ever do is ask a child to keep a secret, and so I had to explain to Maria that I would discuss this with Social Services so her family knew exactly what was planned, which they did. In the event we heard no more about it.

We all enjoyed a lovely Christmas Day at home.

'Do you think he can see everything?' Maria asked, as she fell into bed exhausted from a day full of board games, films, a long walk in the park, plus of course a turkey and Christmas pudding, and plenty of presents.

'It's what you believe that counts, sweetheart. What do you think?'

'I know he does. But why has he let me get presents?'

'Well, lots of people have presents at Christmas,' I said, not quite sure what to say.

'I don't get it,' she said. 'Night, Angela. Thank you for a lovely day.'

And that's the best Christmas present I could have, I thought to myself.

18

'I'm going home'

One Friday night after Christmas, Jonathan and I were getting ready for bed when he called me over to the window to see the snow that had just started to fall. By the time we woke up the next morning, the ground was completely covered in a thick white blanket. For once, Tom, Dillon and Maria all got up early without needing any chivvying or encouragement.

As soon as they were dressed, all three ran out into the back garden and started making a snowman. It was a joy to watch, and when Tom and Dillon announced after breakfast that they were going to meet up with friends for a big snowball fight on the field, Jonathan and I decided to take Maria out sledging.

'Yippee!' she squealed. 'I've never done sledging before!'

Jonathan dug the old sledge out of the shed while I got Maria all wrapped up and ready to face the elements. There were already quite a few other children playing on the slopes beyond the playground by the time we had towed the sledge through the park.

'How about that one?' Jonathan asked Maria, pointing to a

long, gentle slope with an expanse of level ground at the bottom of it, beyond which was a narrow gully and a hedge.

'I'll do it if you'll come with me, Angela,' she said, adding hastily, 'but not because I'm scared or anything.'

'Well, that's good,' I laughed. 'We wouldn't want *two* scared people on the same sledge!'

'Bags I go in front,' Maria called to me over her shoulder, as we followed Jonathan up the hill.

Any anxiety Maria might have had about her first experience of sledging was soon replaced by exhilaration and excitement. It was good to see her laughing and relaxed as we whooshed down the hill together, leaning exaggeratedly from side to side to avoid all the other brightly coloured, snow-suited children and adults on wooden sledges and plastic trays.

After we'd repeated the process a couple of times, Maria decided she wanted to do it on her own.

'It'll go a bit faster without Angela's weight, so you'll have to take it slowly,' Jonathan told her. Then he laughed and added, 'No offence, Angela,' when he saw the expression on my face. 'Although you did enjoy that tin of Quality Street over Christmas, didn't you, dear!'

I hastily picked up a handful of snow and lobbed it playfully at Jonathan's chest, which made Maria clap and laugh.

'Again!' she said, and we both pelted Jonathan with snowballs.

After that Maria pulled the sledge up the slope, while Jonathan and I waited for her at the bottom.

'Why isn't she slowing down?' I said, as she came careering down the run a few seconds later.

'Brake, Maria,' Jonathan shouted, but she either ignored him or didn't hear. 'You need to slow down!'

I could see the other children dragging their boots in the snow to slow themselves down as they neared the bottom, or leaning forwards on their sledges to add to the drag, but Maria was leaning back, feet off the ground, to make herself go as fast as she possibly could.

Jonathan and I could both could see what was going to happen, so he stepped out in front of the sledge to prevent Maria going headlong into the gully. He was sent flying when the sledge crashed into him and I heard Maria shriek with alarm as she fell off into a mound of hard snow. Fortunately, we'd insisted on her wearing a helmet, so apart from a couple of bruises and a few scratches, she wasn't badly hurt. Jonathan came off worse and was very bruised, in fact, but at least Maria hadn't ended up in the gully, as she could have been in a much worse state.

'I'm sorry,' Maria said afterwards, once we'd trudged home and warmed up with mugs of hot chocolate.

'It's OK,' Jonathan said. 'I guess you just didn't have any experience. You'll know better next time.'

'You learn and live,' she said, trying to repeat a phrase she'd read in a book, but getting it slightly mixed up.

'Indeed, and in any case, what are a few bruises between friends?'

Jonathan grinned, but Maria froze and stared at him in horror. We both realised what he'd said and looked at each other, not quite knowing what to do next.

'What I meant is, Maria, I am not in pain. It's not great that

I've got bruises, but I know you didn't mean for me to get hurt. I'm fine, and they will soon heal.'

Maria then started to cry, uncontrollably.

'Can I give you a cuddle?' I said.

'Yes,' she snivelled.

'You can talk to me,' I said. 'I'm here to listen.'

Jonathan indicated that he was going upstairs. 'I think I'll have a soak in the bath,' he said. 'Leave you girls to it.'

I gave him a nod over Maria's head as she sobbed in my arms. She stayed like that for several minutes, not speaking, and then a seemingly amazing transformation took place.

Maria peeled herself away from me, wiped her eyes and said bravely, 'Shall we make some biscuits?'

'Well, yes, why not? Are you sure you're OK?'

'I'm fine!' she grinned. 'There's nothing wrong with me! Jonathan is the one who got hurt. Poor old Jonathan!'

I was pleased to see that Maria had cheered up, of course, but this gave me the strongest feeling yet that she was putting on a brave face. My instinct told me that she was working hard to keep secrets and, I suspected, behaving exactly how Gerry would want her to, even though I knew she didn't like him, he wasn't here to see her and she had no reason to want to impress him.

We reported the sledge incident to our support social worker, and completed the necessary incident report that evening. I also mentioned the tears afterwards, and how the conversation about bruises appeared to trigger them. Maria told her mother about the sledge accident too, as just one of the long catalogue of events she recalled and related during a lengthy phone call they had the following week. Although I had half expected Christine to put in a complaint to Social Services, what she actually complained about wasn't that the incident had occurred at all, but that we hadn't reported it to her ourselves. I just ignored this; it was extremely frustrating that Christine repeatedly refused to accept that Jonathan and I had a duty to report such things to Social Services but not directly to her. Not following the rules could have easily created more trouble, and that was the last thing Jonathan and I wanted.

Maria eventually told Jonathan that evening she was sorry she hadn't done what he'd instructed her to do before she set off, which was to take it slowly.

'I don't want to break anything again, do I?' she commented.

'No, you don't want to break anything again,' Jonathan repeated.

'No. It wasn't my fault last time, but Mummy didn't like it. So it's good, nothing broken, soonest mended! Don't want it to be third time unlucky!'

'Third time unlucky?'

'Yes, I broke my arm twice already.'

This time it was Jonathan who called Social Services. Maria's social worker was on leave, but another social worker answered the call.

'I thought I'd better mention this as Maria clearly said "it wasn't my fault last time" and she said she had broken her arm twice, but we were only aware of her breaking her arm once, when she was about five. We wanted to make sure you were aware of this, if it's true.'

'Oh, it's true,' the social worker said. 'As a matter of fact,' she went on, as she rifled noisily through paperwork, 'I was her social worker when it happened. It's in the notes somewhere. It must have been . . . let me see. I had just come back from maternity leave so it was, let me see . . .'

Jonathan waited patiently as the social worker scanned the relevant pages of the file. It took her a while, and in the end she said she'd call him back.

'Fractured arm,' she said later, after eventually locating the information. 'Fell off a slide. Maria, age three. Couldn't, or wouldn't, corroborate the story. That's how she first came to our attention. We looked into it when the hospital raised concerns, but she wasn't taken into care. There was no evidence to suggest she was being mistreated.'

Throughout her time with us, Maria was meant to have supervised contact with her mother and stepfather once a week at a family centre on the outskirts of town. It wasn't the easiest place to get to, and arranging a time for the contact sessions had always proved difficult. Christine couldn't drive, so the sessions had to be at a time that suited Gerry, who she relied on to take her there. Although Gerry didn't work, it seemed that every time of day on every day of the week that was suggested didn't suit him. This meant that when Maria had been with us for six months I could count on one hand the number of sessions that had actually taken place.

Those few sessions that did go ahead were hard to analyse. When I told Maria she was seeing her mum, or her mum and stepdad, she always said, 'That's great. I'm really happy.' But when I looked at her or tried to give her a reassuring smile she was typically staring straight ahead and the expression on her face didn't seem happy at all.

Jonathan and I were not required to attend the contact

sessions, and a contact support worker called Bessie generally collected Maria and took her there, or we dropped her off. However, on one occasion a temporary contact support worker called Jackie took Maria to the session. Afterwards I reminded Maria to say thanks to Jackie when she was dropped back at our house.

'Oh, yeah, thanks,' Maria called over her shoulder as she bounded up the stairs on all fours.

'It was a good contact session,' Jackie told me. 'Aren't they a lovely family?'

Fortunately, I didn't have to answer her question because all I had a chance to say was, 'Um, ah,' before she continued, 'They're so friendly and loving. I do hope it all turns out well for the little girl and that she can go home!'

I felt glad that Maria was generally accompanied by Bessie, who in my opinion had a much more accurate view of Maria's mother and stepfather, and was not so easily hoodwinked by them. Jackie's influence and optimistic viewpoint seemed to have rubbed off on Maria that day, because after the social worker left she came back downstairs, babbling away about what was going to happen next. Maria seemed excited at first, but I could tell she was also full of trepidation.

'I'm going home,' she said, bending one leg up behind her and holding it by the ankle. 'My mum says so.'

'Your mum said you're going home,' I repeated.

'Yes.' Maria's smile was bright but her lips were stretched into a tight, tense line. 'She said her solicitor told her that Social Services don't have a log to stand on and that the judge will know that the things they're saying about her are all lies. What's for tea?'

'Leg,' I said, buying time. Once again I was concerned by what Maria's mother had told her, but I didn't want to contradict what she'd said.

'Leg of what?' Maria asked.

'The phrase is, "a leg to stand on". And it's chicken casserole tonight. In fact, it's almost ready now. So perhaps you could use your own "logs" to transport you to the bathroom and wash your hands.'

The long-awaited court hearing was finally scheduled for a Thursday morning. When Jess told me about it I felt nervous, as if I was going to court myself and the judgement could affect my own future – which indeed it would.

By this point in time I was feeling extremely torn. I wanted what was best for Maria, but I honestly didn't know what that was. Her mum and stepdad had failed Maria in the past, of that I felt sure, but I forced myself to consider that maybe they had learned lessons and changed. Or was that extreme wishful thinking on my part? What if Maria was forced to live apart from them and it was ultimately the wrong thing? She was still only nine years old – she had half her childhood ahead of her.

The courts would decide between two options: Maria could go home to live with her mother and stepfather, or the voluntary care order she was currently under would be replaced by an interim care order. At that time, an interim care order could last for eight weeks, with four-week extensions to allow more time for assessments and evidence-gathering before the final court hearing, at which a judge would make a decision about Maria's future. The next step could be for a full care order to be put in place. In that case, Christine would then lose her parental rights, and the state would effectively be in control of decisions about Maria's future and who was going to look after her.

On the day before the court hearing, when we were all sitting at the table in the kitchen eating our breakfast, I told Maria and the two boys, 'I'm stripping beds today and taking the washing to the laundrette,' which was something I did from time to time to help support our local precinct shops. (The fact that when I picked up the bed linen later it was all washed, ironed and ready to put away was an added bonus!) 'So who's going to help me make up their bed when they get back from school? Maria? Tom? How about you, Dillon?'

During the silence that followed, I noticed the children glance surreptitiously at each other. Then, almost in unison, they shrugged their shoulders and focused their attention on their toast or bowls of cereal. They still had their heads bent over their breakfast when Jonathan picked up a soft toy belonging to Maria and said, in one of his many funny voices, 'Me! Me! Let me help you, pleeeeease. I'm good at making beds. Please let me help – I'll earn my stripes!' The toy was a zebra, which we'd bought for Maria as a replacement for Benji. Sadly, Christine never did give that particular toy back to her daughter, despite repeated requests. In the end, Jonathan had bought Maria the toy zebra on a day trip to an animal park. She called it Zod and loved it, and thankfully it seemed to go some way towards compensating for the loss of Benji.

I could see that Maria was suppressing a smile as Dillon sighed loudly, shook his head in mock pity, and said gamely, 'Now that *is* something I'd like to see – Zod the zebra making a bed.'

'What's that, Zod?' Jonathan raised the soft toy to his ear and listened as if it was whispering to him, then nodded and said, 'Ah, yes, I can understand that.'

Maria couldn't contain herself any longer and was almost bouncing on her chair as she asked Jonathan, 'What? What did Zod say?'

'He said he's very upset that you don't think he can make a bed,' Jonathan answered solemnly, and Maria grinned.

'Yeah, sure he did,' Dillon mocked rather sarcastically, although he was laughing too, despite himself. 'Anyway, I don't mind making my bed, with or without Zod's help. I'll do it after my club.'

'I don't mind helping either,' Maria piped up. 'Can I choose my sheets?'

Only Tom remained silent. Although he smiled, he continued to munch on his piece of toast. He was a lovely lad, but he was typically reluctant to get drawn into having to do anything around the house.

After the children had left for school that morning, I stripped the beds and did a few other chores in the house while Jonathan opened the shop. When I went into Maria's bedroom, Zod was sitting on the windowsill facing outwards, as if he was watching all the people doing their shopping on the street below. Stacked neatly on the floor underneath him was a pile of bags, which, judging from their bulging sides and half-closed zips, were all full.

Barbara our part-time assistant was having a day off, so I joined Jonathan in the shop as soon as I could and we were busy for most of the day. I was back in the house by the time the taxi dropped Maria off after school, and before Tom and Dillon got home, and I asked Maria about the bags in her room.

'I packed them last night,' she told me. 'Before I went to bed. I told you: I'll be going home tomorrow. I know it's the court case and my stepdad said the judge is going to do what he's told him to do.' She flashed me another bright, tight-lipped smile, and then, before I had a chance to say anything, asked quickly, 'What's for tea?'

'Macaroni cheese.'

'Great!'

This time her grin was genuine when she added, 'I'm so hungry I could eat a house.'

19

'Can I see Nanny?'

It was mid-afternoon the following day when Maria's social worker phoned and told me the result of the long-awaited court hearing.

'We've got an interim care order. I don't know how Maria's going to take the news. Do you want me to tell her, or would you rather do it yourself?'

'I'll do it,' I said, wondering how she would take it and thinking how careless it was of Gerry to claim he could accurately predict the outcome.

'I must admit, now I've heard the news, I'm relieved that she's not going home today,' I found myself saying. 'I think Maria's going to be upset, although I don't know for sure. She says it's what she wants to do, but her expression doesn't always match her words. Sometimes it's difficult to tell what the truth is.'

To be honest, I was really struggling to take the news in myself. We'd waited more than six months for this and it was a momentous day. Of course, we'd have the eight weeks it took for reports to be compiled following the decision to impose the interim care order – and possibly some four-week extensions if needed – before a final decision about whether Maria would ultimately be placed under a full care order would be made. Social Services would continue the process they'd already begun of gathering information from their discussions with Maria's mother, grandparents, teachers, and Jonathan and me, and other details from doctors who had examined Maria. It was still possible she might go home, but now the interim care order was in place this seemed less likely to happen.

My feeling was that Maria would be taken into care long term, but of course that was only my gut instinct. Every case is unique and you never know what evidence is going to be put before the court. Jonathan and I had been surprised by court decisions in the past and so, despite the ruling that day, I had to accept that Maria's future was still hanging in the balance. But, for now, Maria would continue to stay with us.

I felt quite anxious as her taxi pulled up, bringing her home from school, that afternoon. She bounded into the house energetically, saying, 'Well, he was right, wasn't he? I'm going home, aren't I?'

'Maria, sweetheart . . .'

She could tell from my tone of voice and expression that the result was not the one she expected. Her bottom lip dropped and she looked crushed. Perhaps I'd been wrong to think Maria was putting on an act about how excited she was to go home? What she said next surprised me, however.

'But . . . how can Gerry have got it wrong?'

'Well, you never know what a court is going to decide until the decision is announced.'

'But Gerry knew. Gerry has *powers*.'

'I'm afraid nobody has the power to influence a court, Maria.'

'But he *said*! He knows, he knew, he had the power!'

'Maria, you're not going home for the time being, sweetheart,' I said, closing the door behind her as she stepped into the kitchen.

She sat at the table looking shocked and confused.

'What's going to happen?'

'Well, Social Services asked the judge for what's called an interim care order.'

'Yes, I know,' she said, as I'd explained the options to Maria in advance. She narrowed her eyes slightly and looked at me with an expression on her upturned face that I couldn't read.

'Well, the judge did make an interim care order, which means that you'll be staying with Jonathan and me for the time being while . . .'

Suddenly, Maria started jumping up and down, clapping her hands and grinning as she chanted in a sing-song voice, 'I'm staying with you! I'm staying with you!'

'Jonathan and I are really pleased that you're going to be staying with us for a bit longer,' I told her. I was touched, but also confused by her obvious delight and apparent change of heart about going home.

'So, can I stop going to church now?' She paused for a moment, with her hands pressed together in front of her, mid-clap. 'And can I see Nanny?'

'I'll have to ask about church,' I said. 'But you can certainly see your nanny!'

I was delighted and relieved that at long last Maria wanted to see Babs again, and she wanted to see her grandfather too.

'What's changed your mind?' I asked. 'I know your nanny and granddad will be *so* pleased to see you!'

'Nothing.' Maria shrugged and looked evasive. 'I just want to see them now. OK?'

When Jonathan came into the kitchen a little while later, Maria told him excitedly, 'I'm not going home after all. I'm staying with you and Angela! And I'm going to see my nanny and granddad again.'

'We're really glad you're not leaving us, just yet. Aren't we, Angela?' Jonathan said. 'And it's great that you want to see your grandparents. I'm sure your nanny and granddad will be over the moon.'

'Can we phone Nanny now?' Maria was already moving towards the door as she spoke.

'Yes, of course, love,' I said. 'I'll find the number.'

'What was all that about?' Jonathan asked me later that evening, after Maria had talked on the phone to her grandparents and arranged to see them the next day. 'Why has she been refusing even to speak to them for all this time and now suddenly she can't wait to see them?'

'I'm really not sure,' I told him. 'I'm as bemused as you are.'

Jonathan sighed and then added, 'I sometimes think life would be so much easier if we were able to read people's minds – or even to "read between the lies", as Maria put it the other day, remember?'

'I do,' I said, but then I frowned.

'What is it?' Jonathan asked.

'Oh, I might be over-thinking things, but Maria said something about Gerry having powers.'

'Powers?'

'Yes. He seemed to convince her that he could influence the judge to make the decision go his and Christine's way. But now Maria has seen that his powers didn't work, she seems a lot more relaxed. It's like it's freed her up to be true to herself.'

'Interesting,' Jonathan said. 'That would certainly help explain her change of heart. Perhaps it's something we need to ask her more about, when the time is right.'

I agreed, but I imagined this might take some time, as Maria had enough to deal with for one day.

However, at bedtime Maria asked me to help her unpack her bags and reorganise her room, and as we did so she started to talk. It's often the case that a child will open up when they don't have to give you direct eye contact, like when they are in the back of the car and you are driving, for example, and Maria focused on her toys and clothes as she started to chat in the softly lit bedroom.

'When Gerry told me he had special powers I believed him,' she said sadly.

'You believed Gerry?'

'Yes. The contact lady was there, at the centre. You know, that one called Jackie?'

Jackie was the contact worker who'd described Maria's family as 'lovely' and hoped they'd be reunited soon. I felt she was woefully naive and easily taken in by Christine and Gerry, and I was always wary when she was in charge of a contact session.

'Yes, I know Jackie,' I said.

'Well, Mummy was showing Jackie some photos of a trip she'd been on, and while Jackie wasn't looking Gerry told me that I shouldn't forget that he had special powers. He said he had used his special powers to make sure the judge would say no to that care order Social Services wanted, what's it called again?'

'The interim care order?'

'That's it.'

'And Jackie wasn't looking?'

'No, she was busy looking at the photographs.'

Such a basic distraction tactic wouldn't have worked with Bessie, the contact worker who normally supervised the contact sessions. Bessie was aware of every word spoken and every glance exchanged during any contact session. But Jackie was less experienced, and seemingly more easily fooled by the family's pretence of friendly innocence, and she had apparently missed Gerry's strange and inappropriate claims completely.

Over the next few weeks Maria randomly made more revelations, all of which I reported to Social Services.

'I'm so happy I can see Nanny again!' she said again one day, after arrangements were made over the phone for the two of them to meet up. I was delighted too, and of course Babs was thrilled to bits.

'I knew she'd come round,' Babs told me. 'Like I said. Kids, hey? But I knew my little Maria would come round, bless her heart.'

'Well I'm very pleased,' I said. 'I thought it was such a shame when you didn't see each other. Puzzling, too. Still, all's well that ends well.'

After I'd put the phone down I turned round to see Maria standing behind me. It made me jump, as I didn't expect to see her there.

'It *was* a shame,' she said. 'I missed Nanny.'

'I'm sure you did. I know you love your nanny.'

'I didn't want anything bad to happen to her.'

'You didn't want anything bad to happen to her?'

'No. Gerry said if I spoke to her again something bad would happen. Gerry said . . . Oh, never mind.'

'Never mind?'

I said this quizzically, making it clear that I did mind and would like her to tell me what Gerry had said.

Maria took a deep breath, closed her eyes and blurted out, 'He said he would *kill* Nanny if I spoke to her again!'

She then burst into deep sobs that made her gasp for air.

'Sweetheart! Can I give you a hug?'

Maria nodded through her sobs and I gave her a big cuddle. It was a shocking moment and I had no doubt that Maria was telling the truth about what Gerry had said. It all made sense now, and as I held Maria close and let her sob into my jumper I thought about how she'd hidden at the department store, how she seemed scared of even seeing Babs and why she'd supposedly had such a sudden change of heart about her grandmother.

'What an evil, sinister man,' I said to Jonathan later, when I was certain Maria was out of earshot.

'Disgraceful,' he said. 'Remember what I said the first time I met him? He made my skin crawl. I've never had such a bad reaction to somebody. What a terrible thing to say to a young girl. It's absolutely wicked.'

The next day, when Maria was relaxed and sitting in the kitchen drinking a glass of milk, I made it plain to her that she could talk

ANGELA HART

to me whenever she wanted to, and that if anything was worrying her she could talk to me about it. She nodded nervously.

'He won't know, will he, because of his powers?'

I reassured her that nobody has powers like that, to know what other people are doing when they are in a different place.

'I don't even believe in God,' Maria said, and then asked me if she could do some crocheting, as she was making a scarf for one of her teddy bears.

'Of course,' I said. 'I thought you'd given up on it because you haven't done any for a while.'

'No,' she said sadly. 'I just didn't want Mum to know I was doing it, because she said it's only for old biddies to do.'

'Old biddies? Gosh, we'd better not let my mum hear that! She'd be horrified!'

Maria laughed as I said, 'Come on, let's get you set up in the lounge . . .'

When I was alone with Jonathan we talked about the fact Maria still seemed a little uncertain about Gerry's powers and the claims he made. She had clearly sussed out that he had no power over the judge at the family court, but she still seemed anxious about refuting his powers completely.

'It's hardly surprising, is it?' Jonathan said. 'I mean, if you've grown up with someone for years and you're told one thing, it's very difficult to forget all that overnight, isn't it?'

'Of course, you're right. We'll just have to keep reinforcing the message that nobody has special powers like the ones Gerry claims to have.'

This is what we did over the next few weeks. If there was a cartoon on the TV featuring a superhero, or if we saw a poster or an advert where somebody was displaying a superhuman skill,

I made a point of talking about how this was 'fiction' and not real life.

'Are books all lies?' Maria asked one night.

She was reading a book about a magic kingdom, which she loved.

'Lies is not the right word. Authors have a fantastic imagination, which they use to tell stories. It's great entertainment for us, as we can escape into a fantasy world when we read a good book. The writers are not pretending their stories are real. They are fiction, not lies. There's a big difference.'

Maria thought about this, and then she mentioned the fact her mum was supposedly 'psychic'.

'Do you think Mum is lying?' she asked. 'Or can she really talk to "the other side", like she says?'

This was a tricky one, and I chose my words carefully.

'I think your mum really *believes* she has some psychic skills, and your grandmother believes your mum has a "gift" too. They are not lying about what they believe in.'

Maria looked a bit nonplussed and didn't take this conversation any further. My gut feeling was that Christine's 'gift' was very different from Gerry's supposed 'powers', because as far as I was aware she had never used her 'psychic skills' to scare or threaten Maria. Still, I made a note of Maria's questions, as I wanted Social Services to be aware of what was going on in her head.

Several days later Jonathan and I were driving along the road the church was on, with Maria in the back of the car. All of a sudden the penny dropped about what Maria had said more than once. 'He sees everything I do,' she had said. 'He can see me.'

I'd naturally thought she'd been talking about God, but now I realised she was talking about Gerry. The reason she'd been so compliant about going to church and doing her Bible study was that she thought he could see her, and that he would know if she didn't turn up or put the effort in.

'There's the church,' I said, as I wanted to see how Maria would react as we drove past.

'I don't believe in God any more,' she repeated.

'You don't?'

'I never did. I did it because he made me!'

Maria then looked all around her, as if she was checking Gerry's face wasn't going to appear at one of the car windows.

'You can't see me,' she whispered. 'You can't see me, can you?'

She threw her head back and I saw a wide, genuine smile appear on her face.

Eventually I learned from Maria that Gerry had apparently 'proved' his omniscience many times, by saying things to her like, 'Now let me see. You arrived at school at 8.30 this morning and played outside at ten o'clock. Then you ate your lunch in a room at the end of a long corridor that has two windows high up on the wall.'

Maria was too young to realise that the reason he knew those things was that he had been to the school, had seen the corridor and the dining room, and had a general idea of the break times. But because she already lived in an almost permanent state of anxiety when she was at home with her family, it had been easy for Gerry to convince her that he really was watching her all the time, just like he said he was.

As foster carers, Jonathan and I always try to give people the benefit of any doubt when it comes to their motives for doing things that might appear to be inexplicable. We knew, for example, that whenever Maria's grandparents did something that wasn't helpful to her in the long term, it wasn't because they didn't love her. It was simply because their affection for her and their desire for an easy life sometimes clouded their ability to see what was best for her.

Maria's mother's motivation, on the other hand, was often more self-centred than misguided. But it was impossible to find anything positive in Gerry. What he'd done was absolutely wicked, and I dreaded to think what damage his sinister mind games had done to Maria, and what the repercussions would be in years to come. It was hardly any wonder she had been anxious, disruptive, run away and had trouble at school. She had spent years of her young life thinking everything she did, everything she said, and even every thought she had could be seen or heard or somehow picked up by Gerry. It was enough to send a person insane, and was one of the cruellest tricks you could play on a vulnerable young girl. The fact that even the ethical, forgiving folk at Maria's church didn't have a good word to say about Gerry actually said it all.

20

'I want to live with you, Angela'

Unfortunately, even once Maria had seen through Gerry's lies, she found it impossible to stop believing them. The claims he made about his special powers had been so deeply ingrained in Maria that her automatic response was still to believe every word Gerry said and react accordingly.

'Gerry told Colin to tell me that he put memories in my head,' she said one day.

I was so incensed that I said, 'Pardon?' rather abruptly rather than using my usual technique of echoing back what Maria had just said.

'Yes. You know about the bruises and the broken bone.'

'The bruises and the broken bone?'

'Yes. I can't remember how I got them. I thought I did but . . .'

'But?'

'But now I don't know. If he put the memories there, how do I know if they are true?'

I was getting confused myself here, and I took a deep breath and said to Maria, 'Listen, sweetheart, people don't have special powers and people can't put memories in other people's heads.'

'So, it did happen?'

'What did happen?'

'I did have bruises and a broken arm?'

'Yes, you did.'

'But how?'

I waited and then Maria shrugged her shoulders. 'If Gerry told me cows could fly I would have believed him. Ha ha!'

We'd got into a routine of Babs coming to visit Maria at our house for a couple of hours every week, which was agreed by the court. These visits went really well and you'd never have known there had been any break in the contact.

Babs let Maria paint her nails, she asked her about school and she told Maria some stories about when she was a baby. She wasn't what you would call 'hands on' when it came to playing games, reading together or doing anything remotely physical, but Maria didn't seem to mind. Babs would sip tea, eat biscuits and chatter away very easily. Occasionally she'd say something inappropriate, like reminding Maria about the time she tried to eat dried noodles when she was hungry as a child, and telling the story like a funny anecdote rather than the shocking memory it was, but on the whole she was good company, kind and loving, and the visits went well.

Maria always looked forward to seeing Babs, but then one day she asked, 'What if my mum finds out I'm seeing Nanny again? I don't know what she'd say.'

'I'm sure your grandmother would be able to explain to her why it's so important that she sees you,' I told her, 'and I think your mum probably already knows, as Social Services certainly do.'

I was right, because I bumped into Colin outside the shop one morning.

'I saw Mum,' he said.

'How is she?'

'Not bad. I think she's OK with Maria staying here. She told me, "I don't care what she does."'

'I see. Well, I don't think that's a message I'll be passing on to Maria,' I said.

'No, that's exactly what I thought. She doesn't always think before she speaks, my mum.'

That evening Maria announced, out of the blue, 'I hope Social Services gets a full care order when this inter-thing runs out.'

'Interim care order,' I said.

'Yes, that. I want to live with you, Angela. You're always nice to me even though I'm not a nice person and everyone else hates me.'

'No one hates you, Maria,' I told her. 'We all think the world of you.' But although, for a moment, she looked pleased, I knew it was going to take a lot more than kind words – however truthful they might be – to build up her confidence and self-esteem. *Gerry has no idea how much damage he's done*, I thought. Poor Maria had no self-belief and she'd grown up in an environment of fear. She had been physically hurt and mentally abused, and what's more, Gerry had used mind games to play tricks on Maria about how she was physically harmed. It was despicable.

It was another three or four weeks after the court hearing before Maria was able to stop going to church. Even after the interim care order was put in place, her stepfather insisted that she should continue her religious education, and it wasn't until Maria told her social worker very clearly that she really didn't want to go any more that Social Services took the decision to let her stop.

Another good thing that happened once the interim care order had been agreed was that Maria was able to move back to her old school. As the local school was within easy walking distance of our house, there were no more long taxi rides, and as well as picking up most of the friendships she'd had when she was there before, her work improved too.

Unfortunately, Maria continued to have difficulty sleeping and she was often tired in the morning, complaining that she hadn't slept well. This had been an ongoing problem, but now when she woke up in the night, instead of tossing and turning, she would read. She devoured anything, from fiction to comic books to stories about seemingly ordinary people who turned out to do heroic things. She was like a little word vacuum, and as well as expanding her vocabulary and feeding her imagination, she loved learning new sayings and expressions. She still made us laugh by adapting them, either accidentally or deliberately, into things like 'reading between the lies' and 'not having a log to stand on'.

The last couple of reports we'd had for Maria from her previous school said that she was making good progress. But when I'd spoken to her class teacher just before she left there, she'd admitted that it wasn't entirely true. 'We mainly said those things about Maria's progress because we wanted to encourage her,' she told me, 'and because we thought she would read the report herself when she took it home.'

However, at the first parent–teacher meeting we went to after she'd returned to the local school, the comments were considerably more positive. 'I'm very impressed with the progress Maria has made in such a short time,' her class teacher told us. 'She's the best in the class,' her English teacher said, which wasn't surprising, considering how avidly she devoured every book we could provide her with. In fact, although we had a good selection of books in the house, Maria was such a fast reader that it wasn't long before we were visiting the library twice or even three times a week.

As the months passed, it was a real pleasure to watch Maria develop into an articulate, popular little girl with a bit more confidence than she'd had when she first came to live with us. She might have been swapping the healthy lunches I was giving her every day for crisps and chocolate bars – as I discovered later! – but at least she had friends to swap them *with*, and she no longer felt like an outsider.

However, the clock was ticking on Maria's time with us. The interim care order could only remain in place for a limited period, after which a permanent decision would have to be made about whether Maria was going to return home to live with her mother and stepfather or remain in care for the longer term, with the granting of a full care order in place. I couldn't see how she could possibly be allowed home after all the disclosures I'd been passing on to Social Services, but unfortunately as a foster carer you learn to take nothing for granted. Jonathan and I were aware we did not know the full story, and we rarely ever do. We are not lawyers either, and as I've said before we'd been surprised and disappointed by the decisions of the authorities in the past, so who knew what might happen?

21

'Every clown has a silver lining'

It wasn't long after Maria had returned to her old school that her social worker started helping her to put together a book of her life story, which is standard practice for children who are in foster care for any length of time. The life story book helps them understand and remember where they came from, what they have done and achieved in their life, and who the important people are. Typically, the book will record data like the child's place and time of birth, information about where they have lived, details of siblings, pictures from key events like christenings, birthdays and holidays, plus certificates gained at school and clubs and so on.

I am always reading articles and books about child development and I was struck when a feature I read in a fostering magazine quoted Leo Tolstoy, the Russian author who wrote *War and Peace* and *Anna Karenina* in the 1800s. 'Happy people have no history', he said. I thought at first that it was an odd quote to include in the feature but it makes sense when you think about it: people who've had a happy childhood just take it for granted, and there may be no 'stand-out events' they remember, because everything has run smoothly and happily. It's not the same for children who have experienced trauma, and they also tend to develop a view of themselves that's coloured by those traumatic events. This can make for a life story packed with much more 'history' than for the child who grew up in a happy, normal household.

It's important for children who have been subjected to distressing and disruptive experiences to have a record of the *good* things that have happened to them and of all the positive things they've achieved. And as well as being a record of the past, a life story book also provides a means of linking a child's present with their future – a way of filling in the blanks, to make life easier to cope with for the child, going forward.

Jonathan and I always keep a memory book for any children we foster, but that is separate from the life story book, which has to be compiled under the guidance of a trained social worker. This is because it isn't as straightforward as simply listing all the events in the child's life. Sometimes the book will begin with a family tree, which is put together from information provided by the child, their grandparents and other family members, and from any relevant records that can be provided by Social Services. Then maybe the trained social worker will visit the hospital where the child was born, where he or she might take photographs and see if they can discover any information about their birth weight, time of birth and so on.

It's the sort of information children who are brought up by their own parents take for granted, because they can ask about it directly if they want to know. Children who have been adopted or taken into care may have lost all contact with their families and so may not have anyone to provide them with answers to those questions.

Every aspect of a life story book, all the questions and discoveries, have to be handled very sensitively, so that children feel they are in control of the content, and so that they can choose not to pursue a particular line of inquiry that might involve having to rake up and relive unhappy or potentially disturbing memories.

I helped the social worker who was compiling Maria's life story book by going through a pile of photographs that Babs had given her. The idea was that we'd choose a few to go in the book, but it proved less straightforward than I hoped.

I spotted several depicting what appeared to be happy scenes in the back garden of one of the houses Maria lived in when she was much younger. Her mum was there, and Colin and Babs. Inevitably, Gerry was in a few too, though he was typically doing something in the background rather than being at the centre of a family scene.

Maria pushed several photographs away from her, across the table, saying very emphatically each time, 'No. Not that one.'

There didn't seem to be a pattern. I might have expected her to reject all of the ones with Gerry in, even the ones with him blurred on the sidelines, but this wasn't the case. In fact, she even rejected one that just showed a rabbit hutch in the garden, and another of the kitchen, with her mum unpacking some shopping.

I didn't challenge Maria. Unfortunately, however careful you are, you sometimes find that a whole can of worms has been opened before anyone realises what's happening, and a child may discover or remember something that causes them very significant distress. For this reason, I trod very carefully, and as Maria carried on looking through the photographs I simply stayed quietly by her side, to show support without interfering.

My mind wandered back to another child I worked with years earlier. The boy was fourteen, and he worked for several weeks on his life story book, both with us and with his social worker. Although he did occasionally get a bit upset when he remembered some of the things that happened during his early childhood, he really enjoyed drawing his family tree and seemed to be dealing with the whole process quite well.

Then, one day, his social worker came to our house with the finished book, which by now contained everything that was known or had been discovered about his life until the present day. To our surprise, when the social worker handed it over the boy suddenly froze. He already knew about every single thing that was in that book: he'd helped to put it all together himself. But there was something about being handed 'the story of my life to date' that hit a nerve and evoked his frozen response. 'Take it away,' he eventually stuttered, and he didn't regain his composure until the social worker had gone outside and locked it in the boot of her car, promising to keep it at her office for as long as the boy wanted her to.

The following year, the social worker was moving to another part of the country. The boy was still staying with us and she suggested to Jonathan and me, 'It might be a good idea if I give you the book. Put it somewhere out of sight, and leave it there until he asks for it.' So, we wrapped it up carefully, put it in the attic and didn't mention it again.

And that's where it stayed for many years, until he grew up and had children of his own. When he came to visit us one day, he happened to say, 'I wish I'd kept the life story book I did when I was living with you. I'd like to know all that stuff now, so that I can tell my kids about their family and about all the things I did when I was their age.'

It was lovely to see the expression on Jonathan's face as he said, 'Hold on a minute. I'll be right back. I think we can help you with that.' And it was lovely, too, to see the puzzled look on the young man's face quickly turn to delight when Jonathan handed him his carefully wrapped book. We never did find out what had disturbed him all those years before, but it just goes to show that it is worth persevering with something like this, as you never know when the time might be right for a child, or adult, to return to their memories.

Watching Maria sift through her photographs, I couldn't help worrying about the next part of her life story. What would happen to her after the final court judgement was made on her future, and would she be able to confront her past one day, or at least be able to revisit it without feeling traumatised all over again?

Within a few weeks of returning to our local school, Maria was made Student of the Month. Foolishly, in an attempt to encourage her to keep up the good work, I'd said I'd give her £1 as a reward for every test she did well in, which was a promise I was soon beginning to regret!

Jonathan and I had always thought that Maria was a very bright little girl, largely because she was so good at reading. She had a phenomenal memory too, which she had put to good use when she reeled off all those details during the lengthy phone calls she used to make to her mother. It was particularly gratifying to see her work improve so dramatically, and to know that she was both willing and able to make the effort required to reach what we felt was her high academic potential. Now, all we could do was continue to encourage and help her in any way we could, and hope that nothing happened to prevent her from sticking to the new path she had set out on.

We were gradually beginning to learn more about Maria's old life. The journey to and from the local school was a fairly short, safe walk from our house, but I always walked with Maria, just as I had done during her very first stay with us when she was seven. Now she insisted every day that she didn't need me 'tagging along', but I was not changing my mind. Then, one day, as we were walking along the path through the park, she suddenly took to her heels and ran off.

I went after her as fast as I could, but didn't catch up with her until she was almost at the school gate, when she told me angrily, 'You don't have to come with me. I'm not a baby. I can walk to school on my own. I did it every day from our old house when we lived here before, and that's a much longer walk than it is from yours!'

'You walked on your own to school before you moved away to the other school?' It was a cross between a question and a repeat of what she'd just told me. I was shocked about this as Maria would have been very young and I knew the route she would have had to take was across a very busy main road that was notorious for accidents. Parents had been campaigning for years to have a crossing installed, but to no avail.

'Duh, yeah,' Maria answered. 'Mum and Gerry didn't mind! Gerry said he could see if I was going straight there ...' She stopped herself and looked puzzled. It was as if a light bulb had gone on and she realised for the first time that Gerry couldn't actually see her when he wasn't there.

'Well, now you've got me for company,' I said cheerfully, keen to move on and deliver her to school in a decent mood. 'I can't let you go on your own, Maria. I'm not allowed to, even if I wanted to. Not till you're a bit older. Let's make the best of it, shall we?'

Instead of answering, she just shrugged, then swung her backpack off her shoulders and walked in through the school gates, leaving me wondering how on earth Christine and Gerry could have allowed Maria to make her own way to school when she was so very young.

Sometimes, she would say something out of the blue, apparently unconnected to anything that was happening at the time, but presumably because a memory had somehow been triggered, possibly subconsciously. For example, one day when she was helping me lay the table for Sunday lunch, she suddenly said, 'Mum made me put my finger in a match flame.'

I kept my tone of voice as neutral as possible as I said, 'You put your finger in the flame of a match.'

'Yes,' Maria answered, her tone as neutral as mine. 'It was so that I would burn myself.'

'So that you would burn yourself?' I repeated it as a question. 'Yes.'

'I wonder why your mum would want you to do that,' I said, carefully non-committal, without any trace of criticism in my voice.

'I don't know.' Maria spread her fingers, palms upturned, and looked down at her hands, then raised her left hand to her mouth and starting nibbling one of her fingernails.

'I haven't ever put my finger in the flame of a match,' I said. 'But I imagine it would be very painful to do something like that. I don't think I'd do it again if I was you.'

I wrote it all down afterwards in the notes I keep for our six-weekly review, and when I told Jonathan about it later that evening, he was as upset as I had been.

Another day Maria told me that she had invented a story in her head, after reading for ages in her room.

'Are you ready, Angela? Then let me begin!'

Maria cleared her throat and said: 'Once upon a time in a dark, dark house, there was a dark, dark kitchen. And in the dark, dark kitchen there was a stool made of dark, dark wood. And when the little girl was naughty she would stand on the dark, dark stool until the nasty man came to get her. One day, the little girl decided to creep down off the stool and steal a biscuit from the cupboard, because she was hungry! When the nasty man came back he hit her with a big stick. I think it was a snooker cue, as he had been out playing snooker with his friends, but it was dark so I couldn't see.

'"Did you get off the stool?" the bad man yelled.

'"No," cried the little girl. She was very, very scared.

'"Liar!" he shouted in her face. "I know what you did, and I have proof!"

'The little girl trembled and the man switched on the light.

'"Look at the floor! Look at your feet! You are a liar!"

'When the little girl looked down she saw that there was icing sugar sprinkled all over the kitchen floor, and in it were her footprints, leading to the biscuit cupboard and back to the stool.

'The little girl gasped in horror. She knew she had been

caught out and she knew the bad man would throw her down the stairs. The end.'

Maria stared at me when she'd finished her story, looking as if she couldn't quite believe she'd recited it.

'What a story,' I said. 'The teachers at school have commented you have a way with storytelling.'

I stopped there. I almost said the teachers had praised her for having a good imagination, but it seemed fairly obvious this could be based on some truth, and so I memorised as much of it as I could and put it in my notes to pass to the social worker. As I did so I recalled how she'd shrieked and gone very still and quiet for a moment when we were baking biscuits one time, after I spilled a bit of flour on the floor, by her feet. I also thought about one line she had read in her story, which stuck out: 'I think it was a snooker cue, as he had been out playing snooker with his friends, but it was dark so I couldn't see.' There were two odd things about this. The specific detail about the snooker cue (and yes, Gerry and his boys played snooker), and the very obvious use of the word 'I' where really she should have said 'she couldn't see', as she was meant to be telling the story of the little girl.

However many children we foster, Jonathan and I know that we will never stop being surprised, sometimes shocked, by the things they tell us. Over the years, with all the training and experience we have gained, we are now more confident about responding to the disclosures some children make than we were when we first started fostering. But my heart still misses a beat when a child makes any kind of possible disclosure. This is partly because it's distressing to hear, but partly also because I know that what I say in response could make all the difference between them talking about something they really want to talk about or clamming up so that the chance is missed. It's very important the child is aware you are simply listening to them and not judging them. At the same time, we have to be very careful not to criticise the child's family for anything we are told, because any comments we make may well get repeated to them.

On another day I was sitting with Maria in the car outside the house, having the conversation we often had while I waited for her to fasten her seat belt before starting the engine, when she said, 'Well, I don't see why I have to do it up. I didn't have a seat belt in my stepdad's car.'

'You must have had a seat belt,' I said. 'Do you mean you didn't do it up?'

'No,' she answered, heaving one of her long sighs. 'I mean I didn't *have* a seatbelt. Well, not always anyway, 'cos I sometimes went in the boot.'

'You travelled in the boot of your stepdad's car?' I repeated, adjusting the rear-view mirror as I spoke so that I could glance at her face.

'Yes.' Maria met my eyes for a moment, and then looked away. 'There wasn't always room for all of us to sit in the car when his kids and my brother Colin were there. So, as I was the smallest, I had to go in the boot. I hated it though. It was all dark and smelly and sometimes I was frightened in case I used up all the air.'

She paused for a moment and I heard the clasp on her seat belt click shut before she added, 'I suppose wearing a seat belt is OK really. At least it's better than being in the boot. What's that thing they say? I know: every clown has a silver lining.'

'I think it's every *cloud*,' I laughed, somewhat half-heartedly. 'Thanks, Maria, for doing up your belt.'

22

'Dead people talk to her'

We used to go off somewhere most weekends with the children we fostered. Sometimes, we'd go walking in a national park or along a coastal path, or we'd put the bikes on the car and head off to find a cycle route we hadn't explored before, around a lake or along a disused railway line, for example. Maria loved scouting ahead for the arrows that marked the trails, and as time went on she became a very enthusiastic participant in whatever we did.

The activities we do are the sort of things Jonathan and I did when we were children and usually took for granted. However, many of our foster children have never had experiences of exploring, going to the beach and cycling, for example, so we put a lot of effort into making sure they get as many opportunities as possible to enjoy themselves. Not that it really seems like effort: when they're happy, we're happy, and even the most difficult of the children we've fostered over the years have enjoyed doing the activities we've done with them.

We'd had a touring caravan for a few years by the time Maria came to stay with us. A friend of ours who was a foster carer regularly took children camping, until she had a placement whose social worker refused to give permission for the child to go with them because they would all be sleeping in what was, in effect, one open-plan room. That was something Jonathan and I were aware of when we bought our touring van. Its layout was perfect for a foster family that needed separate sleeping compartments. It slept six, when the awning was attached. There were two bunk bed areas at the back of the caravan, with each bunk having its own lighting and a sliding door that could be bolted from the inside – but easily forced open in an emergency.

All the children we took on camping holidays in that caravan loved having their own private space – which soon became christened Tardis One and Tardis Two – not least because it enabled them to read or play Nintendo games into the early hours of the morning without Jonathan and me being aware of what they were doing. In fact, we did know sometimes but we didn't say anything, because that's what holidays are all about: doing things you can't normally do when you have to get up the next morning to go to work or school.

The awning we added on contained two zip-up compartments and a space where we could set up a folding table and chairs, which incidentally we spent several hours clinging on to when a terrific wind threatened to snatch it away one time! The caravan itself had every mod con you could think of – a bathroom, cooker, fridge, television, radio, wardrobe and plenty of storage space. At night, the seating area became a double bed, where Jonathan and I slept behind a fitted curtain I'd made to divide the living area in two and provide us with some privacy if the children got up to use the toilet in the night.

One of the highlights of all our caravan holidays was the many meals Jonathan cooked on the portable barbecue we always took with us. It was an activity I encouraged as it gave me a break from the everyday cooking I did at home, and the children loved helping him, particularly when he cooked what seemed to be everyone's favourite meal of burgers and buns – preferably not 'spoiled by salad'!

We stayed at lots of different campsites over the years, some of them by the sea, others in the countryside, where we would spend the days swimming, walking and crabbing if we were near a beach, then play cards and board games in the evenings.

Maria came away with us for a weekend in the touring caravan during this period, when the interim care order was in place and we were waiting for the final verdict from the court. Her mum complained that she didn't want us to take Maria away for a whole week, but eventually agreed to a short weekend trip when I managed to give a positive response to every criticism she made, such as, 'I don't want Maria sleeping in the same room as Angela and Jonathan' and 'I don't want them touring around places I don't know about.' Via the social workers I provided a full description of the caravan, including pictures showing the layout, and I drew up an itinerary that stated exactly what we planned to do and where. Only then did Christine reluctantly say, 'Go on then, but I'm not paying anything towards it.'

We didn't want any money from her. We wanted to take Maria and the boys on a trip for the pleasure of having a fun and relaxing time together. It was as simple as that.

It was a really good trip. We went walking in the forest, swam at a water park, where Maria must have gone down the water-slide at least a dozen times, and Maria, Dillon and I saw a Disney film while Tom and Jonathan went cycling. Maria was enthusiastic about everything, although she sulked from time to time.

'Can I have Coke?' she asked on the first night.

'Yes, of course. We're on holiday!'

She guzzled the drink in record time, and then unbeknown to me helped herself to another large tumbler full. When I stopped her having a third glass, after realising what she was up to, Maria curled her lip.

'You said Coke was allowed on holiday! You're such a spoil-sport! It won't kill me, you know.'

'Maria, I can't let you guzzle Coke all night. It'll make you ill. It's not good for you to drink too much.'

She huffed and puffed and said, 'Mum told me this would be rubbish! I don't know why we've bothered coming away.'

Unfortunately, Christine had continued to make negative remarks to Maria when she spoke to her, despite being supervised at the contact centre and knowing I could hear her when she talked to Maria on the phone. It was something Jonathan and I had reluctantly learned to live with.

I ignored Maria's comment, and that tactic seemed to work. Maria didn't have any tantrums and she didn't run off once, although I made sure she was never out of my sight, of course. Maria was at the age where she liked to be doing things all the time, and I think the fact we had plenty to do kept her mind off other things. She seemed happy, and she liked being busy and involved in whatever activity we did, so I don't think it crossed her mind to run off, as that was typically something she did when she was in a bad mood and needed to vent her dissatisfaction.

However, there were a couple of incidents that meant the trip wasn't perfect. On our second evening the people running the campsite organised a barbecue, and when the food was ready I called Maria over from the nearby play area, which I could see clearly from where I was sitting.

I was happy to see that Maria had made friends with another little girl. They were walking towards us, laughing, and then Maria appeared to freeze. It was as if she was suddenly rooted to the spot, staring at something with an expression on her face of pure terror. When I followed her gaze I saw that she seemed to be transfixed by a man drinking a can of beer. He wasn't drunk – no one was; they were all families with children and it wasn't that sort of gathering. The thought crossed my mind that perhaps she knew the man, which would have been a huge coincidence as we were miles from home, but not impossible.

However, before I had a chance to react, Jonathan had sprinted across the grass and positioned himself so that he was standing next to Maria, blocking the man from her view. Then he gently touched her arm and, after a brief hesitation, they walked back together to where I was waiting for them, holding her plate of food. Jonathan pointed to something on the other side of the campsite to distract her and give her time to relax again.

A similar thing happened later that night and again the next day, and Jonathan and I came to the conclusion that the trigger seemed to be someone drinking beer from a can. Each time it happened, Maria would go into a sort of trance and just stand there, staring at whoever it was, clearly very frightened, until

192

Jonathan or I noticed and did something to divert her attention. There must have been some reason for it. Maybe it was the way her stepfather took his drink, although drinking wasn't encouraged by his religion. Or maybe some unpleasant incident had occurred related to beer that had created a subconscious link in her mind? We never got to the bottom of it, and Maria never spoke about it.

On our last morning, we all went on a long walk together, and unfortunately Maria fell and cut her knee open quite badly on a rock that was jutting out of the nature trail path. It was a nasty cut and it must have hurt a lot, but she didn't cry. Apparently, 'being a baby' was something her stepfather didn't tolerate, and Maria always tried very hard not to cry if she hurt herself, although she didn't always succeed.

Fortunately, we weren't too far away from the car so we took her straight to A & E at the local hospital, where they cleaned up the wound and put a butterfly stitch on it. Maria was very brave and good about it all, and I think that when the initial pain wore off she rather enjoyed all the sympathy and special treatment.

We filled out an incident report and let Social Services know what had happened. As every parent and anyone else involved in childcare knows, you can take every sensible precaution to protect children, but unless you wrap them in cotton wool and make them walk sedately at your side until they're eighteen, it isn't possible to stop them hurting themselves in some way, by falling over or bumping into something as Maria had.

Sadly, when Maria's mother found out what had happened, she made an official complaint to Social Services because we hadn't told her about the incident ourselves, although it wasn't our responsibility to do so. As I've said before, it was up to Social

Services to decide what Christine needed to be told. Despite this Christine was very annoyed, and she was angry with Maria too, because she had forgotten to mention it when they subsequently spoke on the phone, although she had told her grandmother and showed her the wound when we got home.

Though Tom and Dillon were happy to come away in the caravan, they were equally happy to stay at home, especially as they were at an age where they could entertain themselves at weekends. Sometimes they helped out in the shop to earn some extra pocket money, which we encouraged as we felt it was a good way for them to learn some life skills by dealing with the public. They also spent their money more wisely when they earned it themselves!

Dillon was keener than Tom, who usually preferred to spend his spare time doing things with his friends. One of the things Dillon seemed to enjoy most of all was setting up the shop in the morning and making sure the displays looked as eye-catching as possible. He had a very creative streak and was excellent at art at school, as well as technical drawing. Dillon still hadn't worked out exactly what he wanted to do for a job, but he loved designing things, and he was also very interested in fashion and textiles, and in fact anything that let him use his broad imagination.

The window displays he created were always much admired by our customers, who started asking for particular colour combinations of flowers based on how Dillon put the vases, baskets and bunches of flowers together.

It was actually one of Dillon's ideas that solved a problem that had been troubling many of the locals for quite some time.

The issue was that rabbits had started eating the flowers that were placed at graves in the local cemetery. Someone would put a beautiful display of flowers on a grave, then go back the next day to find nothing but a bunch of chewed stalks. It was very distressing for people; one poor woman came into the shop and burst into tears while she was telling me about it. It was a topic that was often discussed by our customers, and although people did come up with various suggestions about how to stop it happening, including using only rabbit-resistant flowers such as asters or delphiniums, only a few of the methods that were tried really worked.

Then, one day, Dillon was helping out in the shop when he put a display of imitation flowers on the counter and asked me, 'What do you think?'

'It's beautiful,' I told him. 'But why in a grave vase?'

'Because that's what it's for,' he said, taking a step back from the counter and looking at the arrangement critically, with his head on one side, before apparently deciding that he liked it too. 'You'd have to be a very hungry rabbit to want to eat that!'

'What a brilliant idea.' Jonathan had just come back into the shop after carrying some bouquets out to someone's car. 'Why didn't anyone else think of that? It's the perfect solution.'

We obviously weren't the only ones who thought Dillon's specially designed grave-vase displays were lovely, and of course practical. They were an instant hit with our customers. We always encourage youngsters to have ambition and something to strive towards when they are older, so we were very pleased when Dillon decided to start his own little business with this idea, which he ran within the flower shop.

'I think it's what's called a win-win situation,' Jonathan told

Dillon one morning when he was checking his bank statement and exclaiming excitedly about how much money he'd saved from the profits he was making. 'Unless, of course, you're a rabbit!'

'I think you're right,' Dillon laughed. 'I hear I'm public enemy number one among the rabbits. But I can live with that. I'm going to be an entrepreneur and run my own business when I'm older.'

'And I've no doubt that it will be a great success,' Jonathan said, 'whatever you decide to design or sell.'

Maria came in on the latter part of this conversation.

'I'm glad they don't put the rabbits in hutches,' she said. 'I don't like rabbit hutches.'

This rang a bell, but it took me a moment to remember why.

'Oh, you had a rabbit, did you, Maria?' I asked gently, as I remembered seeing a hutch in the photographs Babs had given us to look through for Maria's life story book. It was in one of the photos Maria had rejected, rather forcefully.

'No rabbit, just a hutch,' she said.

I imagined she'd been disappointed as a child to have a hutch and no rabbit, but I didn't want to open old wounds and so I left a gap in the conversation, giving Maria the space to say whatever she wanted. Looking at the grave vases, she then said, 'Do you think the dead people like having flowers on their grave?'

'Well, I think it's more about the people left behind. They want to put the flowers on the graves to show their loved ones they still care, even though they have passed away.'

'But dead people can see. Mummy said dead people talk to her.'

'Is your mum *psychic* or something?' Dillon asked, flicking his head around.

'Yes. And so is my stepdad. He can see through walls too. And he can talk to ghosts. He's telepathic. It's *an-noy-ing*.'

Dillon burst out laughing. 'I don't think so, Maria,' he said. 'It sounds like he's been winding you up! Nobody can do those things. Ha ha, it sounds like he's been watching too many spooky films!'

Jonathan and I looked at each other uncertainly. We didn't want Maria to be upset, but then again we didn't want to stop her making any disclosures that might be important for Social Services to know about.

'Well, Dillon, perhaps it's best not to pass a verdict about something when you don't know all the facts,' Jonathan said diplomatically.

'It's OK,' Maria said, and then added defiantly, 'but I know things that would make your hair twirl!'

'Make you hair curl, you mean,' Dillon said. 'Maria, you're so funny!'

That was the end of the conversation, and Jonathan and I were left feeling confused and uneasy. We thought Maria had seen through Gerry and the claims he made about his so-called special powers, but apparently not. It seemed that whatever nonsense he'd fed to Maria, backed up by Christine and her belief she had a psychic gift, had had a deep and lasting impact on Maria.

23

'I can't learn stuff like that'

Maria was continuing to do well at school, although she still hated PE, which was unfortunate as I had noticed that she'd started to gain a little bit of weight.

'You know what I think Maria needs,' I said to Jonathan.

He raised his eyebrows.

'A trampoline.'

'Why a trampoline?'

'Well, it would help her keep fit, which I think she needs to do as she's still not taking part in PE at school as often as she should. Also, exercise is good for the brain.'

I read somewhere that a study in America had shown that doing a particular exercise plan for three months had led to a thirty per cent increased blood flow to the part of the brain that's responsible for memory and learning. I told Jonathan about this study, adding, 'I know there is nothing wrong with Maria's memory and learning, but that doesn't mean she can't benefit mentally as well as physically from doing more exercise. And as we know, the key to successful exercise is that you need to find something you enjoy, so you do it without it being a chore. I think she'd love it!'

Jonathan scratched his head. 'Well, it sounds like you have this all worked out, Angela. And I think it's a very good idea. Tom and Dillon will love it too, I'm sure, as will whoever else comes along in the future.'

The final decision on Maria's care order was now possibly only a matter of weeks away. I really didn't want to think about her leaving. I would miss her, and I worried about how she would cope with all the inevitable upheaval she would face, whichever way the court decided.

There was nothing I could do but make the best of the time we still had. The weather was good and I felt that Maria could get great use out of the trampoline while she was still with us. As Jonathan pointed out, it would be a good long-term investment that plenty of other children would benefit from, so we agreed to make the purchase. We ordered a trampoline from a catalogue store and assembled it as soon as it was delivered to the house a few days later.

'If she feels fitter and healthier, it can only help with her self-confidence,' I said to Jonathan as we sat down on a couple of garden chairs, admired our handiwork and had a welcome rest.

'Yes, I hope so,' he replied. 'She still needs help in that area, doesn't she?'

We said this because Maria still frequently said things like 'I can't do it,' 'I'm rubbish!' or even 'I'm too thick to do that!' whenever we suggested she try something new or had a go at a task she didn't readily enjoy. Having Maria learn to crochet with my mum had helped show her that when you put your mind to something you can do it if you want to, however unfamiliar or unappealing it may be, or even if you think you are going to fail. However, I think she was so used to feeling inadequate that she found it hard to change her mindset.

'If you are physically hurt by the people who are meant to be looking after you, I imagine you really lose faith in yourself,' I said. 'It must be so difficult.'

'That's right,' Jonathan said, very knowingly.

I looked at him and realised he was remembering his own childhood, growing up on a farm with his three older brothers. Jonathan was the smallest and thinnest of all the boys and his father always treated him like the runt of the family. For instance, when Jonathan wasn't strong enough to chop the wood his father hit him with a belt and berated him for being a 'useless weakling'.

Inevitably, this impacted on Jonathan's self-esteem, and it wasn't until he was grown up and had forged a career for himself away from the farm, working in the city, that he truly began to believe in himself.

'The damage lasts a long time,' he nodded. 'When you are repeatedly told you are no good you believe it, especially when you are told it by your parents. However they treat you, you know they are in charge and you think they have to be right. It's how the mind works when you are a child. You accept things that are told to you by figures in authority, even when what they are saying doesn't seem right or fair. And once your mind has been set it is hard to reverse the negative patterns created in your brain.'

I squeezed Jonathan's hand. We'd talked about his past many times, and as we'd become more knowledgeable about psychology and child development through our training, he had learned and understood more about himself and his past. It was painful to think of Jonathan being treated badly by his father, but when I looked at him that day I also felt flooded with optimism. If he could not just get over what had happened to him but also become the loving, sensitive and self-aware foster carer he was, then there was hope for all the children we fostered. Granted, Maria had been subjected to far worse physical and emotional abuse than Jonathan ever had, but that did not mean she couldn't overcome the difficulties of her early childhood, did it?

The next time my mum came over I asked her if she might now teach Maria to knit, as a step on from the crocheting she had mastered.

'Of course,' Mum said. 'It would be my absolute pleasure!'

Mum has always had very good relationships with the children we've fostered. Perhaps one of the strongest bonds she has had was with a lad called Ian who came to us for respite care when he was fifteen. Ian had a speech impediment that made him anxious and frustrated, and as a result he found it very difficult to make friends. My mother used to sit with him for hours, reading to him, listening and encouraging him while he read to her, and playing board games with him. I think she was the first person who had ever really spent as much time with him as he needed and, as well as helping to improve his self-confidence, she really helped him with his speech too.

Jonathan took a photograph of the pair of them one day, sitting on the sofa in our house, their heads together, absorbed in whatever they were reading at the time. When Ian gave a copy of it to Mum, she framed it and put it on a table in her living room. And every time we took Ian round to her house with us he would pick it up and show it to us proudly, each time as though it was the first time we'd ever seen it. He's an adult now, and he still visits Mum regularly.

Anyhow, after we'd had dinner together that evening Mum offered to teach Maria how to knit.

'I can't learn stuff like that,' Maria told her.

It was clear to me that Maria's response was almost automatic, as it really wasn't an accurate thing to say. She'd crocheted various items for her teddies and had even made me a cushion cover, which I put on the cushion on my favourite chair. If she could do that 'stuff' then it was obvious she'd be able to knit.

'Oh, why's that?' Mum asked, looking confused. 'If you can crochet I'm sure you can knit!'

'Because I'm stupid,' Maria answered, twisting a strand of hair around her finger and looking embarrassed.

'Stupid! Who told you that?' Mum exclaimed. 'Well, whoever it was, they need to have their head examined.'

Not having had the training Jonathan and I have had, Mum didn't always react to things the children said the same way we would have done. But Maria seemed pleased by my mum's response, even if she wasn't entirely convinced that what she'd said was true.

'Of course you can learn to knit, Maria,' Mum insisted. 'Come on, let's go in the living room and I'll show you.'

'No,' she said, chewing her fingernail anxiously. 'I can't do it. I'm too stupid.'

'Maria,' I said. 'You are not stupid. You're nervous. Everyone gets nervous when they try to do something they haven't done before. I remember being nervous when Mum taught me to knit.'

'Really?'

'Really,' I said. 'I've been nervous about lots and lots of things when I've thought I couldn't do them or felt a bit scared, but once I've got started I've generally found that I can do it, even if it's not perfect.'

'Like what?' Maria said suspiciously.

'Well, I was a bit scared about sledging. Do you remember I told you that when we went sledging together? And I can still remember the first job interview I ever had to do. I was so nervous before I went that I could hardly breathe, and my dad said, "Just sit there and smile, then take a deep breath and remember that all the people interviewing you have had first interviews themselves. At some point in their lives, they've all gone through exactly the same thing you're going through now – they've all been nervous about something at some time. So just remember that you're not the only one and then do your best. I know you can do it."'

Maria hadn't ever had that sort of encouragement growing up. She was used to her stepfather telling her, 'You're no good. You're a bad person. A waste of space. Can't you ever do anything right?' So she believed that she felt the way she did whenever she was faced with something new or potentially difficult because she was stupid and wouldn't be able to do it.

Fortunately, having Mum there to reinforce my positive encouragement really helped. She was patient and tolerant and she also offered a story to inspire Maria, about a time when she felt she couldn't possibly get a Brownie badge she wanted.

'You were a Brownie?' Maria laughed. 'That's so funny! I didn't think they had Brownies in the olden days!'

Mum, who was in her seventies, smiled and didn't take any offence. 'I think you're funny, Maria,' she laughed, 'and also rather cheeky! The olden days, honestly!'

It was nice for Maria to see that someone who didn't have any reason for being involved with her – who wasn't a family member or a foster carer, for example – actually enjoyed her company. Mum thought the world of Maria, in fact, and when the two of them presented me with a knitted yellow square some time later, it was hard to tell who was the more proud, Maria or Mum.

The trampoline was a hit too, incidentally. Maria loved it and was soon learning how to do tuck jumps, half-twists, backdrops and straddle jumps.

'Watch this, Angela!' she'd call to me as I watched from the kitchen window, or when I kept an eye on her as I pottered around the garden, usually doing some weeding or hanging out the washing at the same time.

'Look! You missed it! Watch now! And again! Look, I did it! I'll do another one!'

When Jonathan was with me, we would swap amused glances, as if to say, 'What have we done? No peace for the wicked!'

24

'Are you jealous or something?'

Maria continued to have the weekly calls with her mum, or at least they were scheduled to take place – Christine wasn't always available. When the calls did go ahead as planned Maria still seemed to be on high alert a lot of the time, choosing her words carefully and racking her brain to provide details of her daily life that hopefully wouldn't bring any criticism. More than once I saw Maria visibly sigh and drop her shoulders in relief when the call ended.

One day Gerry phoned up, out of the blue. It was around the time of day when Christine was due to speak to Maria, and as I recognised the phone number on the digital display I told Maria she could answer the call. She had been in a really good mood, but the moment she lifted the receiver I saw her shoulders shoot up to her ears and the colour drained from her face.

'Gerry!' she said, sounding nervous and shocked.

When Christine called I always pressed the speaker button straight away, as Social Services asked me to do and Maria knew to do the same, but I had no instructions for dealing with Gerry. I didn't want to antagonise him by taking the phone off

Maria or have him hear me tampering with the phone by switching it to speaker mode, and so I decided to just stay close by and listen to Maria's half of the conversation. That way I felt I was protecting her as best I could without potentially causing trouble.

'Yes,' Maria nodded. 'No. No, I didn't know that. I am not sure I believe in . . . what? How did you know?'

Maria was as white as a sheet, and I said loudly, 'Are you all right, Maria?'

'I've got to go!' she said hastily. 'Bye Gerry!'

Her little hand was trembling as she replaced the receiver back in its cradle.

'Are you all right?' I asked again.

'Fine, all fine!' she said breezily. 'Gerry is fine! All good!'

'It's unusual for him to phone up, are you sure?'

'Oh yes, he's only looking after me, Angela! Are you jealous or something?'

I let this go. I had no idea what Gerry had been saying but all the signs were that he was playing with Maria's young mind, and I wasn't going to allow myself to be sucked into his games.

We were looking after another little girl that day, so that her foster carer could go to a funeral. Amelia was a couple of years younger than Maria, and they had seemed to be getting on quite well until the phone call from Gerry.

The girls had been playing a computer game together, and when Maria went back to it she suddenly started bossing Amelia around, telling her she wasn't allowed to play the game because she was stupid and she'd break it. 'You're too thick to play it,' Maria told Amelia, then started chanting, in a sing-song voice, 'Amelia is useless. Amelia's a fool.'

When Jonathan and I told Maria to stop calling Amelia names and leave her alone, she ignored us and continued to taunt and tease her, until eventually Amelia got so upset she screamed at her, 'I am *not* stupid. Leave me alone. I *do* know how to play this game. We've got it at home.'

I touched Maria's shoulder to attract her attention and told her again, 'Please, Maria, leave Amelia alone.'

'You're all stupid,' she shouted, spinning round on her heels and then storming out of the room and up the stairs. 'Gerry is right! Stupid and jealous and he's cleverer than you! He knows you talk about me behind my back!'

Had that been the purpose of Gerry's call? To slyly try to turn Maria against us in her final few weeks? He would know all too well that Jonathan and I *did* talk about Maria between us. That was part of our job, to discuss the children in our care, support one another and hopefully share information that would make children's lives better. I had no idea why he would use this fact to try to undermine us at this stage. Maria would be leaving us soon whatever the verdict of the court, so what was he worried about, and why was he meddling like this?

'Some people are just plain nasty, I'm afraid,' Jonathan said, when we talked about it later. 'There is no reasonable explanation why anybody would want to fill Maria's head with nonsense about us, or nonsense of any kind. But Gerry is not reasonable, is he? We know that, unfortunately.'

I discovered later that when Maria went upstairs she told Tom I'd hit her. I didn't confront Maria about this but just made a note of it in my daily log. Maria's social worker spoke to her about it the next day, and Maria admitted I hadn't actually hit her and that she'd just said I had because she was in a bad mood after speaking to her stepfather.

I can remember my father telling me when I was a child that he was often told as a little boy that 'children should be seen and not heard'. It was not something he agreed with, and his willingness to sit down and talk to me about anything that was troubling me is something I have always remembered, and it's something I try to do with all the children we foster.

What was also very much a factor in raising children when my dad was young was the commonly held belief that children 'need to be taught to behave'. I suppose that's true to the extent that there are certain codes of behaviour that are acceptable in the society we live in, which children don't have any innate knowledge or understanding of, and so have to learn about. But trying to teach children to behave when they have experienced the sort of emotional abuse that Maria had been subjected to, which was reflected in her frequent outbursts of anger, was not the answer. Maria's behaviour was driven by her emotions, over which she had no control. So before she could be 'taught to behave', she had to learn how to deal with her feelings. That is why I didn't confront her about telling Tom I'd hit her. Instead, I waited for the next opportunity to ask her how she was feeling and to make it clear to her that she could talk to me any time she liked.

I find the training Jonathan and I did on PACE – playfulness, acceptance, curiosity and empathy – very helpful in situations like Maria's.

Jonathan was good at the *playfulness* part, and could usually raise a smile from Maria when she was sulking by 'acting the goat' and singing the silly song he made up about a girl called Maria, which had become her signature tune ever since the first time Jonathan sang it when she stayed with us when she was seven. Maria would blush and tell him to 'stop it', but it was obvious that she enjoyed the attention, which was kind and positive and in stark contrast to the unkind, negative attention she was used to getting at home.

We always *accepted* what Maria told us about her past, which she often did by mentioning some incident in an apparently nonchalant tone of voice while we were busy doing something else, so that she didn't need to make eye contact with anyone. And whenever she did tell us something, we responded in a similarly matter-of-fact tone, were never judgemental and always told her, 'It was not your fault'.

We would be *curious* by asking her, 'I wonder why your stepdad did that,' when she told us about the nasty 'games' he played on her. Then we would *empathise* by telling her, 'I think you are very brave, Maria, the way you are learning to deal with all the things that have happened to you.'

'I like it when you listen to me,' she told me one day, not long after this incident with Amelia, and Maria telling Tom I'd hit her. 'I tried to tell *him* once that I was feeling sad about something, but he said,' she mimicked a man's deep, angry voice, '"I don't want to hear about your *feelings*. What are you trying to do? Bore me to death? Don't come whingeing and whining to me. Just deal with it. Go on, sod off, crybaby!"'

It was understandable that, having never been allowed to express her feelings before, it was some time before Maria began to realise and accept the fact that she wasn't alone any more, that we cared about her and that it was OK to feel whatever she felt. By explaining to her, either explicitly or by example, that although she would be held responsible for her behaviour, she *wasn't* responsible for the emotions that elicited it, we gradually helped her to start learning to deal with, communicate and accept her own feelings in a way she had never previously been able, or allowed, to do.

Maria could be quite a clingy child, sitting very close beside me on the sofa when we were watching television, for example, and often trying to get my attention whenever I was talking to someone else. One of her complaints when she was in a sulk was that, 'No one cares about me.' It didn't matter how many times we told her, '*We* care about you, Maria,' she still didn't believe it. Part of the problem was that the message she'd been receiving until then was that she didn't deserve anyone's care and affection. We knew it was going to take a very long time to persuade her otherwise.

One day, when she was in a temper, she locked herself in the bathroom and wouldn't come out for ages. We tried coaxing her. Then we sat in silence for a while, hoping that her protest would lose its dramatic appeal if she thought we'd left her to it and that there was no one there to witness it. I don't remember what triggered that particular tantrum – it could have been something, or nothing. But when she did eventually come out of the bathroom, she was still sulking, 'Because nobody cares about me.' I gave her a cuddle, and we talked about how she felt until she cheered up again.

We've fostered many children whose reactions, at times, seemed to be out of all proportion to the events that precipitated them. I was interested to read recently about some research that's been done which indicates that, for a child who has always had to be alert to the signs of trouble kicking off, an incident that might appear to be insignificant to anyone else can trigger a response in a part of the brain that's constantly on red alert. The brain then responds as it would to the threat of being attacked – hence the out-of-proportion reactions we sometimes witnessed.

There were certain triggers that made Maria behave as if she were being attacked, including one that she was particularly sensitive to, which was the word 'bad', I think because her stepfather always told her she was a bad person. One example of the effect it had occurred when she was at her grandparents' house one day, playing with a cousin who was about the same age as she was. The two children were squabbling mildly as they played and eventually Maria's aunt – the little boy's mother – said, not angrily at all apparently, 'I don't know, Maria, you and your cousin are as bad as each other.'

'It was as if a switch had been flicked inside Maria's head,' Babs told me later. 'She'd just been grumbling and sulking a bit before then. But she suddenly flew at the poor little lad and started hitting him.'

It had taken the combined efforts of her aunt and grandmother to pull Maria off her cousin. When everything had calmed down again, she told her grandmother, 'It's true what Mummy says about you, you're not really a nice person. You just pretend to be.'

It was always a big issue to Maria, the dilemma about whether she could trust people. She seemed to suspect that people who seemed to be nice were just pretending and were really as 'bad' as she believed she was. I think that believing she was 'bad' was also one of the reasons why her tantrums could sometimes be prompted by something as simple as someone being nice to her: the trauma and hurt she'd experienced as a young child had taught her to be defensive as a means of self-protection, and her instinct when anyone threatened her defence was to react with anger.

I discovered that, at the school she had gone to when the family moved out of the area, Maria had been due to see a child psychologist because of the way she behaved, but had left before an appointment could be arranged for her. This was a shame, as it's very difficult to get access to mental health support for any children, not only those in foster care, and the opportunity didn't arise again.

Unfortunately, there just aren't the staff available to deal with even a fraction of the number of children who would benefit from psychological intervention. In our experience, they usually have to be in crisis before they can get an appointment.

Sometimes, when Maria got upset about something and ran away, and Jonathan had to sprint after her and bring her back, I would try to encourage her to talk about what was wrong. But her usual response was either a sullen, 'No one cares about me,' or 'You wouldn't understand if I told you.' The truth was, of course, that she didn't understand it herself.

When she was angry with us for some reason that we couldn't put our finger on, we would say something like, 'You sound angry and upset. Are you?' Or sometimes I'd say, 'Look at me, Maria. Now, take a deep breath and count to ten.' I always found that useful when I was growing up, and I still occasionally do it now, and I would tell Maria this.

'Yeah, right,' Maria would say. 'I don't believe you.' Or she'd respond by saying something to us that wasn't very nice, and we'd tell her, calmly, 'Try saying that again, but this time in a nicer way.' Then later, when she had calmed down, she would sometimes say, 'I don't know how you can be so calm with me. I know I wouldn't be able to do it if I was you.'

'We can all say things in the heat of the moment that we later regret,' we'd tell her.

In fact, though, Jonathan and I have learned over the years not to speak our minds, however sorely we're tempted to do so in some situations. Your thought processes are always clearer when you've had a chance to step away, mull over what's happened or been said, and maybe have a good night's sleep too. It's never a good idea to let off steam and respond in the heat of the moment, whereas positive comments made after some thought can actually be useful.

Sometimes, your automatic response to a situation has less to do with what's happening at that particular moment and more to do with other things that are going on in your life – how much sleep you've had; what's happening within your own family. But it's not so much what you feel as how you handle your feelings that matters in a potentially confrontational situation. So, if you do speak without thinking, particularly when you're angry or upset, you might end up saying something that makes everything worse.

We have supervision with our support social worker every six weeks, which is very useful in that respect, because it enables us to talk about things that have happened, which is something foster carers can't do with anyone else, not even their family or close friends. Jonathan and I have also learned that when things are not running smoothly, which they don't always do in any fostering household, you have to take care of yourself without feeling guilty about doing so. That's why we like to go out together occasionally for an evening and spoil ourselves, which we can do thanks to my mum's willingness to babysit.

Eventually, more by accident than design, I did find one way of helping to defuse some of Maria's angry outbursts. A girl we'd fostered a few years earlier was into all kinds of art, and after she gave me a set of glitter tattoo pens as a Christmas present, I got quite good at face painting – for the children we fostered, I hasten to add, not for myself! When Maria told me one day that she wanted to get a tattoo as soon as she was old enough, it gave me an idea. The next time she was angry, I offered to do a tattoo on her arm, in glittery, washable pen.

The combination of her focusing on watching what I was drawing and having one-to-one time with me seemed to help her to self-regulate and deal with her feelings. And, after that first time, she often asked me to do a tattoo for her when she was angry or upset.

'If only they'd taught us that at foster training years ago,' Jonathan mused one day.

'I thought the same myself,' I laughed. 'But having said that, I'm not sure it would work on every child. I can't really see Tom and Dillon parading around with glitter tattoos, can you?'

Jonathan laughed too. It was moments like that that often rescued the day and helped me stay positive when the going got tough.

25

'I wonder how Maria will take it'

As the legal process dragged on, Christine not only continued to make numerous complaints about things she thought Jonathan and I should or shouldn't have done, but she also started being blatantly obstructive and refusing to talk to us, or even look at us, during the couple of meetings she came to at the Social Services offices in town. Then she stopped coming at all.

We would always wait for a while, in case she was held up, before carrying on without her. When she didn't show up she would always be informed afterwards of everything that was said and decided at the meetings. Copies of the notes taken would be sent to her and there was usually something that required her consent. But Christine rarely answered the letters she was sent by Social Services either. When she did, it was usually just to complain about something else. For example, once she criticised us for telling Maria she couldn't have her ears pierced. In fact, we'd told Maria this was not a decision we were able to take, and that she would have to talk to her social worker and Christine herself. Had we allowed Maria to have her ears pierced without Christine's consent, I'm sure she would have had a lot more to complain about, and quite rightly so.

When Christine was challenged by Social Services about why she didn't attend the meetings she said, 'I'd prefer to go to the house,' meaning our house.

Jonathan and I have to gauge on an individual basis whether it's appropriate for a particular parent to come to our house. And although Maria's mother had been a few times before the interim care order came into effect, and her grandmother came often to see Maria and have a cup of tea, we never hosted the organised meetings at our house, and in fact we had reached the point where we did not want Christine in our home.

When a foster child comes to live with us, our house is their new home, for however long they stay, which might be for just a few days or, in some cases, for years. For some children, our house might be the only place they've ever lived where no one shouts or is unkind or cruel to them. Once they begin to feel safe there, we need to make sure nothing happens to change that. We learned this lesson the hard way, when a very vindictive mother flew into a rage one day and said some terrible things that left her child in tears. We realised after the experience that meetings at which sensitive issues might be discussed are best held elsewhere.

Another reason, of course, is that if there are other children living in the house at the time, their opinion of a particular child might be coloured by the fact that he or she has a mother or father who they've heard swearing and shouting. It can make things very difficult for a child in that situation if the other children think the mum or dad is 'horrible', because however badly they've been treated by their parents, most children still love them, and it's very hurtful to them if other people are critical. That's why, whatever Jonathan and I know about a child's background and the sometimes unspeakable experiences they've been subjected to – which might include sexual and physical abuse – we have to work with their parents, and we are always nice to them. So we continued to be civil to Maria's mother, however infuriated we were by some of her complaints and actions, but we did not agree to any meetings with her in our home.

Another of the complaints Christine made to Social Services was about something that had been said by Dillon. Normally, Dillon and Maria got on very well, but one day, after he'd seen her chatting with a boy on the playing fields behind our house, he teased her about it and asked if it was her boyfriend. It was just a bit of fun, but her reactions could be unpredictable, and on that occasion she flew into a rage. Then the next time she spoke to her mother, she told her what Dillon had said, and Christine complained to Social Services.

You couldn't be a very effective foster carer if you weren't able to bite your tongue when something like that happens. What was irritating in this particular case, however, was that Maria's mother had complained about some harmless teasing by a lad who had been nicer to her child than almost anyone in her own family had ever been.

'My stepdad said that if Dillon does it again, I should deck him,' Maria told us later.

'Did he now?' Jonathan's tone was ironic. 'Well, as I expect you realise, there are quite a few reasons why that wouldn't be a good idea. I'm not sure whether top of the list would be because hitting someone is *never* the solution to any problem or because Dillon is a strapping lad, and you're . . . well, you're not!'

'My stepdad says I'm so feeble that anyone would know I wasn't his kid,' Maria said quietly.

'You're not *feeble* at all,' Jonathan retorted hastily. 'That wasn't what I meant. But Dillon is a big teenage boy . . .'

'My stepdad used to tell Frank and Casey to punch me,' Maria interrupted. 'Then he'd tell *me* to hit them back. He always got really angry with me because I didn't do it. But they're much bigger than me, and I was scared that if I did try to hit them, they'd really hurt me. And I knew *he* wouldn't have done anything if they had.'

'What your stepfather did was not nice and should never have happened, Maria,' I told her. 'As Jonathan said, it's always wrong to hit someone. You did the right thing and we are very proud of you for not hitting back.' I was unafraid of speaking so bluntly about Gerry because I believed what Maria was telling me and I wanted to get the message across to her that physical abuse, and inciting physical abuse, is never acceptable.

Fortunately, Maria had only told her mother that Dillon had teased her because it was something to say, so she wasn't influenced by the fact that her mother had complained about him to Social Services. It would have been a shame if it had affected her relationship with Dillon, because they generally got on very well and she looked up to him, and to Tom.

I think the relationship between children fostered in the same home has quite a special and unique dimension, because they are in the same boat and understand what life is like for one another. I suppose it's similar to us talking to other foster carers: only someone who has had the same sort of experiences as we've had can really know how we feel.

When we were introduced to the first child we ever fostered, I can remember looking at the photographs we'd been sent of her and thinking, 'She's going to be our child.' It was a very special feeling, particularly because Jonathan and I hadn't had any children of our own. But, of course, the children who came to stay with us weren't, and wouldn't ever be, *our* children. They already had parents and other family members, and most of them wanted to be with their own families, who, unfortunately, couldn't, wouldn't or weren't allowed to look after them at that time.

It was a few years after we fostered that first girl that we discovered we couldn't have children of our own, and since then a friend who is a member of a local church has told us many times that it was God's will for us to look after 'damaged' children – 'Because you're so good at it,' she says.

What Jonathan and I have both realised since then is that although we care *for* the children we foster to the very best of our ability, and we care *about* them too, our role in their lives will only ever be peripheral and temporary. Becoming emotionally attached to the children you look after is a risky business for a foster carer. We would do anything we could to support them, both during and after the time when they're actually living with us. But we try not to allow ourselves to become too deeply attached, because however long children may live with us, if we allow ourselves to forget that we are not their parents we could very easily get hurt. We put our heart and souls into fostering, but trying not to be entirely *whole*hearted as a foster carer is really just a case of self-preservation.

That said, we certainly care about them very deeply, and

however much we want to protect ourselves from being hurt, ultimately the truth is that we can't help but love the children.

Yet another complaint from Christine was that Maria had started referring to her stepfather by his name, Gerry, instead of calling him Dad, as Christine told her to. I think she did still say 'Dad' when she was speaking directly to his face, but Babs had apparently told Christine that she didn't do it when he wasn't actually there. Christine complained to Social Services, although I'm not sure what she thought they could, or would, do about it.

Of course, even under the extended interim care order, Christine had every right to say if she wasn't happy about some aspect of her daughter's care. The problem was that although she complained, she didn't ever do anything herself to try to make things easier for Maria – or for us, although we didn't expect her to care about that.

Finally, on a dull, wet day when Jonathan and I were going about our business as usual in the florist shop, we got the news we had been waiting for.

'It's Jess,' the social worker said, and I could tell immediately that she was itching to pass something on. 'Can you talk, Angela?'

The shop was empty of customers, and I said, 'Yes, I can talk.' With that I walked with the hands-free receiver to the storeroom at the back, just in case somebody came in.

Jonathan gave me a nod as I said, 'What is it, Jess? Is it the court decision?'

'Yes. The final judgement has been made.'

It had taken more than six months since the interim care order for this verdict to come through and I think I'd thought about it every single day, but now the moment had arrived I almost didn't want to hear it.

'And?' I was holding my breath.

'Maria is being placed under a full care order. We will be fixing up a long-term foster home for her as soon as we can,' Jess said.

I exhaled. Feelings of relief seeped through me, but I also felt a grip on my heart. Poor Maria. This judgement meant that the state believed her mother and stepfather were not fit to look after her. Finally, Christine had lost her parental rights. I thought about what this really meant. The full care order effectively meant that the state had removed Maria from her mother, and all decisions about her care and wellbeing would be made by the local authority. In that moment I found this very sad, and very worrying, in terms of what evidence must have been presented to the court. I also thought about Maria's birth father and wondered if he had been involved in the court's decision process. I suspected not, seeing as from the little I knew there appeared to have been a dispute about who Maria's biological father was. That upset me too; it was such a desperately sad situation.

I thanked Jess and relayed the news to Jonathan in a deadpan way, as I was still trying to absorb it.

'It's shocking, isn't it?' he said. 'What a lot to take in. I wonder how Maria will take it.'

Fortunately, it was almost the end of the school day, so we didn't have long to wait to find out.

I collected Maria at the gate and walked her home. She seemed to be in a fairly good mood, chatting about a lesson she'd had on Australia, and telling me how she had been the only one in the class to recognise the Australian flag.

'What a clever girl!' I said. 'I'm not sure I would have known that when I was your age!'

Maria giggled. 'I learned it from one of the jigsaw puzzles I did with your mum,' she said proudly.

As soon as we were home I sat Maria down, as Jess had asked me to, and explained that the decision about her future had been made at long last.

'What is it?' she asked nervously.

'A full care order,' I said. 'You know what that means, don't you?'

By now Maria knew all the terms used by the local authority and Social Services, as her social worker had explained the system and process to her several times to make sure she understood exactly what was happening, and she'd heard plenty about the process from Babs and Christine too, not to mention Gerry.

'Yes,' she said, and then she allowed herself a little smile.

'How do you feel about that, Maria?'

'Happy,' she whispered. 'I'm safe now.'

Maria then took the smile off her face. Despite everything, she loved her mother and I think it felt to her like treachery to be so relieved when she knew she wouldn't be going home again.

'It's all right, you are allowed to tell me how you feel,' I said.

'Thanks. He can't hear, can he? He can't see me?'

'No, Maria. You are safe here.'

With that she asked me to cuddle her, and then she sobbed quietly in my arms for quite some time.

*

A phone call had been fixed up between Maria and her mum, and this was to be the first one since the news of the full care order had come through. It was obviously going to be a bit awkward, to say the least, but Maria told me she was 'looking forward' to talking to her mum.

'I won't tell her what I told you,' she said.

I listened, knowing she meant the comment about being 'safe' now.

'I think I'll just tell her what I've been doing at school and things.'

'I think that's a good idea,' I said. 'She likes to hear all about the things you've been doing, doesn't she?

'Yes,' she smiled. 'And now she can't tell me what to do!'

It was a bittersweet moment. I could tell that Maria felt an element of relief that her mum no longer had control over her life. It was as though a protective barrier had been put up, and she felt safe behind it. I was pleased about this, but at the same time I felt the sadness of the situation. Despite everything Christine had done to make life difficult for Maria, and for Jonathan and me, at the end of the day she was a mum who had just had her child taken off her. Of course, there were very good reasons for this, but I still felt Christine's pain, or at least the pain I imagined she would be feeling.

Maria approached the call bravely, launching into a list of the activities she'd been doing at school and telling her mum about her being the only one in the class to recognise the Australian flag.

'Australian flag? How did you know?'

'From doing a jigsaw with—'

Maria stopped herself from saying 'with Angela's mum.'

ANGELA HART

'A jigsaw?' Christine snorted. 'Aren't you a bit old to be doing *jigsaws*? Jigsaws are for little kids!'

Maria let this go and started to tell her mum what she had for breakfast, how many days her class teacher had been off sick, how one of her friends' mums was having another baby, and finally how we had some flowers in the hallway.

'Angela brings them from the shop when she can't sell them any more,' she explained. 'There are some pink ones, yellow ones and white ones and they are in a blue vase with a picture of a bird on the side. They smell nice and they look pretty, but I prefer the kind of flowers Nanny has. Nanny's are *much* better!'

Babs had vases of artificial flowers dotted all around her home and Maria had confided in me once that she didn't like them because they 'smelled of dust'. I thought what a shame it was that Maria had to work so hard during these conversations. It must have felt like walking a tightrope. I was just listening in, not taking part in the conversation, but even I felt anxious that Maria might make one false move that could lead to a big fall.

I did not expect what happened next, and clearly nor did Maria.

'I'm going to put Gerry on, and Frank and Casey,' Christine said.

Before Maria could reply all three had come on the line to mutter hello. I was perplexed about why Christine had put them on the phone, as they didn't have anything to say, and seemed to be going through the motions of talking to Maria just because Christine asked them to. Frank and Casey had never spoken to Maria on the phone while she was staying with us, so it all seemed very odd. Maria looked wary, and my guard was up too, as this felt wrong.

Then Christine came back on the phone.

'Did you wonder why they all wanted to talk to you?' she asked, somewhat triumphantly.

'Yes, Mum. Why?'

'Well, it's because I thought it might be nice for you to speak to them for the last time. And it's the last time you'll speak to me too, because we're cutting you out of our family. Bye.'

It was honestly that short, and that brutal. The line went dead and Maria stood rooted to the spot, still holding the phone receiver in her hand.

I stepped gently up to her.

'Shall I take the phone off you?'

She handed it to me, slowly, clearly in shock.

'Can I take your hand? Come on, let's get you a drink. Come here and sit at the kitchen table . . .'

Maria let me take her hand and I guided her like you would a blind person.

She sat down and stared into space as I tried to talk to her. 'Maria, I'm sorry that just happened. Can I get you a drink? We can talk about it, if you like?'

Maria couldn't speak.

Eventually I asked, 'Shall I call Nanny? Would you like that? I'm sure she'd love to see you.'

Maria managed a nod and I called Babs and told her what had happened.

'What in the name of God?' she exclaimed. 'I swear my daughter isn't right in the head sometimes. What did she say that for?'

'I have absolutely no idea, Babs.'

Babs came rushing round. Maria was still rooted to the spot

at the kitchen table, and now she was chewing her nails and biting her lips, looking as though she was trying hard to hold back the tears.

'Mummy doesn't mean it,' Babs said. 'She's just upset about the care order, because it means she can't make decisions about the things that affect you any more. She'll change her mind, though. You've still me and Granddad, and Colin, Angela and Jonathan too. Everything will be all right. I promise.'

Maria did calm down eventually and even managed a smile at bedtime when one of the boys told a funny story about something that had happened at school. She was still very quiet though, and said she just wanted to read a book and be on her own.

The next day, Christine apparently told Maria's grandmother, 'If Social Services don't think I'm fit to be a mother, then why should I bother to try?'

26

'Gerry used to play this game'

'If I was naughty,' Maria told me one evening, 'Mum made me eat chilli sauce.'

I was changing the sheets on her bed, while she sat on the floor twiddling the knobs of an Etch A Sketch, and for a moment I paused and glanced towards her, then quickly turned away again and started folding the pillowcases I'd just removed. I didn't want to make eye contact or stop what I was doing, in case this put Maria off saying anything else. It was only a few days after that awful phone call with her mum, and I wanted to tread extra carefully.

'Your mum made you eat chilli sauce when you were naughty,' I repeated, unfolding the pillowcase and then folding it up again.

'Yes.' She paused for moment. 'Chilli sauce is really hot. It makes you cry when you eat a whole spoonful of it. Not cry like when you're sad, though. It makes your eyes water and your mouth feels like it's burning. And *then* you cry because it hurts.'

'It must taste horrible,' I said, sitting down on the chair beside Maria's bed and looking at the pillow I was holding on my lap. 'I think I would have been sad too, if it had happened to me.'

'And sometimes . . .' Maria shook the Etch A Sketch and erased the picture she'd been drawing. 'Sometimes Gerry put honey in my hair and made me sleep in the cupboard where he said ants and spiders would come in the night to eat it. I don't think they did though, because the honey was still always there in the morning, and my hair was all hard and sticky.'

'Maria,' I started, but she ignored me and carried on talking, which I was glad about. 'Gerry said that if I didn't behave myself he would make me sleep in the rabbit hutch. I told him I didn't care because at least I would be out the house, but he told me he would come outside and scare the living nightlights out of me, and that he'd be able to see if I tried to escape.'

'The living daylights.'

'Yes, that's it. "I'll scare the living daylights out of you, Maria, do you hear?"' She said this in a deep, gruff voice.

Then, before I could say anything, she did what she often did in those situations and changed the subject without even pausing for breath. 'Can I have crisps for my lunch tomorrow?' she asked.

I wished I could say, 'Yes, Maria, you can have anything you want!' but I had to be consistent, so I said that no, she couldn't have crisps for lunch, but she could have some tomorrow evening, after her meal, if she was still hungry.

'OK,' she shrugged, even though she usually threw a little tantrum whenever we returned to this same argument.

'He used to lock me in my room,' Maria then said. 'I wasn't allowed out, even to go to the bathroom. So I used to pee my pants and he'd be really angry and shout at me like this.' She held her hand a couple of inches away from her face and shouted into it loudly, "'You're dirty! You're a crybaby!'"

'Then he'd get this slipper and hit me on the bottom, really hard. He said it was to teach me not to be a baby, because only babies wet their pants. But I didn't do it because I was being a baby. It was because he locked the door.'

The more Maria told me, the more I understood why she had so much anger and resentment bubbling away inside her, and why it sometimes seemed as though the smallest, most insignificant incident could trigger a full-scale meltdown. She clearly felt safe now, and as she made disclosure after disclosure I could sense the tension escaping from her body.

'I'm glad I can talk to you, Angela,' she smiled. 'It feels good to talk. You believe me, don't you?'

A look of worry suddenly shot across her face.

'Maria, of *course* I believe you.'

She sighed deeply and smiled again. 'Good. I hope my next foster carer is as nice as you, but I'd rather stay here. Can I stay here?'

I was very heartened to hear Maria say she'd like to stay with us, but of course the plan was for her to move to a long-time foster carer, freeing Jonathan and me up to take in another teenager who we might be able to help using our specialist knowledge.

I explained to Maria that we would love to have her stay with us for longer, but that it was not our decision, as it was up to Social Services to make the arrangements. It was difficult, as I had no idea how quickly Maria would be moved. She'd had so much uncertainty in her young life, and it wasn't over yet.

*

'Gerry used to play this game,' she told me the next day, as we were walking to school. 'He put a big hankie over my eyes and tied it behind my head, really tight, so it hurt and I couldn't wriggle my face to push it up and see underneath it.'

She scuffed the toe of her shoe on the path and sent a pebble skittering along it in a cloud of dust.

'Your stepdad made you wear a blindfold,' I repeated.

'Yes,' Maria said. 'Then Frank and Casey and Gerry used to play this game where I had to walk from the back door in the kitchen to the far end of the living room. If I bumped into anything, I had to go back to the kitchen and start again. But Frank and Casey used to stand in front of me, or jump out and scare me, and they put things on the floor so that I'd fall over them. Then they'd laugh at me and say I was stupid.'

'That doesn't sound like a game at all,' I told her.

'He used to play lots of horrible games,' she said. 'Now that they've got this full care order, does that mean I can get my hair cut without having to ask Mum first?'

'I'll check with the social worker,' I answered, following Maria's lead in changing the subject. 'But I'm sure the answer will be yes.'

Maria was now almost ten but her morning ritual still included trying to tame her tangled hair. Though she didn't call out in the night any more, she often told me that she had bad dreams, woke up several times in the night and was scared of the dark.

'I couldn't stop turning and tossing,' she said.

'Tossing and turning? Oh, that must be why your hair is in such a terrible tangle again! Come here, let's get the spray out and see what we can do with this haystack.'

'I thought you said it was a bird's nest?'

'It used to be, but I think it's grown!'

Maria had asked me several times if she could have her hair cut to a more manageable length and style, but to date her mother had always refused to give her permission. Now, though, it was up to the local authority to make that sort of decision, although as a courtesy they would always approach the mother first. A few days later, Maria emerged from the local hair salon with her hair cut into a neat, shoulder-length bob, and 'tackling the bird's nest' became a thing of the past.

'That's a set of weights off my shoulder,' she said, as she walked down the street.

'I can imagine it is,' I said, smiling at how she'd not quite got the phrase right once again, but also thinking what a symbolic statement it was.

It takes a long time for an abused, anxious child to learn to trust anyone again. Coming to terms with childhood trauma is a subject I've studied over the years, as scientists have learned more and more about the workings of the brain. Several recent studies have discovered that traumatic experiences in early childhood actually cause areas of the brain to develop in ways that it can take years to reconfigure, if it's possible to do so at all. There still hasn't been any conclusion to the nature–nurture debate – about whether our personalities are dictated primarily by our DNA or by our early experiences. What is known, however, is that the nature part of the equation, which involves the DNA, is set in stone and can't be altered, but that there are parts of our genetic make-up that *can* change as a result of the experiences we have as babies, or even while we're still in the womb.

When babies and young children are exposed to stress-inducing events, their bodies produce excess amounts of the stress hormone cortisol, which has a damaging effect on the development of the brain. There seems to be some indication that the 'magic age' in terms of brain development is three, because although high levels of cortisol do more damage before the age of three, any damage that is done can also be more easily reversed before that age. However, it is thought that as children get older it takes much more time and effort to reconfigure the 'abnormal' neural pathways.

Some studies have suggested that what's 'normal' has been established in a baby's brain by the age of six months. So a baby who has been subjected to fear, anxiety or any other kind of abuse will grow up to accept levels of stress other people would find very difficult to deal with. A knock-on effect of that is that it takes a very high level of stimulation to make the child react.

I find it very interesting to read about these studies, especially the ones that help to explain some of the issues we've faced with the children we've cared for over the years. I have learned that it takes a very long time for the nerves in the brain to develop new pathways. And until that happens, you can't expect children who have lived their entire lives in threatening, abusive, frightening environments to learn within a matter of months, or even years, to behave differently.

Having that knowledge makes it much easier to understand why a child like Maria can sometimes switch from good humour to full-blown temper tantrum at the slightest provocation. Instead of processing the message with the cool, reasoning part of her brain, it goes to the so-called 'hot' part and she responds to the perceived threat by overreacting. That's why children like

Maria need a lot of support. Children don't *choose* to behave badly. They react in certain ways to certain triggers because they've been neurologically primed to do so. So they have to be taught a different way, and by repeating something to them over and over again, you can help them to create new neurological pathways that they can then follow automatically. I think of it like finding a good, new, hazard-free route through a forest and using that same route for long enough to create a new path. I know from experience that it works, but it takes a *long* time.

The question was, now that Maria's time with us was coming to an end, how would she fare in her next foster home? And how long would it take for her to become a more balanced, stable and happy young person?

'Do you think she'll ever be able to get over what she's been through?' I said to Jonathan when we talked about the implications and practicalities of her full care order.

'Honestly, I don't know. I have a horrible feeling Maria will always be haunted by her past, to a greater or lesser extent.'

'Haunted,' I said thoughtfully. 'Unfortunately that's a good word to use. Gerry is spooky, isn't he? He has scared the living daylights out of Maria.'

'Yes, and Christine is, well, I suppose she's a bit of a ghostly figure, isn't she?' Jonathan replied. 'I mean, she's not quite there, as a mum. She's appeared in Maria's life when she's felt like it and then – poof – it's like she's disappeared into the ether. It has been so unsettling for Maria, not knowing if her mum is going to be there for her.'

I gave an involuntary shiver. 'Sorry, my skin just crawled,' I said.

'I know that feeling,' Jonathan replied.

In time, after many weeks, Christine did phone her daughter again, telling her she'd changed her mind about cutting her out of her life, but giving no explanation as to why.

'That's good,' Maria said, looking as if she didn't know whether to smile or cry. Instead she chose to run, as soon as the call ended, dashing out of the house and across the field. Jonathan gave chase, to make sure she was safe, but luckily Maria didn't go far.

'Sorry,' she said when he caught up with her. 'I couldn't help it. I just did it, without thinking.'

'It's all right, you're safe, Maria.'

'Am I?'

'Yes,' Jonathan said. 'You are safe, Maria.'

She nodded uncertainly and they walked back to the house together.

27

'I thought it was him!'

Jess, our social worker, informed us that it may take 'a little while' for Maria to be found a new long-term foster home, and of course we told her we'd willingly look after Maria for as long as necessary.

'We love having her,' I said. 'And in fact she has already asked if she could say, so I know she's not in any rush.'

'That's a great compliment to you,' Jess said. 'It's a shame that can't happen, though. You know how much we need to be able to call on you for help with the teenagers, Angela.'

'I totally understand, and it's right that Maria moves on to the right type of foster home. I wish you luck in your search.'

While Jess and her colleagues were working behind the scenes to find a permanent foster home for Maria, Jonathan and I were working hard on making sure she enjoyed her remaining time with us.

One weekend we went to a theme park – the one Maria had tried to win tickets for at the local festival when she first stayed with us – and it proved to be a great success. Maria went on all the rides for younger children, while Tom and Dillon went off together to try out all the faster, scarier rides.

Maria hadn't ever been anywhere like it before and she loved every minute of it, particularly the 3D cinema, which was her favourite activity. When the chairs moved and water shot out of the seat in front of us, I was taken by surprise and screamed, which made Maria hoot with laughter. And Jonathan and I laughed too, as we watched her reaching out to try to touch things she thought were actually there, becoming more and more bemused when she couldn't find them. In fact, she enjoyed it so much that we ended up going back to the 3D cinema twice, although after the first time she sat on the step that didn't move, so that she didn't get wet. Tom and Dillon were not so careful, and when we eventually caught up with them we found them to be soaked to the skin after going on every log flume and water ride they could find.

We had such a good time that when the children spotted a poster for a Halloween camping event near the same park, Jonathan and I readily agreed we could return and stay over for the weekend in the touring caravan. There was to be a fancy dress party at the campsite, and Maria cracked us all up laughing when she decided she wanted to be a 'little devil'.

'Is that what you call typecasting?' Dillon laughed.

'Why are you laughing? What does typecasting mean?'

'He's laughing because it's so appropriate,' Tom said, 'because you *are* a little devil, Maria!'

She took this in the good spirit in which it was meant, and when we got home we set about making the Halloween costume. It was easy really – a pair of black tights and shoes, a red dress that Mum and I made out of some cheap satiny material and then frayed the edges, all finished off with a pair of red horns attached to a hair band, plus a devil's fork, picked up at the local supermarket.

The fun started at breakfast on the Friday morning of the camping weekend, when Maria could hardly contain her excitement. By the time I got back from school with her that afternoon, Tom and Dillon were already home and, as soon as they'd all had a drink and a snack, we began to pack up the caravan. By 6.30 that evening we were finally ready to leave.

Just half an hour into the journey Maria started asking, 'Are we there yet?'

'No, love,' I told her. 'We've got about another hour's drive.'

'Oh.' She sighed and settled back in her seat – for about five minutes. Then she asked again, 'Are we there yet, Angela?'

'No,' Dillon replied, before I could say anything. 'Angela just told you it'll be another hour yet.'

Maria hadn't ever been to a fancy dress party of any kind before and she was far too excited to be patient. After she'd asked for the fourth time, I suggested, 'Let's play a game.'

I think Tom and Dillon were as relieved as Jonathan was by the prospect of doing something to try to take Maria's mind off what otherwise promised to be a question asked on a continuous loop, and all three of them answered in unison, 'Good idea!' and 'Yes, let's!'

'OK. You all choose a colour of a car and the winner is the first one to spot five cars of their chosen colour. But they have to be driving towards us. Cars parked in side roads don't count.' It was a rule I had added after having been caught out before by children apparently spotting cars in side roads that no one else had seen.

'I'll have silver,' Tom said immediately.

'Which is probably the most popular car colour,' Dillon said sarcastically.

'Oh really? How odd,' Tom answered. 'I chose it because I thought it would be almost impossible to spot any silver cars at all. Duh.'

'OK, I'll have blue,' Dillon laughed.

'I want silver,' Maria said.

'We can't both have the same colour,' Tom told her, 'and I've already chosen silver. You'll have to pick something else.'

'But that's not fair.' I didn't have to turn around to know that Maria was pouting. 'It's my favourite colour. Can't you choose another one?'

'OK, I'll have white.' I saw Jonathan catch Tom's eye in the rear-view mirror and smile at him for having deflected what would probably have been a full-scale sulk. In fact, his good deed was rewarded when it suddenly seemed that every car that passed us was white.

'That's not fair,' Maria said again, when Tom won after she had only seen one silver car. But at least Maria had been distracted for a while from asking, 'Are we there yet?' And it wasn't long before we were.

The campsite where the Halloween event was being held was a farmer's field, and there was a toilet and shower block quite close to where we set up our caravan. Despite having done it many times before, nothing seemed to fit when we tried to attach the awning to the side of the caravan. At first we couldn't work out what the problem was, and it wasn't until several

people had scratched their heads and tried to help that someone finally realised we'd threaded the awning back to front. So
then we had to start all over again, and by the time we finished
it was past Maria's bedtime.

Tom was sleeping under the awning, which he always liked
to do, having spent many nights camping – in all weathers –
with the Scouts. Maria and Dillon were in the bunk beds that
each had their own private cubicle.

'I want to go in this one,' Maria said.

'They're both the same,' I replied. 'Can you take the other
one as I've already put your bedding in there?'

'*I* want this one,' Maria insisted, tiredness making her sullen.

'That's fine,' Dillon said, removing his bedding. 'I don't mind
at all.'

'That's very nice of you, Dillon,' I told him, grateful to him for
being so amenable. 'Isn't it, Maria?'

'I suppose,' Maria said, before something made her add,
'Thanks. I'm sorry. I *am* a little devil, aren't I?'

'No, sweetheart,' I said. 'You are tired. Sleep well.'

There were games organised for the following day like egg-and-
spoon races, three-legged races and an obstacle course, which
involved having to jump over little gates, slide through tubes
and eventually sprint to the end.

All the races were divided into age categories. Being competi-
tive, Tom and Dillon were obviously a bit put out when they
didn't come in the top three of their group, and I don't think
they were convinced when I told them later, 'It's the taking part
that counts. Not the winning.' Their scepticism wasn't helped
by the fact that Maria came third in the under-elevens and was

so excited she spent the rest of the day – and most of the next one – showing us the medal she had won.

Unfortunately, Maria went into a mood when she didn't win a prize in the fancy dress competition, and there was a rather disturbing incident when she saw one child dressed as a famous character from a horror film.

'What's *he* doing here!' she screamed, running to hide behind Jonathan.

'Who?' Jonathan said.

'That thing!'

We all looked over to see a boy wearing a Ghostface mask from the movie *Scream*.

Tom chuckled. 'It's not the real character!' he said. 'It's just a boy dressed up.'

'I didn't think it was the real character!' Maria snapped. 'I thought it was him!'

She started looking all around, as if anxiously checking whether or not she was being followed or watched.

'Can I have a glow stick, Angela?'

'Of course you can, sweetheart.'

I took her by the hand to the stall, and while we were waiting in the small queue, Maria whispered, 'Gerry used to put on a mask like that, just for fun, to scare me!'

'For fun?'

'It was fun for him, and Frank and Casey. But not for me.'

My heart sank. It was awful to think of Maria being scared like that and I wondered how *anybody* could take pleasure from frightening a little girl, least of all her own stepbrothers. Seeing Tom and Dillon treating Maria so well only added to the sadness

I felt. Why could Frank and Casey not have been the caring big brothers Maria so desperately needed?

Despite the mask incident, it was a really good weekend, topped off with a day back at the theme park. On the journey home late on the Sunday afternoon, all three children chattered excitedly about everything they'd done.

'We'll have to plan the next trip,' Dillon said. 'Didn't you have a magazine from the Caravan Club, Angela?'

'Yes, it's here,' I said, fishing it out of the glovebox. 'Good idea; they list all the events where you can take the caravan.'

'Can I come?' Maria asked, rather nervously.

I turned around just in time to see her bottom lip wobble.

'Sweetheart, I can't make any promises,' I said, chastising myself for being a bit slow here, not pre-empting this as soon as Dillon mentioned the 'next trip'. 'I hope so, I really do.'

Maria had put the glow stick from the previous evening around her neck, like a necklace, and now she suddenly took it off. It still had a faint pink glow, and I wondered what she was going to do with it. To my surprise she opened it up until it made a half moon shape and put it in front of her face, making it look as if she was wearing a big, bright smile.

'I hope so too,' she said. 'I would have a smile this big if I could!'

241

28

'We'll take legal action'

Social Services had been advertising for suitable carers for Maria and eventually came up with four possibilities. One couple sounded as though they would be particularly suitable, and I think they had got quite a long way through the assessment process when something cropped up and we were told they weren't going to be accepted as foster carers for Maria after all. None of the other three sets of potential carers were accepted either: every time it looked as though things were going well, something seemed to come to light that resulted in another couple being dropped from what is, quite rightly, a very rigorous process.

The first step to becoming a foster carer involves filling in a detailed application form. Then there's an initial visit by a social worker, who looks at where you live and how many bedrooms and communal areas you have. They ask you questions about your understanding of what's involved in being a foster carer and about your reasons for wanting to foster children, and answer any questions you may have. If you get through that part of the process, the Form F assessment begins, which is carried out by a specially qualified social worker who might visit you anything between half a dozen and a dozen times.

Everyone aged eighteen and over who lives in the same household as someone who wants to become a foster carer is included in the assessment, which involves what used to be called a Criminal Records Bureau (CRB) check and is now a Disclosure and Barring Service (DBS) check, as well as a local authority check and a medical examination. At some stage during the assessment process, potential foster carers also have to participate in a two-day or three-day Skills to Foster training programme.

If they pass all the checks and examinations, they attend a fostering panel, at which they're asked questions by panel members who have a broad range of knowledge and experience related to childcare. Having examined the Form F and compiled their own report, the members of the fostering panel will then make a recommendation about the individual's suitability as a foster carer. And when the local authority or an independent fostering agency has looked at all the evidence and information, the person concerned will either be approved as a foster carer or not.

Jonathan and I had gone through the lengthy process many years earlier, in the late eighties, but it was still fresh in my mind because I was nervous and extremely keen to be accepted. Fostering felt like something I really had to do, even for a short time. I imagined that it might be something Jonathan and I did until we perhaps had children of our own, but of course life doesn't always turn out the way you expect.

I think the worst thing for Maria during this time was the

uncertainty of not knowing where, and with whom, she would be living for the next few years of her life.

'How do they "advertise"?' she asked me one day, as she had heard a social worker talking about the process when she came to visit us at home.

My heart sank. It seemed dreadful to imagine a child being advertised, and even worse to have that child standing in front of you, wide-eyed, asking what it meant and how it worked.

'Oh, they just write out a little bit about you, so they can match you with the right foster carer.'

'And they read it and see if they like me?'

'It's not if they *like* you, it's if they feel you would fit happily into their household.'

'Oh.'

Thankfully she didn't ask any more, and when I later saw that Social Services had placed an advert in the local press and relevant magazines, I was of course incredibly careful to keep it out of Maria's sight, just in case she recognised herself. The advert gave her age and read:

Described as lively and alert, will challenge if not happy. The foster family she joined a year ago enjoy looking after her, saying she is generally well behaved, and she has a healthy appetite. She seeks hugs and cuddles. Attends mainstream school, having recently changed school, where she is now thriving. She has made excellent progress over the past year, and has also thrived since joining the family. Needs firm, clear boundaries.

A white two-parent permanent family is needed, living in the local area, so contact with extended family can take place. She is very close to her grandmother. Ideally she should be the youngest child by about three years, or the only child.

Contact: Supervised contact with birth parent to continue, decreasing to four times a year; weekly contact unsupervised with grandmother to continue.

Status: Full Care Order.

Generally, there is desperate shortage of potential adoptive parents and foster carers, and there was not a rush of carers coming forward to offer a home to Maria. This was a problem, as Social Services had already exhausted all the contacts they had on their books, so they were forced to consider the possibility of looking out of the area.

When Babs got wind of this, she hit the roof, got a solicitor involved and told the local authority: 'If necessary, we'll take legal action to stop you moving Maria out of this area.'

Although she couldn't look after Maria full time herself because of Stanley's poor health and whatever the historic 'issue' was that prevented Maria from being allowed to live with her grandparents, it was understandable that they didn't want her to go and live somewhere miles away, where they might only see her a handful of times a year, if that.

Babs's threat to take legal action left Social Services stumped. They couldn't find anyone suitable locally, and now they couldn't move Maria anywhere else without having to fight a legal battle that would potentially cost the local authority a great deal of money, and which they might well end up losing.

It was at that point that Jonathan and I were asked if we

would consider being matched with Maria long term. Of course, this had crossed our minds in the circumstances. We cared very deeply for Maria and it seemed exactly the right thing to do, not least because Tom and Dillon were both approaching sixteen and would be moving out shortly, leaving room for us to take in other teenagers. Until now Jonathan and I had not pushed ourselves forward, as we were repeatedly reminded by Social Services that they would prefer us to foster another teenager who would benefit from our specialist training.

'What do you think?' Jonathan asked me, when we had some time to ourselves to talk about it. 'It makes sense. Shall we do it?'

'Well, we said from the outset that we'd be happy for Maria to stay with us for as long as she wanted to be here,' I said. 'And I still feel the same way. I really would like to be able to help her to become the sort of person she so clearly has the potential to be.'

'I feel exactly the same way,' Jonathan agreed.

Our conversation was that brief, and when I told Social Services we were happy to keep Maria on, I think it's fair to say they snatched our hands off.

All that remained was for me to tell Maria that we would like her to stay with us until she had finished school. She was still only ten and in her last year of primary school, so this was a long-term commitment and I felt nervous when I prepared to pass on the news. It was one thing Maria wanting to stay with us until our next camping trip, but how would she feel about staying for the next six years?

'You're joking,' she said when I told her the plan. There was no reaction on her face at first; I think she was completely surprised.

'No, I'm not joking. What do you think?'

She ran into my arms and hugged me, and then she began dancing around the room singing, 'I'm *stay*-ing. I'm *stay*-ing.'

For some children, having to move from one foster home to another can seem like an endless journey of rejection. It doesn't matter how many times it's explained to them that the reason they're being moved on again has nothing to do with them; they still believe it has, particularly if they've come from a home where they feel unloved and unlovable. I think Maria had always believed that no one wanted her – after all, even the grandparents who loved her couldn't have her to live with them permanently. When she knew that we wanted her to be part of our extended family and that she was going to be staying with us until she was old enough to live independently, I think that, perhaps for the first time ever, she considered the possibility that she might not be totally unlikeable after all.

I had already explained to Maria that Tom and Dillon were soon to be placed in supportive lodgings nearby, which were shared houses or flats supervised by Social Services, provided in those days as a stepping stone for foster children once they reached sixteen. One of the first things Maria asked when she knew she was staying was whether the five of us could still go on the caravan trip that we had planned.

I reassured her that we could fit in the weekend break before the boys moved out, as that had always been the plan, and not long afterwards we had an absolutely brilliant time at a campsite on the coast. Maria tried her hand at wakeboarding and loved it, commenting very memorably that she'd had the 'best time of my life.'

On our way home in the caravan Tom and Dillon asked if they could still come for Sunday lunch sometimes, once they had moved out. Of course I said yes, as this is something I always encourage the foster children to do, and Maria cheered. It was wonderful to see that she'd formed a bond with Tom and Dillon and seemed so content. The weekend before the boys moved out we had a farewell meal, as we always do, which everyone enjoyed. Our household would not be the same without the boys and I knew Maria would miss them, but nevertheless we would still be able to give her as much security and continuity in her life as possible. It was the very least she deserved, and Jonathan and I were delighted to have Maria with us long-term, at last, without the uncertainty of any further court decisions hanging over us.

29

'It makes it all worthwhile'

We all missed Tom and Dillon. The house seemed very quiet and there was a lot less cooking to be done, except of course on a Sunday, when they usually joined us for lunch, often along with my mum. Both boys were doing well in the supportive lodgings and had left school and embarked on college courses, which they were thoroughly enjoying. If anybody asked me if I was sorry to see them go I found myself saying: 'Yes and no'. Of course I missed having them around, but my overriding feeling was one of pride that Jonathan and I had helped get them to the stage where they could stand on their own two feet and take on responsibilities. That is our job, and we see it as a positive when children grow up, become more independent and do well for themselves.

Before we took in any other teenagers or children, Jonathan and I decided it would be nice to take Maria on a holiday abroad. This would finally give her the break Social Services had agreed they would pay for after Maria didn't come to Portugal with us when she was younger, due to her habit of running away.

Before we mentioned the idea to Maria herself, I rang Maria's latest social worker, Emily.

'We'd like to take Maria on holiday to Menorca,' I told her. 'She always loves the weekends and holidays we have in the caravan. So we thought it would be nice for her to have a *real* holiday, somewhere where the sea is warm and sunshine is pretty much guaranteed. But I just wanted to see what you thought about it first, before we make a formal request for permission from Social Services.'

'It sounds like a great idea,' Emily said. 'I know all the other kids you've taken on holiday have thoroughly enjoyed themselves and had experiences they might never otherwise have had. I'm sure Maria would enjoy it too.'

'I'm sure she would,' I agreed. 'The other thing is, you weren't working with us at the time, but when Maria came to live with us when she was nine, Social Services were going to pay for her to go to Portugal with us. That didn't work out, because she was going through a phase of running off and it was deemed unsafe, but we were promised Social Services would defer the payment until next time.'

'Leave it with me,' Emily said. 'I'll put in a request, in principle, for Maria to go on holiday with you and for Social Services to pay her share of the cost of flights and accommodation.'

When Emily phoned back a couple of days later, she spoke to Jonathan.

'Emily said it's OK for Maria to come to Menorca with us,' he told me later that morning, as he handed me a cup of coffee. 'We just have to let her know the details when we have them. Unfortunately, though, Social Services are now saying that they won't pay anything towards it. Emily said to tell you she's sorry, but there's nothing she can do as they don't remember ever promising to pay for her holiday. She said she has put all this in a letter to us.'

'What did you say?' I asked him, feeling annoyed on Maria's behalf.

'I told her not to worry and that we'd pay for it ourselves.'

Jonathan was frowning, and I caught his hand and gave it a squeeze. 'Of course you did,' I said. 'As if we wouldn't. We promised we'd take her, so we will. It's just a shame Social Services don't feel the same way about *their* promise.'

Jonathan's frown turned into a smile and I knew that he was thinking the same thoughts as me. There was no point in wasting time or energy on arguing with Social Services about their broken promise. Now it was time to look forward, not back.

Jonathan and I have always been happy to cover the additional costs incurred when we take children on holiday. Social Services sometimes give a small extra allowance, and we've had the odd occasion when relatives have contributed, even if that has simply meant providing some extra spending money or just a few pounds for souvenirs. Generally, though, Jonathan and I cover the cost of holidays ourselves. It's lucky we have our business, which earns us a comfortable, regular income and fits very well around our fostering commitments. Our view is that as long as we have enough to get by on ourselves, we are very happy to spend what we can afford on the foster children. With no children of our own, we don't have to think about leaving an inheritance behind. Life is for living, and if we can share what with have with the children we foster, then all our lives are enriched.

'Maria's going to love Menorca,' Jonathan said. 'Imagine

what she'll think when she feels how warm and soft the sand is there, and sees the colour of the sea.'

I was sitting with Maria and Jonathan at the kitchen table having dinner when Jonathan asked her, 'How would you feel about coming on holiday with Angela and me, to Menorca?'

'Are you serious?'

Maria looked at him steadily, her head tilted to one side, then turned to look at me as she asked, 'To Menorca? Is that Spain?'

'Yes. Well, not mainland Spain,' I told her. 'We thought it would be nice to go to Menorca, which is one of a group of Spanish islands called the Balearic Islands, in the Mediterranean Sea. We'll show you on a map after supper. It's got a really . . .'

But Maria was no longer listening to what I was saying. Pushing her chair back from the table, she jumped up and flung her arms around my neck, then did the same to Jonathan, almost deafening us with shouts of, 'We're going to Menorca!'

'First, though,' Jonathan said, when she had calmed down enough to eat the rest of her dinner, 'we need to get you a passport.'

In fact, getting a passport for Maria proved to be fraught with difficulty, not least because Christine had changed her daughter's surname unofficially twice, so that the name Maria was known by at that time wasn't the name that was on her birth certificate. In the end, we had to get a letter from Social Services explaining the discrepancy. And then we were good to go.

Jonathan was right: Maria did love Menorca. She loved flying in an aeroplane for the first time, she was brimming with excitement on the taxi ride from Menorca Airport to the apartment complex we were staying at, and she was ecstatic when she saw the swimming pool and the sea.

When we settled into the holiday, Maria enjoyed being able to choose what we did a lot of time, and not having to share our attention. She told us she missed Tom and Dillon, and I think this was true, as when they subsequently came to visit us she always looked forward to it and thoroughly enjoyed seeing them. However, she wasn't exactly pining for them, and I think the benefits of being an 'only child' for a while really quite appealed to her, especially on holiday.

The apartment we'd booked turned out to be even nicer than it looked in the photographs. It was on the first floor of a low-rise, whitewashed block and had two bedrooms, a small kitchen, a wet-room bathroom and a living room with a balcony that looked out on to the shared swimming pool and to the harbour beyond.

It was a real pleasure to see Maria enjoying herself, and although she did have a couple of sulks while were there, there were no temper tantrums, and no running away – that had gradually become a thing of the past, thank goodness. Every morning, after we'd eaten our breakfast in the apartment, we walked down to the harbour and along the sea wall to a beach. The water was warm and so clear that you could see the fish swimming around your feet.

On the second day we were there, we bought Maria a mask and snorkel in a little supermarket near the beach and, after Jonathan taught her how to use them, she spent the rest of that morning – and almost every other morning for the next two weeks – floating face down in the shallow water, totally absorbed by the life on the seabed. Then we either went back to the apartment for lunch or ate in one of the many cafes that lined the narrow road beside the water. After lunch, we sat in the shade and then swam in the pool.

Whenever we took children on holiday with us, Jonathan and I always insisted, 'No sunscreen, no sun'. It was a rule we were particularly careful to stick to with Maria, who had fair skin that would have burned very quickly. She sighed and rolled her eyes heavenward every time I handed her the plastic bottle of factor-30 sunscreen and asked her to apply a fresh layer, but she never refused to put it on.

Maria made friends easily with the other children staying at the complex, and Jonathan and I were sitting by the pool one afternoon, watching her splashing around with some of them, when a shadow fell across my sun lounger and I looked up to see a woman standing beside me. I didn't recognise her until she smiled, and then I realised it was a woman I had seen talking to Maria in the pool a few minutes earlier.

'I'm sorry to disturb you,' she said, 'but you *are* Angela and Jonathan, aren't you?'

'Yes,' I replied, returning her smile and leaning back slightly so that Jonathan could see her too.

'Well, I just wanted to say that the little girl – Maria – was telling me what fantastic foster carers you are and how lucky she is to be able to live with you.'

'Oh, thank you,' I said, surprised by the lump that suddenly seemed to have formed in my throat.

'Anyway, I expect she's told you that herself,' the woman continued. 'But I was so struck by the positive way she talked about you, I just wanted to let you know what she'd said. She was telling me about all the nice things you do with her and that, although she wasn't very happy before she was taken into care, she likes her life now. And she thinks Menorca must be the best place in the whole world!'

'We like it too, don't we Jonathan?' I laughed.

'Yes,' he answered. 'Thank you. It was nice of you to think of letting us know what Maria said.' And from the way he cleared his throat as he spoke, I realised that he was as affected as I was by what the woman had told us.

It was interesting that Maria had been open about the fact we were foster carers. A lot of children in her position don't want to reveal any personal details about themselves, especially not the fact that they've been taken into care. If asked, 'Is that your mum and dad?' most would probably say, 'Yes,' and leave it at that. Similarly, Jonathan and I wouldn't ever correct someone who referred to one of the children as 'your son' or 'your daughter'.

What made it even more surprising, however, was the fact that Maria hadn't ever said anything like that to us. There had been several occasions in the past when she made a point of telling us that we weren't her family and never would be – a statement that was usually made in response to us asking her to do something she didn't want to do, and that was invariably followed by something along the lines of, 'So *you* can't make me.' Jonathan and I knew Maria said such things more in the hope of getting her own way than to cause us hurt, but nevertheless we were still quite taken aback by what the woman said. It was wonderful, in fact, to hear what Maria had told her about us.

'It makes it all worthwhile,' I said to Jonathan that night.

Maria was fast asleep and we were sitting on the balcony chatting.

'It does indeed. I don't think I've ever been paid such a big compliment!'

He was positively beaming, and we both agreed that taking on Maria long-term had been exactly the right decision.

30

'You don't care about me!'

Maria had finally had her ears pierced, for her eleventh birthday, which was something Social Services ran past Christine, as a courtesy. Thankfully she agreed without a fuss – unfortunately she still tried to criticise Jonathan and me and cause trouble sometimes, despite the fact she no longer had the final say on any decisions relating to Maria's care.

Maria was delighted to have pierced ears and Jonathan and I were pleased too, as we felt that, at eleven, she was now old enough to look after them and cope with having pierced ears. However, Maria then decided she wanted to have a second piercing in each ear. She had started secondary school by now and had made a new set of friends, which I was very pleased to see. However, she claimed that 'everybody' in her group of friends had two lots of piercings, and she asked me about this one morning over breakfast.

'No,' I said. 'I think you're too young for that.'

'But that's not fair!'

'Maria, I am not changing my mind.'

She was furious, and she then asked Jonathan the same

question. To Maria's fury he gave exactly the same response, which set her off on a rant she had had in the past, about how we were 'telepathic' as we both knew what the other was saying.

'It's not fair!' she repeated over and over again.

'We're not changing our minds,' we chorused, which irritated her even more.

'I hate you!' she said. Then, out of the blue she shouted, 'My mum says you got paid by Social Services to take me on holiday and that you didn't pay for it yourself. So you should be giving me more money! Then I can pay for my own piercings!'

I was very taken aback by the accusation, particularly after we'd had such a lovely holiday, but I was incensed by it too, and there was no way I was going to let it pass unchallenged.

'Hang on a minute,' I said. 'Social Services did *not* pay for your holiday. We paid for it ourselves, because we wanted to take you with us, so that you'd have a nice time.'

'Oh yes they did!' she snapped, standing in front of me with her hands on her hips and fixing me with a defiant glare.

'OK, I'll prove it to you.' Sidestepping Maria, I unlocked the drawer of the desk where I kept her file, handed her a letter and said, 'Read that.'

It was the letter from the social worker stating that Social Services would not be able to pay for the holiday and unfortunately had no recollection or record of ever promising to do so.

'We did ask, because they had already offered, but when they refused we were perfectly happy to pay for you ourselves. See?'

'Oh,' Maria said, very quietly, after she'd read it. 'Well, Mum said . . .'

*

The next time Christine called Maria took the phone cautiously, and looked deep in concentration as she listened to what her mother was telling her. Christine told Maria she had split up with Gerry and also said, 'Did you know, Maria, Angela and Jonathan have lied about paying for your holiday.'

Maria gave a little shrug, went very quiet and looked sad. She had seen the proof about the holiday with her own eyes, and on this occasion Christine's lies had been well and truly exposed.

'Do you want a cuddle?' I asked when the phone conversation was over.

She nodded, and we stood in the hallway for a few minutes together silently, having a hug. There was no need for words. I could see that Maria felt hurt and I felt very sorry for her. It was completely beyond me how a mother could lie so cruelly and unnecessarily to her own daughter, but it was all part of the on-off injections of antagonism that we had come to expect from Christine.

'So she split up with Gerry? I said eventually.

'Yes. Good ribbons to him.'

I smiled sadly. 'Good riddance.'

'Whatever, that's what I meant. I'm glad he's gone, psycho!'

Unfortunately, even though Maria knew that her mother's claim about us lying over the holiday money wasn't true, she started to become fixated by the idea that we were getting more money for looking after her than we were spending on her. Nothing could have been further from the truth. Jonathan and I looked after children for the love of the work we did, and because we wanted to help them grow into happy adults who could function well in society and lead a full and meaningful life.

Although foster carers are paid, it is a not a huge amount, and Jonathan and I manage financially because we also run a flower shop. Without that, there would be no holidays or any of the variety of other 'extras' every child needs. It's one of the paradoxes of fostering: if it was well paid, it would probably attract people who are more concerned about money than they are about the wellbeing of the children in their care; but as it isn't well paid, some aspects of the welfare of these children is reliant on the altruism of their foster carers.

Sadly, Jonathan and I could see that it was very easy for Christine to make Maria feel insecure about our motives for fostering. Even though she'd come on in leaps and bounds since she first moved in with us, Maria still had low self-esteem, which was regularly stoked by things her mother told her.

Incidentally, Christine never did give any reasonable explanation or apology for telling Maria she was being cut out of the family. She simply invited herself back into her daughter's life when it suited her, prompting Jonathan to once again compare her to a ghoulish, shadowy figure. 'What did I say?' he said one time, when he was feeling particularly riled. 'She's like a ghost, I swear. Boo! Now you see her, now you don't.'

He tried to say it in a jokey way, but once again the reference gave me the creeps, as it was a bit too close to the truth.

Christine's constant complaints began to prompt aggressive behaviour from Maria. For instance, she threw a shoe down the hallway one day when I asked her to hurry up and be on her way to school. She went on her own now that she was at secondary school and was always leaving at the last minute, which made me feel anxious as I was trying to teach her the importance of punctuality.

'What does it matter to you? I'm not your kid! What do you care?' The shoe knocked over a vase of flowers, and water splattered all over the floor.

On another occasion, she kicked the hubcap on Jonathan's car because he'd told her he wasn't going to be able to give her a lift to her friend's house, as he had work to do.

'You don't care about me! I'll walk then. I'll probably get murdered but you wouldn't care, would you?'

After that particularly upsetting comment we asked if someone from Social Services could have a quiet word with Christine. Fortunately, whatever was said to her seemed to have the desired effect for a short while, although it wasn't long before she found something else to complain about.

One of her gripes was that we didn't spend enough on Maria's Christmas presents that year, which was extremely rich seeing as the previous year, when Gerry was still on the scene, Maria wasn't supposed to have had any Christmas presents at all!

It may simply have been sour grapes on Christine's part, because Maria had been so obviously pleased with what we'd bought for her, while her mother had given her something someone had given to *her* and she didn't want. In fact, though, Maria's mother rarely gave Maria any presents at all, for Christmas or birthdays, even after Gerry left and Maria was no longer expected to follow his religion.

Jess, who was still our support social worker, was livid when she heard that Maria's mother had complained about the presents. Maria was very upset about it too, and it was heartbreaking to see that her pleasure had been tainted by anxiety when she told us, 'I didn't complain about the presents you gave me.

Honestly I didn't. I was really happy with what I got. Then I showed them to my mum and she went on the internet and worked out what everything had cost. But I think she made a mistake because . . .'

'It's all right, Maria,' I said. 'We didn't think you complained to your mum about your presents. And the only thing that really matters is that you like them.'

'I really do,' she said. 'They're the best presents anyone has ever given me.'

Christine and Gerry got back together for a short time, then split up again. They were obviously leading a very tumultuous life, always falling out, having horrendous rows, then making up only to break up again.

'I'm so depressed I'm going to have to go into a mental hospital, Maria,' Christine told her daughter one night.

At this point I was no longer required to listen to Christine's side of phone conversations – I think because Maria was now a little older, and also because Christine had complained bitterly about this being a breach of her 'human rights' – but Maria had developed a habit of relaying all the key pieces of news she heard from her mum. I didn't mind, as it helped Maria unload, which she very nearly always had to do these days.

Although we were cautious about what we said to Maria, as we didn't want to criticise her mother, Jonathan and I found it very uncomfortable when Christine passed on details about her relationship bust-ups and mental health. Sometimes I felt it was right to pass on certain information to Social Services, and when I heard about the depression and the mental hospital I did mention this to my support social worker. It was a relief when I subsequently learned that it was a complete lie that Christine was having to go into a mental hospital, but I was angry nonetheless.

'It was a despicable thing to say to Maria,' I vented privately to Jonathan, feeling very protective of Maria. 'Imagine what that does to a child's brain – first the anxiety because she thinks her mother's ill, then the confusion when she inevitably finds out it was just some story she had made up?'

Jonathan and I also became increasingly frustrated with Christine's inability to move on from Gerry. It felt as though she was gradually abandoning all attempts to sort her life out. She allowed herself to be sucked back into all the rows, drama and aggressive behaviour that revolved around, and were encouraged by, Gerry.

'There must be reasons why Gerry turned into an angry bully of a man,' I said to Jonathan one day, when Gerry and Christine had got back together yet again. Maria had recounted a story about a bad argument they had, which her mother had given a blow-by-blow account of.

'Yes, but I'm not sure what they are,' he said. 'Sometimes you get a sense with people that their aggression is a learned response or that they hide behind it when they're feeling out of their depth. But Gerry just seems to be a really angry man, all of the time. What makes someone like that? I find it really worrying.'

It was clear there had to have been something seriously wrong in Gerry's life to cause him to behave the way he did. Part of me wanted desperately to find out more about the man, and part of me was afraid of what secrets he held.

'What on earth causes a person to be so cruel and nasty all the time?' I said.

As I spoke, Jonathan and I exchanged glances. Of course, our years of fostering had taught us that a person could experience all kinds of unspeakable, unthinkable horrors in their life that can affect their behaviour. Time and again it had been reiterated to us in the regular training sessions we attend that it is not the *person* who is bad, but the *behaviour*, and that the behaviour is typically a reaction to life events the person has been exposed to.

The social workers had never given away any private details of Gerry's life over and above the bare minimum they had to pass on to us when we took Maria in. Babs had never given any meaningful insight into the man's character either, so all we could do was listen to our gut feelings and hope that we never had to deal with Gerry again. More importantly, we hoped that Maria could be protected from his negative influences on her life as much as possible.

31

'It's just the way I am'

Christine came back to live in our town again, after splitting from Gerry 'once and for all'. It had been a violent parting of the ways, from what Babs told us, and although we did ask her not to say anything unnecessarily detailed to Maria about what had apparently happened, we weren't sure if she would be as diplomatic as we hoped.

Maria eventually started having authorised contact with her mum at her nan's house for an hour every Saturday morning. A support worker, who arrived before Christine did and left at the same time, always supervised it. So we knew nothing could have been said during any of those meetings that could upset Maria, unless of course it was coming from Babs, who might inadvertently say too much.

Unfortunately, despite the steps that had been taken to protect Maria from any unnecessary upset, it seemed that her mother's return did cause her distress. Suddenly, as soon as Christine was back on the scene, Maria started getting report cards from school for bad behaviour. Then I was called up to the school urgently one day, after Maria had received detentions three days running.

'What have you done to get the detentions?' I asked.

'Nothing. It was just stupid Mr Parsons picking on me. I'd had enough, I had!'

'What do you mean, you'd had enough?'

It turned out that Maria had been losing her temper then running out of the classroom whenever she got into trouble. The reason the school wanted to see me as a matter of urgency was because they were concerned she might run off the premises, which of course could have serious implications for the school, as well as Maria's safety and wellbeing.

'Has she ever done this kind of thing before?' the teacher asked. He had clearly had no information passed to him from other members of staff who were aware of Maria's background.

'Losing her temper and running away?' I asked. 'Yes, I'm afraid she has, for as long as I've known her.'

We discussed a positive strategy for helping Maria deal with her temper within the classroom, which involved her being moved to sit at the back of the room to 'cool down' if she became agitated. It would be made clear to Maria that if this didn't work she would then be taken to the 'chiller', which was a supervised room where disruptive pupils were taken for detentions, 'time out' and so on.

I felt relieved that the school was very understanding and had invited me in to discuss Maria's behaviour in this way, and with such a positive strategy. It seemed to work too. After she was moved to the back of the class a few times to cool down, Maria soon decided that she didn't like the attention this brought her and began to regulate her temper on her own much better.

Whenever I saw an opportunity, I gently attempted to get Maria to open up about what was causing her temper to flare up so dramatically, and so frequently. Clearly, I didn't want to put words into her mouth about how her mother's move had affected her, but I did ask, 'Is there anything that has happened to you, recently, that has upset you? Has something changed? Has somebody said something? You know you can talk to me, if you need to.'

'It's just the way I am,' she said. 'It's the way I've always been. I'm bad-tempered, that's all. I'm not going to change, you know!'

'No, Maria, you are not a bad-tempered *person*, you are a person with a bad temper at the moment, and there's a big difference,' I told her. 'You are a lovely girl, but your temper is spoiling things for you. We need to work out why that is.'

'It's nothing! Leave me alone, will you! I've had enough of everyone!'

I thought there had to be some explanation for her change in attitude, either directly or indirectly linked to Christine, but Maria simply refused to discuss it. I was also aware that, as she was soon to become a teenager, she had her hormones to deal with too, and I talked to her about how this might affect her.

'I know all this!' she said sulkily. 'I'm not a little kid any more!'

One day Maria announced that she wanted a mobile phone.

'No, not yet,' I said. 'You're still only twelve. You'll have to wait until you are a bit older, until you're thirteen.'

'Thirteen? Are you serious?'

'Yes, Maria.'

'No way! That's ages! Only the losers don't have a phone! It's not fair! Why are you so mean to me? Can't you ask Social Services to pay? Is that what it is? Are you too mean to pay for it?'

'I'm not discussing this any further,' I said, turning on my heel and climbing the stairs to run myself a bath. 'That is the rule and that is the end of it.'

Setting the age at thirteen was a rule Jonathan and I had established in the house some years earlier, as it was a topic that often came up with children of Maria's age. There was no practical need for a child any younger than thirteen to have a mobile phone, as the only place they went on their own was to school and back.

Though many of the children we had staying with us chose to get the bus to and from the local secondary schools, they were close enough to our house to make the journey on foot. This meant that there was no argument that a child needed a phone in case they got stranded because the bus hadn't arrived, for example. Ultimately, our biggest concern was to put their safety first, and make sure they were old enough to use the phone in a sensible way.

I found out later that, while I was in the bath that evening, Maria asked Jonathan the same question, without mentioning our conversation at all and knowing we hadn't had a chance to discuss it.

'Not again! I swear you two have a secret way of communicating!' she huffed when he gave her exactly the same answer, almost word for word. 'You're a pair of psychics, that's what you are!'

Jonathan tried to defuse the situation by turning a glass

upside down on the kitchen table and saying, 'Spirit of Angela, are you there? I know you can hear me, wherever you are . . .'

Maria froze, and Jonathan knew instantly that he'd triggered something in her. He immediately felt guilty, and foolish. He knew Christine claimed to have a psychic gift, and while he certainly hadn't done this to mock her or indeed make fun of anybody who believed in that sort of thing, Jonathan realised too late that his silly joke would inevitably make Maria think of her mum and her supposed connection to the spirit world.

'Are you all right, Maria?' he asked.

She appeared to stare straight through him.

'I was only joking. I didn't mean to scare you, if that's what's happened.'

'I'm not scared,' she said eventually, but continued staring, glassy-eyed, in Jonathan's direction.

'That's good to hear.'

Moments later Maria let out a deep breath.

'You know what?' she said. 'I hate you, Jonathan! Just give me a mobile phone, you're so tight!' Then she stomped off upstairs to her room, leaving Jonathan open-mouthed at her sudden shift in behaviour, and at her rudeness.

I went to see her after my bath, when she'd had a chance to calm down.

'I'm sorry,' she said. 'Mum's ghost used to get on my nerves.'

'Mum's ghost?'

'Yes. Night, Angela.'

A couple of days later, I had a phone call from Maria's social worker, sounding as rushed as she typically did.

'Hi, Angela. How are things?' she said, barely waiting for me to answer before continuing, 'It's just a quick call to say please do *no*t buy Maria a mobile phone. She's been on to me about it and I've told her it's a definite "No".'

'Don't worry,' I laughed, 'she's already run the idea past us and had the same response. I suppose she was hoping you'd overrule us.'

'Well, I'm glad we're on the same page with this.' Her voice had relaxed a bit, and I could imagine her ticking off another item on what I knew would be a very long 'to do' list that every social worker always had.

As far as I was concerned, after that phone call the matter had been dealt with, and I had forgotten about it by the time Maria's grandmother dropped her off the following Sunday morning and told me, 'Maria was asking about getting a mobile phone, and her granddad's told her he'd be happy to buy one for her.'

'Oh dear, she hasn't given up then,' I sighed. 'She asked us too, and we said to wait a while. In fact, her social worker's adamant that she shouldn't have one, particularly because one of the stipulations of her care order is that all phone calls with her mother are supervised, which obviously wouldn't be possible if she had her own phone.'

'I see,' Babs said, nodding her head slowly and looking thoughtful. 'Oh well, in that case, we won't then.'

32

'It didn't seem fair'

The very next weekend, Maria came home from her grand-parents' house with a smile on her face. Normally, when Babs brought Maria home, she walked straight through the front door and into the kitchen without even waiting to be invited in. On this occasion, however, Babs seemed to be avoiding looking directly at us. She said, 'Can't stop,' then turned and scuttled away down the path.

As soon as she'd gone we realised the reason why. Maria had a brand-new mobile phone. It was an expensive model, and Maria was very excited about it as she showed it off and told us about all the different functions it had. I could see that Jonathan was biting his tongue as determinedly as I was, trying not to say something that might cause a row or inflame the situation.

I called Babs later that evening, as soon as I had the oppor-tunity to do so in private. Keeping my tone of voice as neutral as possible, I asked her, 'Did you forget that I'd explained to you why Social Services don't want Maria to have a mobile phone?'

'Oh. No,' she said, 'no, I didn't forget. But she'd really set her heart on having one and I couldn't bring myself to disappoint her. It didn't seem fair.'

I knew there was no explaining to Babs that what was *really* unfair on Maria was allowing her to have and do things that weren't in her best interests. It was a recurring battle we faced throughout the time Maria lived with us, and although we kept on fighting it – with tact and patience – I already knew by the time the mobile phone incident occurred that it was a battle we were never going to win.

When I saw my chance, in a quiet moment before bed, I reminded Maria of what we'd said about the phone, but she just shrugged and reminded *me* of something.

'You're not my mum, so you can't tell me what to do.'

I didn't rise to this.

'No, I'm not your mum, Maria, but I do care very deeply about you and your safety and wellbeing,' I said calmly.

I then talked about phone safety, and how she should be careful not to give out her number to people she didn't know and trust.

'I know all this,' she said, cutting the conversation short and rolling her eyes. 'We've had a talk about it at school, because *everyone* has a mobile phone, remember?'

I let this go too, even though I knew it was untrue. At that time it was absolutely not the case that every child had a phone in secondary school – in fact it was still quite unusual in the nineties. Nevertheless, I simply reminded Maria not to be rude to me. I told myself that she wasn't really to blame for this behaviour. Any twelve-year-old child is going to be more focused on what they want than on the reasons why it isn't a good idea for them to have it. This is exactly why it was so annoying that her grandparents so often did what was easy and indulgent rather than what was right for Maria herself.

Once Maria had been given the phone it was her personal property and Jonathan and I didn't have any right to take it away from her. We knew Social Services had no power to remove it from her either, as it belonged to her and was not technically a 'dangerous' item, which is the only thing we would have been able to confiscate.

This meant that all we could do was report what had happened to the social worker, who spoke to Babs. Then we were asked to monitor the calls Maria made, which was not easy and certainly not foolproof. We insisted Maria left the phone downstairs when she went to bed at night, so that at least we knew she wasn't using it when she should have been asleep.

Of course, Maria wasn't very happy about these rules, but every evening before bed she did show me her call and text list to let me see me what she had been up to. Usually Maria hadn't made a single call beside the odd short one to Babs or me, to let us know she was on her way or going to be late. All the texts were to friends I knew or recognised. Clearly, Maria could have been clever and deleted her history, but I didn't feel this was the case as I trusted her to be telling me the truth.

'I'm impressed,' I told Maria. 'You're managing it really well and being very sensible.'

To be honest, I was surprised that Christine's number hadn't cropped up on the phone, and I was still trying to work out how and why Maria's behaviour had taken such a turn for the worse. Surely seeing her mum at her grandmother's house, during a supervised contact visit, couldn't upset Maria in the dramatic way it seemed to have done?

It was a weekday afternoon when a woman came into the flower shop who I knew to be a friend of the wife of one of Jonathan's brothers, and also a neighbour of Maria's grandparents. After spending a few minutes examining all the flowers with what I noticed was very intense concentration, she came over to the desk where I was sitting, picked up a gift card from the display, opened it, read what was written inside, then turned it over and read the print on the back.

'Is there something I can help you with?' I asked at last.

'I couldn't decide whether to come in,' the woman said. 'Not to buy any flowers . . .' She looked flustered for a moment, then added hastily, 'although they *are* all lovely. I just . . . It's about the girl you're looking after. I know her mum, a bit. God, she'd kill me if she knew I was telling you this. But I thought you ought to know something.'

'I see. What is it?'

'Erm, well, I'm afraid that after Christine leaves Babs and Stanley's house on a Saturday with the social worker, she goes back.'

'What do you mean?' I stuttered.

'Christine. She goes back into Babs's house, to see Maria unsupervised. You won't say I said anything, will you?'

'Not to Christine, no, of course not,' I said, hopefully sounding a lot more calm than I felt. My blood was pulsing around my body and I could feel a tightening around my heart as I said, 'I'll have to report this, but I won't tell anyone how I know. Thank you very much for telling me.'

As soon as the woman had gone, I called Jonathan in from the stockroom to watch the shop while I went into the house to phone our social worker.

'But Maria's grandmother *promised* she wouldn't let her daughter into the house while Maria was there except for that one hour when her visit is supervised by someone from Social Services,' Jess said, sounding bemused. 'I must say, I'm really surprised. I know the family has problems, but I thought Maria's grandmother was the sort of person who would keep her word. She really does seem to be genuinely attached to her grand-daughter.'

Of course, I knew from long experience that Babs was capable of saying one thing and doing another – all with good intention, which was unfortunately often misguided. I didn't want to accuse Babs of being a liar, but I had to speak out. I said as diplomatically as I could, 'Well, the person who told me is absolutely certain about it, and I can't think of any reason why she wouldn't be telling the truth. Perhaps Babs can tell you more? Maybe there is some kind of explanation?'

'I'll speak to Maria's grandmother,' Jess said with a sigh. 'If it *is* true, it might explain why Maria has been less settled at school recently.'

'You might be right,' I agreed, as this thought had inevitably occurred to me too.

It wasn't that I thought Christine was necessarily mistreating Maria at those meetings, but rather that I was concerned about what Maria might be hearing about Christine's break-up from Gerry, her personal life and goodness knows what else. Most of all, I knew that if Maria was being asked to keep her mother's visits secret, this would put her under a great deal of strain.

I imagined it was the sneaking around that had probably caused Maria to have behaviour issues, because it's very tough on a child to ask them to keep a secret like that. For Maria, I think this kind of thing was particularly destabilising because she'd gone to church and had Bible-reading classes. During that period of time she had taken on board the basic message she was taught, which she told me herself one day was, 'You shouldn't lie or steal, because if you break the Bible rules, you'll go to the devil.'

It turned out that Babs was fully in support of the clandestine meetings, and she had told Maria, 'It's a secret, not a lie. Don't say anything about it to anyone or you'll get your mum into trouble.'

Clearly this must have created a pull in Maria's mind. She was a bright girl, so she would probably have been able to see that sometimes 'a secret' is just a lie by another name, and she wouldn't have liked having to hide the truth from us or anybody else. And when Maria was confused and upset, or faced with a situation she didn't know how to deal with, her default response was to have a tantrum or run away, as we'd unfortunately seen many times.

When Jess confronted Babs about all this she had said she 'felt sorry' for Christine and that she felt it 'wouldn't do any harm'. She didn't seem to understand that in trying to be kind to Christine and Maria by giving them unsupervised time together, she was causing all kinds of problems for the granddaughter she loved dearly.

I had no doubt that in her own way Christine loved her daughter too, despite what had gone on in the past and the way she was behaving now. Why else would she risk being caught by

Social Services to spend time with Maria like this? It was a mess, it really was. Neither woman could see how their actions were wreaking havoc in Maria's life, and that unsupervised time arranged like this was incredibly damaging and destabilising.

Social Services stopped all visits from Christine while they worked out a way forward, and for the time being Maria was not allowed to go round to her grandmother's house. Jess said the probable solution, in the future, would be to fix up supervised visits for Maria and Christine in a contact centre. However, before this was arranged Christine moved out of the area once more, with no plans in place to have any contact with Maria.

After her mother had moved, Maria eventually told me one day that she was sorry about what had happened.

'It's OK,' I said. 'It's dealt with now.'

'But I lied to you.'

'Maria, you were asked to keep a secret by your mum and nan and so you did. I understand what happened, and that it can't have been easy for you.'

'No,' she said. 'I don't like secrets, but Mum does.'

'Your mum likes secrets.'

Maria sighed deeply. 'She had to keep secrets when she was a girl, because she was visited by her spirit guide.'

'Visited by her spirit guide?'

'Yes, he is an old Irish farmer and he is the one who lets her talk to the people on the other side.'

'The people on the other side?'

'Yes, the ghosts. She kept them secret too, but she has lots of ghost friends. And they aren't all good.'

'I see.'

'Yes, they tell my mum to do stuff. Stuff that gets her into trouble.'

'Stuff?'

'You know, the stuff she did when I was little. The stuff she let Gerry do. It wasn't her fault. The ghosts made her.'

33

'I don't care'

After Maria's mother moved out of the area again Maria seemed to become more settled at school, and both her behaviour and her work showed a marked improvement. In time, we heard that Christine was in a relationship with a new boyfriend, and eventually Babs told us that Christine was expecting another baby, a little girl.

'Isn't that good news!' Maria said, a little unconvincingly.

I couldn't work out if she was putting on an act or not, but something was off about her reaction.

'It's probably a shock,' Jonathan reasoned. 'I mean, what must Maria think about her mum having another daughter, when she hasn't exactly raised Maria?'

I felt Jonathan was right. It's a big deal for any sibling when a new baby is on the way, and it must have been difficult for Maria to grasp how her mother could raise another child while Maria herself was in care. I made a point of telling Maria she could talk to me about this or anything else that might be worrying her, but she told me flatly she was 'over the moon' about the new baby.

ANGELA HART

Maria's visits to her grandparents had been reinstated by this time and one Sunday, when Babs had brought her home and we were sitting in the kitchen drinking a cup of tea, Maria said, 'My mum says that as soon as she gets a new place, I can go and live with her and my baby sister, and then . . .'

'Goodness, are you all right?' I asked Babs, who was suddenly coughing loudly and seemed to be choking on the mouthful of tea she'd just swallowed.

'Yes. Fine, thanks,' she said, as soon as she was able to speak. 'But, well, that's not um . . . That's not right, is it Maria? Your mum didn't *say* that to you, did she? She *wrote* it in that letter she sent you.'

If I hadn't already suspected that something was wrong, I certainly did now, looking at the anxious expression on Maria's face as she hastily corrected herself.

'That's what I meant,' she said, glancing at me sideways and then quickly looking away again. 'Mum said it in . . . in a letter.'

It was clear to me then that Maria was having some form of unsupervised contact with her mum, either on the phone or in person. I was confident she wasn't speaking to her from our home phone, as I monitored all the calls and phone bills, and I had no evidence she used the mobile phone to talk to Christine either. I suspected, from the way Babs behaved that day, that despite the fact Christine had moved away, she might still be sneaking round to Babs's house when Maria was visiting. However, I had no proof of that either.

Jonathan and I talked about it later, when Maria had gone to bed, but there wasn't really anything we could do except report the conversation to our social worker and try to encourage

280

Maria to focus on her schoolwork, which, along with her behaviour, was suddenly beginning to go downhill again.

Another issue that was concerning us was Maria's weight. She had always been fairly slight at primary school, but now she had started putting on quite a lot of weight. We knew she didn't have the healthiest diet in the world as we still had to regulate the amount of crisps and Coke she consumed, and she also much preferred to eat a chocolate bar than a piece of fruit, which I understood but couldn't let her get away with, except as a treat.

What we hadn't realised, however, was that Maria had started to eat vast quantities of junk food, including multipacks of crisps and Coca-Cola by the litre, when she was round at Babs's house. We found this out from Maria herself, but unfortunately not before she had already gained a lot of weight.

'I can have what I want at Nan's house,' she began to tell me, crossly, whenever I wouldn't let her have something unhealthy she wanted to eat or drink. I suspected that Babs gave Maria whatever she wanted partly because she was trying to make up for all the negative, hurtful things that had happened to her, and partly because it made for a more peaceful life if she and Stanley said yes rather than no. The problem was that although Maria was happy to eat the food, she was becoming very unhappy about the weight she was gaining, which only served to reduce her already low self-esteem.

We discovered much later that what was also contribut-ing to Maria's weight gain was that the dinner money we gave her every day to pay for her lunch at school was actually being spent on sweets. Apparently, she had been sneaking over to her grandparents' house for a cooked lunch every day and spending her dinner money at a sweet shop she passed on the way. Although Maria wasn't allowed to leave school at lunchtime, unbelievably it seemed her teachers weren't aware that it was happening any more than we were. In hindsight, all of these bad habits helped to explain why Maria continued to gain weight despite the healthy food we gave her for her evening meal every night, and in spite of our best efforts to get her walking and doing other physical activities.

As her weight increased we noticed that the trampoline Maria had loved when we first got it hadn't been used by her for months and months. We had other children staying with us by now, filling the rooms vacated by Tom and Dillon, and they loved the trampoline, and often asked Maria to go out and jump on it with them, but she always refused. She avoided PE like the plague, to the point where we got a letter from the school saying that the next time she didn't participate in PE she would be put in detention.

I can't remember now how many letters we received about it, or how many detentions she was actually given, as there were so many of them. Nothing the school or we did to encourage her to do PE made a difference, unfortunately, and in the end the school simply gave up. So, from the age of about fourteen, Maria didn't ever do PE again.

It was a vicious circle, I suppose, and probably a common one among adolescents: because Maria ate unhealthy food – far more than we realised – she put on weight; as she got heavier and less fit, she didn't want to expose herself to teasing, or even bullying, at home by trampolining with other children or at school by doing PE; then when she stopped doing PE, she put on more weight and became even more reluctant to do any sporting activities.

It's hard enough being a teenager with low self-esteem, but at that time it seemed as though all the models in the magazines aimed at teenage girls were Photoshopped, and the images portrayed by pop stars and the like were completely unattainable and ultimately demoralising to a girl like Maria. I think today we are far more aware of Photoshopping and so we can discuss this with teenagers, but back then it was more of a hidden practice, and people generally believed what they saw and felt inadequate by comparison. The catastrophic result was that insecure girls like Maria thought along the lines of, 'I can never look like that, I'm fat and therefore I'm a failure.'

Jonathan and I tried everything we could think of to help improve Maria's physical health, including buying her a fantastic new bicycle, which she rode to her grandparents' house once and then we never saw again, despite their repeated assurances that *next* time they brought her home in the car, they'd bring it with them. Incidentally, I never understood why they ever drove Maria home, as it was easily close enough to walk to our house.

In the face of her grandmother's apparent belief that 'loving someone means never saying no', we knew we were fighting a losing battle in our attempts to help Maria get fit for the sake of her physical and mental wellbeing. Babs was overweight herself but she did nothing about it, and I couldn't help but notice that she always ate more biscuits or a bigger slice of cake than I did.

'I won't have another,' I'd say sometimes, as I was always trying to lose a few pounds and hoping to drop a dress size by the next holiday or the next 'do' I was going to.

Babs would snort and look me up and down.

'What are you, Angela? A size fourteen?'

'Well, sometimes a fourteen, sometimes a twelve depending on the cut . . .'

'I ask you,' she'd say, 'I don't know why you're denying yourself the odd treat. It won't kill you. Life's for living, Angela. You look great!'

That summed up her attitude to a tee: what was the point in saying no? The fact something wouldn't kill you was her benchmark, and I wondered how many times Babs had lazily indulged Maria and justified it with that reckless attitude.

Despite being hindered by Babs's influence over Maria, Jonathan and I didn't give up and continued to encourage her to go on walks with us or take part in fun activities like ice-skating, albeit with ever-decreasing success. Sadly, Maria admitted, 'I don't care. I don't want to be slimmer. What's the point?'

As a younger child, Maria had often told us that she believed she didn't deserve to be liked.

'Gerry told me that,' she had told us more than once. 'I don't deserve anything in his eyes.'

Of course we tried to repair the damage, but I was afraid that now it already looked like it was too late. Unfortunately, I think it was probably fair to say that Maria's soaring weight was possibly another symptom of the mental abuse she'd suffered as a child, and I was starting to become as worried about Maria's mental state as I was about her physical size.

'It seems obvious to me that another aspect of her low self-esteem is that she doesn't think she *deserves* to look nice,' I mused to Jonathan one day. 'She doesn't deserve it, and she doesn't care. It's extremely worrying.'

'How sad,' he replied, and then in typical Jonathan style he added generously, 'but the daft thing is she does look nice. I know she is overweight, but she has a lovely face and she could look really good if she tried. Imagine how much better she'd feel if she was happy with how she looked?'

It was incredibly frustrating. I agreed with Jonathan but he was talking from the point of view of a normal, ordinary person who hadn't suffered the way Maria had and was lucky enough to have a balanced, optimistic outlook on life.

Despite Babs's well-meant but frankly dangerous overindulgence, I still felt that in the circumstances Maria was very fortunate to have the love and support of her grandmother. Babs was supportive of us in many ways, too, and was always quick to offer to help if she could and the need arose. We had a good relationship with her and with Maria's granddad Stanley in the main, which we were careful to maintain – sometimes by taking deep breaths and counting to ten, particularly when we discovered some new deception that had been thought up to enable Maria to have something she wanted.

I think Jonathan sometimes found it even more difficult than I did not to say anything on those occasions. What also frustrated him – although he was always civil and offered her a cup of tea – was Babs's habit, every time she brought Maria back after a visit, of coming into the house and heading straight for the kitchen without waiting to be invited. She usually stayed for at least an hour, and I must admit that I did sometimes wonder whether, if I were to clutch my chest and then slump sideways on my chair, she would finish what she'd been saying before phoning for an ambulance.

I often called in to have a cup of tea with my mum on Sundays, and sometimes I didn't get back until after Maria returned from visiting her grandmother. Even if Jonathan was there on his own, watching sport on TV, Babs would still come in, hear that the television was on and head straight for the living room. Then she would settle down on the sofa and talk to Jonathan about people he'd never met who had done things he didn't really understand, while Maria disappeared upstairs to her room.

We were both sympathetic to the fact that Maria's grandmother was a bit lonely. Stanley tended to keep himself to himself and was rather a curmudgeonly character. But in our house, peaceful moments are quite rare and don't last for very long, so when you do get the chance to relax, you want to make the most of it. For Jonathan, that often meant watching sport.

There was one Sunday afternoon when he was just settling down to watch a football match he'd recorded the previous day when Babs came bustling into the living room saying, 'Oh, that was a good game. Arsenal won that 2–1.' On occasions like that, after having managed to avoid finding out what the score was all day, it was understandable that Jonathan felt as though his patience was being sorely tested.

Another Sunday soon after, I had arranged to pick Maria up from her grandparents' house on my way home from my mum's, but Babs must have forgotten what I'd said and she brought Maria back herself, before I was due. When they got to our house, Maria went straight up to her room to do her homework, while Jonathan took a deep breath and returned to the living room, where Babs was already sitting on the sofa.

Jonathan was very tired that day, and the whole point of my

saying I'd pick Maria up was so that he could watch the match in peace. So, instead of offering her a cup of tea, as he would normally have done, he sat down and watched the match, while she sat there in silence for a few minutes and then left.

'I do feel a bit bad about it,' he told me later, after he'd explained what had happened. 'It doesn't take much effort to be polite to someone. But, to be honest, I'm having one of those days when it feels as though the tank is empty. It was a game I'd been looking forward to seeing. I suppose there was a silver lining to this particular *clown* though, because at least she didn't know the score this time.'

I sympathised with him. 'Really, Babs is the only one at fault here,' I said. 'She should know better than to behave the way she does, but unfortunately she doesn't seem to tune into situations the way we'd like her to.'

'You're right,' Jonathan lamented. 'Frustrating, isn't it? I feel like our good nature is being exploited, but I know it's not deliberate. If it was anyone else I'd feel able to have a civilised chat about it and explain that I just wanted to have some relaxation time to myself in my own house. Anybody else would understand, but I know Babs would take offence.'

His guilt and irritation turned to indignation, however, when our support social worker rang a couple of days later to say that Christine had complained to Social Services that Jonathan had been rude to her mother. This was particularly galling as we hadn't heard a peep from Christine for a long time. Thankfully, Jess smoothed this over by explaining the full story to Christine and making it clear that Jonathan did not intend to cause any offence. Christine apparently accepted this without any further fuss or complaint. She'd had the baby by now, but there had

ANGELA HART

been no official talks with Social Services about arranging for Maria to meet her sister, despite whatever promises Christine had made to Maria in her clandestine conversations or meetings.

We had finally sussed out by now that Christine's attitude towards us tended to be related more to what was going on in her own life than to anything we did or didn't do in relation to Maria. And the numerous complaints she made about us to Social Services were usually an expression of a generalised resentment of 'the establishment', which of course, in her mind, included foster carers like us.

The complaints Christine made about us didn't ever have any significant impact, apart from being a bit aggravating. What really mattered was how her behaviour affected Maria, whose progress at secondary school seemed to soar when her mother was off the scene and plummet whenever Christine re-entered Maria's life.

34

'Something is very wrong'

Although Maria was still sometimes very angry as a teenager, and generally found it difficult to express her emotions, thankfully she did occasionally talk to us about how she felt. A lot of children who've had experiences similar to hers won't talk about them to anyone, and there's little point trying to encourage them to do so until they're ready and able to start compartmentalising the different parts of their life and all the things that have happened to them.

Some children might benefit from professional counselling and therapy, which, unfortunately, are rarely offered to them, primarily due to lack of funding. The other problem is that when professional help is given, it isn't always as useful as people hope it will be. For example, one boy who was with us for a few months as a teenager told me after he'd had a session with a therapist, 'I'd been talking about something my dad did and she suddenly said, "I know exactly how you feel." It made me really angry when she said that, because she can't possibly know how I feel. Has she been through the things I've been through? I doubt it.'

Of course, it's possible that his therapist had had similar experiences as a child, although even if she had, she couldn't have known 'exactly' how that particular boy felt. What was more likely, however, was that she didn't mean it quite the way it sounded. But the boy was right to protest, because everyone's experiences are unique. Although you might be able to *imagine* how a child feels, you can't ever *feel* what they're feeling, which is one of the reasons why you always have to be so careful about what you say.

Another child we looked after, a little girl who stayed with us for a few months while Social Services were looking for a long-term foster home for her, was given several appointments with the Child and Adolescent Mental Health Services, or CAMHS as we called it. That in itself was proof of how serious her problems were, as the service is always so overstretched that therapy sessions are usually reserved for only the most acutely ill children. The sessions appeared to help the child a great deal, as she always returned in a calmer, more positive frame of mind, even if she had been extremely angry and aggressive in the car on the way to her appointment.

As I've said before, you never know what will trigger a memory for a child who has had bad experiences; I never expect or assume they know themselves. And although Maria did sometimes talk to us about the things that had happened to her, I'm sure there were many more horrific incidents we aren't even aware of.

One day, when she was sitting beside me on the sofa watching television, she suddenly blurted out, 'Whenever I think about my stepfather, my face gets really hot and I feel sort of . . . tight.

As though, if he was standing in front of me, I'd punch him in the face.'

Maria was nearly fifteen by now. Her love of reading had persisted throughout her time with us, and as well as reading a lot of fiction she had also started to read some self-help type books, the ones about improving your life and happiness and that sort of thing. This started after she had a lesson on psychology at school, which really interested her. I imagined her reading encouraged her not just to think about the past, but also to start to articulate her feelings about it.

I didn't really know how much impact the self-help books were having on Maria, and I wasn't exactly sure what to do or say about them. As is often the case with the children I foster, I was walking on eggshells to a certain extent. I didn't want to question Maria directly about how she felt and I was wary of saying the wrong thing. Eventually, after the remark about punching Gerry, I picked my moment and asked her, 'Would you like to talk to someone professional about how you feel? Someone who could help you to deal with your anger so that it doesn't build up inside you and make you miserable?'

'Yes, I think that would be a good idea,' she said, looking relieved. 'I know I can't really hit my stepdad or punch him in the face, so sometimes, when I get really angry, I'm afraid I might end up hurting someone else.'

Maria had been going through a bad patch for a while before we had that conversation. There had been a few spats at school with teachers and other pupils, but she refused to discuss what they were about. Then Christine phoned one evening out of the blue. Even though Maria was older and I no longer listened to the calls, Christine was meant to call at specific times, and this was not one of them.

On this occasion, Maria had a blazing row with her mum. I had no way of finding out what Christine had said unless Maria told me, but I heard Maria scream, 'Why did you let that happen?' This was followed by several outbursts like, 'What sort of answer is that? I want to know the *reason*. What was going through your head? You're mad, d'you know that? Psycho!'

When Maria came off the phone she barged past me, her face like thunder, and ran up to her room, where she stayed for several hours.

I spoke to her social worker about my concerns and Maria was put on a waiting list to see someone at CAMHS. 'The services are massively overstretched,' the social worker told me, unnecessarily, 'so I'm afraid it's going to be a long wait before Maria is able to see someone.'

'I understand. I'm just glad she's on the waiting list. I think it's essential she gets the right help. I am afraid that not only is she struggling with her anger issues, but I'm concerned she also has depressive tendencies.'

I went on to talk about Maria's weight problem – something I had kept Social Services very well informed of – and made the point that she did not seem to care about how she looked, which to my mind was a very worrying indicator of her state of mental health. I had also mentioned her weight to her GP at the last visit, when Maria went for her annual medical check.

I heard nothing for weeks, during which time my concerns for Maria's mental health became more acute.

Maria had a habit, when she was sitting at the table in the

kitchen, of tipping her chair onto its back legs and reaching behind her to get whatever it was she wanted out of a drawer or the fridge.

'You're going to tip that chair right over and end up inside the fridge yourself one of these days,' I'd said to her many times.

'You're just jealous because you can't do it,' she would retort, and then carry on tipping her chair.

'I mean it, Maria! I don't want you falling!'

She did it one night when we were having a nice meal, with a lot good-humoured banter being exchanged. I didn't want to spoil the atmosphere so I gently chided, 'Maria, if there was an Olympic medal in balancing on two legs of a chair, I think you'd win gold.'

'Very funny,' she said, rolling her eyes.

'Well, I don't want you to get hurt, sweetheart,' I said.

'I know, I know,' Maria tut-tutted.

As she spoke I noticed that the sleeves of her top had risen up her forearms, as she'd twisted round in her chair and reached awkwardly to get a bottle of water out of the fridge. To my dismay I saw that there were lots of red marks on the insides of her wrists. Suddenly my words 'I don't want you to get hurt' took on a whole new meaning.

If this was what I feared it might be, it certainly wasn't the first time I'd dealt with a child who self-harmed. Unfortunately, self-harm is a very common problem. It's thought around thirteen per cent of young people may try to hurt themselves on purpose at some point between the ages of eleven and sixteen, but the actual figure could be much higher as very few teenagers tell anyone what's going on. In 2014 figures suggested a seventy per cent increase in ten- to fourteen-years-olds attending A & E for self-harm-related reasons over the preceding two years. Inevitably, the children I cared for were even more likely to be at risk from self-harm than those without specialist needs, so Jonathan and I had dealt with many incidents over the years.

I said nothing to Maria at that moment and tried to join in the chatter around the dining table, but my mind was whirring. I wondered how long this had gone on for, and to my horror I realised I couldn't remember the last time I'd seen Maria with bare arms. After she gave up PE and gained all the weight I'd never seen her in a short-sleeved top, and in fact she usually wore baggy sweatshirts or a long-sleeved top with a big hoodie layered over it. You could barely see what shape she was, let alone the skin on the underside of her wrists.

I waited until later in the evening, when Jonathan and I were alone in the living room and Maria came in to say goodnight, before asking her, 'What are the marks on your arms, sweetheart?'

'What marks?' she replied, instinctively pulling down the sleeves of her sweater beyond her wrists.

'I saw them when you were reaching to get a bottle of water out of the fridge at dinner tonight. All those red lines on the inner surface of both of your arms.' I tried to maintain eye contact with her as I spoke, but she looked away.

'Oh, *those* marks,' she said, hunching her shoulders and pushing her hands into the pockets of her trousers. 'They're nothing. We were playing this stupid game at school today, where you flick each other with elastic bands to see who can hold out longest.'

'That doesn't sound like much fun,' said Jonathan, who was fully aware of my concerns.

'I know,' Maria laughed. 'You're right. It wasn't. Well, anyway, goodnight.'

I wanted to believe this was the truth, and the way Maria said it did make it sound just about plausible, but of course I couldn't be sure and I was very worried. I made a note of it in my diary to show the social worker and debated whether to put in an emergency call to them first thing in the morning. After sleeping on it, I wasn't sure. I didn't want to cause undue alarm just yet, so instead I decided I would be extra vigilant and would keep a close eye on Maria to see if I could spot any more marks or other signs that something was badly wrong.

She seemed chirpy enough over breakfast the next morning. When I asked her if the red marks had gone down she said very convincingly, 'What marks?'

'The ones on your wrists.'

'Oh, those,' she laughed. 'Forgot all about them! Yes, no problem.'

Even though I decided to hold off on calling Social Services, I couldn't get the marks out of my mind, and I thought about ways to talk to Maria. By the afternoon, after talking things through with Jonathan during quiet moments in the shop, I decided I was going to casually ask Maria to show me her wrists, just so I could make sure she didn't need any cream on them or anything to soothe them after the 'elastic band game'.

Unfortunately, when she came in from school my plan changed, as Maria had little specks of blood on the back of her hands.

'What has happened there?' I asked, taking her hands in mine.

She wriggled free and pulled her sweatshirt down so that only her fingertips were visible.

'Oh, I've been in the wars again!' she said. 'Forgot all about that. It was just another game at school, mucking around.'

'Oh dear. What kind of game makes you bleed like that?'

The 'explanation' Maria gave this time was that she and her friends at school had all been writing their names on their hands with pins. This seemed much less plausible than her elastic band story, and I told her I was a bit worried about this 'game'.

'Why?' she said, immediately retreating out of the kitchen, even though she usually helped herself to a drink and a snack as soon as she got in from school.

'I'm going to do my homework, got loads. What time's tea ready?'

'But I'm worried . . .'

Before I could finish my reply, Maria was already heading up the stairs, saying as she did so, 'Oh, Angela, didn't you ever do any silly things at school? I bet you did! You're just so old you can't remember.'

She said this playfully rather than rudely, and she was out of earshot before I had time to give any answer at all.

Standing alone in the kitchen, I knew I had to take action. *Something is very wrong*, I thought. *I don't like this one bit.*

35

'I don't want to talk about it'

As soon as I heard Maria's music go on I phoned her latest social worker, Suzy, and told her of my concerns.

'I'll talk to her,' Suzy told me.

'Good,' I said. 'I'll leave it with you. My instincts are telling me this is self-harm, I'm afraid, so I hope you can talk to her very soon.'

'I understand. I'll prioritise Maria, even though my diary is packed. I know you don't make calls unless you think they are necessary, Angela, and I trust your instincts.'

Suzy was quite young and inexperienced, but she was very friendly with a couple of the older social workers who Jonathan and I had worked with for years. I knew they had all been talking, as Suzy had popped into the shop one day when she was off duty and buying flowers for her sister's twenty-first birthday.

'I've been hearing all about you and Jonathan, and all the children you have fostered over the years, and I just want to say I admire you,' she had said sweetly.

I was taken aback as I hadn't expected a compliment like

that. I appreciated her kind words, and I was pleased to have Suzy on our side, as that could only be a good thing for Maria.

Unfortunately, by the time Suzy did speak to Maria, things had escalated. I'd noticed knives going missing out of the drawer in the kitchen, and when I checked Maria's room one morning after she went to school I found blood on towels and bedding and a stash of blades that looked as if they had been pulled out of pencil sharpeners and razors. Jonathan and I were extremely careful not to leave sharp objects lying around, and we only kept essential knives in the kitchen and all razors were stored out of harm's way in our own bathroom. It's very difficult to remove every single sharp object from around your house, which as foster carers we're told we should do. We did our best, but clearly it wasn't good enough. Plus, of course, Maria was old enough to walk into a shop and buy scissors or razors if she really wanted to.

When Maria came home from school that night, I asked her outright how she was, and told her I had found some blood in her room when I went in to fetch the washing. I didn't want her to think I'd been snooping, but I did want her to know I'd found evidence.

'I'm fine,' she said quietly.

'Are you?'

'Yes.'

'Can I check your arms, then, because I'd like to be sure.'

Maria froze, and then looked at the floor. 'I'll be all right,' she muttered. 'Leave me alone, OK?'

Then she ran to her room.

It was a very difficult situation.

'Maybe Maria can be moved up the CAMHS waiting list?' I asked Suzy at the first opportunity.

'I'll do what I can,' she told me. 'But they really are incredibly overstretched, and I think everyone else on the waiting list has a problem at least as urgent as Maria's.'

It was obvious there was no point in Jonathan and me trying to talk to Maria about what she was doing, as it only made her retreat to her room. She was clearly in denial about it, and she became very defensive and took great care to keep her arms well covered. I did some research and read that self-harming is a way of releasing overwhelming emotion and can be linked to depression, and that if the problem isn't addressed very promptly, as soon as it becomes apparent, it can become a compulsion.

I knew Suzy would let us know as soon as Maria reached the top of the CAMHS waiting list, but I still couldn't stop myself asking her every time we spoke if she had heard anything. The answer was always the same, and I think Maria might have waited a very long time to see a psychologist if she hadn't done something that brought everything very abruptly to crisis point.

As well as self-harming, Maria was incredibly moody and lost her temper more often and more easily than she had done for some time. It's difficult enough for any child having to deal with everything involved in becoming a teenager and Maria seemed to be struggling, particularly, to cope with the changes in her body. She was having yet more problems with her mum too. Christine was having trouble in her new relationship, and whenever she phoned up, Maria shouted on the phone and got upset.

'Do you want to talk to me about what the problem is?' I asked one time.

'No. Mum makes me think about when I was little, and Gerry. That's all. I don't want to talk about it. I don't want to even *think* about it.'

However, one day Maria did open up to me, about an issue I least expected her to talk about – her anxiety that she might be gay.

'This girl at school keeps laughing at me and telling everyone "Maria loves girls",' she told me. 'I get really angry and tell them that I don't. But the trouble is, I think it might be true. There's this girl in the class above me that I really like. I think about her a lot and try to think up ways of getting her to notice me. So maybe I *am* gay.'

'We've talked before about why some people say unpleasant things about other people,' I said. 'About it often being because they've got problems of their own. But, actually, it doesn't matter if it *is* true. Being a lesbian isn't the end of the world, you know?'

'I know that,' she said, miserably. 'At least, I know it in my head. But being gay is like anything else that makes you *different*: it just makes everything even more complicated than it already is.'

'It might just be a crush,' I told her. 'Lots of girls your age develop crushes on older girls. But as there's nothing you can do about it if you *are* gay – and nothing you *need* to do – why not just wait and see? And try not to worry. It *will* be OK, either way. But I'm sorry if you're being a given a hard time at school by someone who doesn't know any better. Perhaps if you ignore her, she'll get bored and turn her attention to doing something more useful.'

Then we talked a bit about coping strategies, and although there didn't seem to be anything I could say to persuade Maria to believe that she wasn't the inadequate person she thought she was, at least she seemed to become a bit less anxious about her sexuality.

A few days later, after spending Saturday night with her grandparents – something she had been allowed to do for a while now – Maria had come back in time to have Sunday lunch with my mum, which she always really enjoyed. In fact, she was in such a good mood after we'd all eaten that she helped clear the table and stack the dishwasher without having to be asked, pointing out cheerfully as she did so, 'Many hands make light work.'

Then, as Jonathan, Mum and I were all settling down in the living room with a cup of tea, Maria put her head round the door and said, 'I'm going round to Meg's house this afternoon. We're going to play a new computer game she's bought. It's a really good one.'

'Just for a couple of hours, then,' I told her. 'Didn't you say you've still got some homework to do? What do you think? Back by four?'

You never knew how Maria would react when you said something like that to her. Sometimes, she'd sulk and mutter about it not being fair, how all her friends were allowed to do fun things at the weekends, so why wasn't she? It was a rhetorical question, of course, and it was pointless telling her, 'Because you've been "chilling out" since Friday evening and now you need to do some homework.' She didn't get into a mood on this occasion though; she just said sarcastically, 'Thanks for reminding

301

me, Angela,' and then, in a more conciliatory tone, 'OK, I'll be back by four.'

It had been one of those weeks when, for one reason or another, Jonathan and I seemed to have spent every day cooped up either in the shop or the house, and as it was a lovely sunny afternoon we decided to walk Mum back to her house. We had two other children staying with us at the time and they were both out visiting their families, so it was a good opportunity for Jonathan and I to spend time with Mum on our own.

We had a look around Mum's garden and she picked some of her fresh vegetables for us – I love the smell of fresh, garden-grown tomatoes. Then we had another cup of tea and Jonathan and I got home just before four, followed within minutes by Maria, who kept the hood of her sweater pulled up so we couldn't see her. Then she went straight upstairs without speaking to us.

A little while later, after the other children had also returned and were in their bedrooms, we could hear banging and crashing around in the bathroom. We both knew it had to be Maria, as the other children were quietly trying to do some schoolwork.

'It sounds like our peaceful weekend has come to an end,' Jonathan said, raising his eyebrows and sighing with mock despair.

'It's such a shame, isn't it?' I sighed. 'Maybe she and Meg had an argument. If only she could learn to deal with frustration in some other way. I know she has every reason to feel angry at life, and I'm worried that one day she might let her temper get the better of her and do something she regrets.'

'I know,' Jonathan said, with a worried expression on his

face. 'I'll be glad when CAMHS finally come up with an appointment for her. Their psychologists and psychotherapists must have a lot of experience, so maybe they'll be able to help her develop some strategies for dealing with her anger.'

'It sounds as though she might be dealing with it by breaking things now,' I said, looking up at the ceiling when there was another loud thud.

'I'll go.' Jonathan put his hand on my arm as I was pushing myself up out of my chair.

He was just reaching for the handle when the door opened and Maria stumbled into the living room. I leapt to my feet as soon as I saw her, but Jonathan had already caught her and was helping her into the chair he'd just vacated. She looked terrible. There were dark marks under her eyes that looked like bruises. For a moment I thought she'd been beaten up. Then she rested her head against the back of the chair and whispered, 'I've been really sick,' and I realised that the dark marks weren't bruises after all; they were a sign that she was very ill.

'Have you got a pain anywhere?' I asked her, crouching down beside the chair.

'Everywhere.'

She closed her eyes for a moment and when she opened them again, she was the little girl she had been when she came to stay with us briefly at the age of seven. 'I took some tablets,' she said. Then she started to cry.

36

'Two packets . . . and some more'

I glanced at Jonathan and knew his heart must be beating as fast as mine, as I put my hand on Maria's shoulder and asked, 'What tablets did you take, Maria? Do you mean that you took some tablets because you've got a pain?'

Although I kept my voice calm and even, I was very worried by the peculiar, creamy-grey colour of her skin and by the fact that she now seemed to be on the verge of losing consciousness. 'Can you hear me, Maria? Can you tell me what tablets you've taken?'

'Paracetamol.' Her voice sounded weak.

'How many?'

I could feel the panic expanding inside me.

By the time she answered, 'Two packets and . . . and some more,' Jonathan was already dialling 999.

I stayed with Maria while Jonathan went out on to the road to flag down the ambulance when it arrived. It felt like hours before I finally heard the sound of a siren – in the distance at first, then gradually getting louder as it got closer – but it was probably only about ten minutes since Jonathan had made the phone call.

Although Maria was still conscious when the paramedics arrived, she didn't seem to understand anything that was said to her. They spoke to her quietly, explaining what they were doing as they lifted her out of the chair in our living room and placed her in the one they would use to carry her down the stairs. I walked beside her, holding her hand, as they wheeled her out of the house.

'I'll go with her in the ambulance,' I told Jonathan.

'OK. I'll follow in the car,' he said, thinking out loud about calling my mum to come and babysit the other foster children we had staying with us. 'Yes, I'll ring your mum, sort things out here, and then I'll come in the car as fast as I can.'

His eyes were searching mine as if he were trying to gauge whether I knew the answer to the questions neither of us wanted to say out loud: How serious was this? Had Maria tried to kill herself? Most importantly, was she actually going to survive this?

'Maybe being sick helped,' I muttered desperately. It was what Maria would have called 'gasping at a straw', which was a thought that brought tears to my eyes as I climbed into the back of the ambulance and sat down on the narrow seat beside her.

Maria was lying very still now, and while the paramedic attached monitors to measure her blood pressure and heart rate, I tried to work out how many tablets she could have taken. 'Two packets and some more,' she'd said, which I reckoned meant more than thirty-two tablets. Even if I hadn't seen the concern in the paramedic's eyes when I told him what Maria had said, I knew enough from training and first-aid courses to understand that this quantity could kill. I also thought about a very nice woman who used to come into the shop. She took twenty-seven tablets, and she had died before the ambulance arrived at her house.

It was horrible, just sitting there, watching helplessly as we sped through the town, siren blaring. Maria slipped in and out of consciousness, and I stroked her hair and told her I was beside her, and we were getting help. As soon as we arrived at the hospital Maria was whisked away, so I went back outside and phoned her grandparents.

When Babs answered the phone, I explained, as gently as possible, what had happened, telling Babs softly but plainly that Maria had taken a dangerously large overdose of paracetamol.

'Oh dear. Paracetamol?' Incredibly, Babs didn't sound distressed or even upset. In fact, she sounded as if she didn't grasp the seriousness of the situation at all. 'Well, give her our love, won't you, and tell her I hope she feels better soon.'

I was shocked and bemused by Babs's reaction, especially as I'd explained that the quantity Maria had taken was very dangerous, and potentially life threatening. Now I was torn between wanting to make sure Babs understood what I'd told her, and not wanting to upset or alarm her unnecessarily. Maybe her response was some form of self-protection, so that she didn't have to face the very real possibility that Maria might die?

Babs abruptly ended the call with an almost breezy, 'Keep me posted, Angela!' I stood there staring at my mobile phone for a few seconds outside the hospital, wondering whether to phone Babs back and tell her that if she didn't come right away, it might be too late. In the end, I decided not to. I'd told her as plainly as I could what the situation was, so what more could I say? Besides, I wanted to get back inside the hospital, so I dashed back inside to find out what was happening to Maria.

By the time Maria had been treated in A & E and then taken to a ward, Jonathan had arrived at the hospital, so we went in to see her together. As we walked up to her bed, the first thing that struck me was how small she looked, like a little girl, lying there dressed in a hospital gown and with a drip attached to her arm. Her normally rounded cheeks looked hollow, as if they had sunk into her face, and her skin was so pale I reached out my hand instinctively to feel for the pulse in her wrist, just to make sure that she was still alive.

As I've said before, we're not religious people, but as we sat in silence beside her bed I think Jonathan and I were both silently praying. I know that in that moment I didn't believe that Maria was going to make it. Because she had taken so many tablets and some time had elapsed before she was treated in hospital, I was also afraid there was a risk that, even if she did survive it, Maria could suffer lasting liver damage.

'It's probably best if you go home and get some rest,' a kind nurse said a while later.

She had reassured me that Maria was stable now. She wasn't going to die, as I'd feared, and so Jonathan and I agreed to go home, even though we were still worried sick.

'Will she make a full recovery?' I asked. 'I mean, will her liver be all right?'

'I can't tell you that,' the nurse replied. 'The doctors will need some time to do tests, I would imagine, before they can tell you exactly what has happened internally. Don't worry, though.

Maria will be monitored throughout the rest of the night. She's safe with us here. You've done all you can.'

Jonathan and I drove home in a daze. The experience was surreal, in fact. I felt as if I was living somebody else's life as it seemed so unbelievable that Maria had taken those pills, could have killed herself and was now lying in a hospital bed. How had it come to this?

'It's not our fault,' Jonathan said, reading my mind. 'You know that, don't you?'

I nodded.

'Good. That's important, Angela. We have looked after Maria well. We have not only given her a safe and comfortable home, we have been vigilant about her mental health, and we have been meticulous in reporting everything to Social Services that we have felt needed to be shared.'

'I know, I know,' I said. 'But she's still in hospital, isn't she? Is it good enough to say "we did all we could", when we both know that Social Services are so strapped that they can't necessarily act on the information we give them.'

Jonathan thought about this for a moment. 'You have a point,' he said. 'But all we can do is our best, and we *do* do our best. You are a dedicated foster carer and you have nothing to feel guilty about, or to blame yourself about.'

'But . . .'

'No buts, Angela. Our job is hugely important. You do it brilliantly but unfortunately you cannot be responsible for the actions of others; only those of yourself.'

'Thanks,' I said quietly. I appreciated Jonathan's words, but nevertheless I still had tight knots around my heart and in my stomach. I don't think I'd have been human if I hadn't felt absolutely dreadful about this.

Maria ended up staying in hospital for a week while she had intravenous treatment with something called acetylcysteine, which protects the liver cells against the toxins in paracetamol. Jonathan and I visited her every day while she was there.

'Thank you,' she said feebly the first time she spoke to us. 'You saved my life.'

Maria still looked younger than her years, and now she had a guilty expression on her face.

'We're both really sorry you felt so bad, that you were in such a bad place.'

'It's not your fault.'

'Still, we are truly very sorry.'

'Don't be. It's fine now. How is the shop?'

We made chit-chat about the shop. Jonathan bought a newspaper from the trolley when an auxiliary came round, and then we discussed a local news story. We asked Maria if we could fetch her anything from home, to bring in on the next visit.

'Lip balm,' she said. 'That nice strawberry one I have. And crisps, if I'm allowed?'

I smiled. 'Back to normal I see!' I teased. 'Prawn cocktail flavour, as usual?'

We made the best of the visits, trying to keep Maria's spirits up. We were her only visitors, and some time during that week I came up with the only possible theory I could about why Babs was keeping out of the way: she felt guilty.

I came to this conclusion because, a couple of weeks earlier, when Maria's grandmother had dropped Maria off after an overnight stay, I'd offered her a cup of tea, as I usually did. While she was drinking it I was sitting across the table from her, peeling vegetables for supper and trying to follow the complicated story she was telling me about one of her neighbours. 'Her husband suffers from depression,' she had told me, which was when the idea just popped into my head for some reason to ask her, 'You do keep all medicines under lock and key, don't you?'

'Oh yes, of course,' she replied.

'Good,' I said. 'It's a good idea. You know all foster carers have to have a locked medicine cabinet, and I think it's a very good precaution for anyone with children in the house.'

I don't know if it was some instinct that had made me say this to Babs, or maybe it was simply because I knew Maria had been a bit depressed recently and I was feeling extremely protective towards her. However, it didn't actually cross my mind that Maria would ever try to take her own life – I would never have predicted that.

As we discovered later, however, Maria had taken at least one packet of paracetamol from the cupboard in the bathroom at her grandparents' house. It contained sixteen tablets, and she had also bought a packet of sixteen in the local supermarket. She'd hidden them at her friend Meg's house, together with two tablets I had given her a couple of days earlier when she complained of having a headache, and she took at least two more she'd got from somewhere else, making a total of thirty-six tablets. If she hadn't come back to our house after taking them all that Sunday, I don't think she would have survived. The medics told us as much, praising Jonathan for calling 999 the moment he did.

*

Needless to say, the whole sorry episode was a horrible experience for Maria. Quite apart from whatever it was that made her feel so miserable that she decided to try to take her own life, she had to endure some very unpleasant hospital treatment over the week she was kept in. And the incident highlighted that she was obviously more distressed and disturbed than even we had realised. Jonathan and I were very relieved when, having spoken with a psychiatrist while she was in hospital, she had her first appointment with CAMHS within days of coming home.

Christine did not visit Maria at all, incidentally. Babs told us she was 'too busy with the baby', but sent her love and hoped Maria got well soon. I half expected her to put in a complaint to Social Services about Jonathan and me, perhaps blaming us for what happened, but I'm very glad to say she didn't get involved at all like that.

During this period, Jonathan and I looked back and tried to make some sense of how it had come to this.

When Maria was younger, we were busy doing things with her almost every weekend – caravanning, walking in the countryside, going on bike rides, having barbecues and so on. It meant she didn't really have time to dwell on all the horrible things that had happened to her when she lived with her mother and stepfather. But as she got into her teens, she became more introspective and started spending more time on her own in her bedroom, when she must have tried to make sense of some of the things that didn't really make any sense at all.

I think we only ever knew a very small part of what Maria had experienced before the age of nine, when she was primarily living at home. At least, now that she was going to be getting some professional help, she might begin to understand that she wasn't to blame in any way for the cruel treatment she'd been subjected to.

In fact, I'm very happy to say that the psychotherapy she received through CAMHS helped Maria a lot. She stopped self-harming and her life became relatively stable – for a while.

37

'Oh, that man!'

Jonathan and I did everything we could think of to motivate and encourage Maria with her schoolwork. Overall, she did do well – well enough, in fact, that by the time she was working on her GCSEs her teachers started telling us that if she continued to do the excellent work she had been doing, she would be able to go to university.

One day, when I'd been trying to encourage her to study, she told me, 'Nan says no one in our family has ever been to university, so I'd be the first.'

'Wouldn't that be great,' I responded. 'I think you'd enjoy it. And a university degree gives you more choice, too, about the sort of jobs you can do.'

'Maybe I'll be a lawyer,' she laughed. 'Or a headmistress – then I could open a school for witchcraft and wizardry, like Hogwarts!'

Maria absolutely adored Harry Potter, and had read all the books several times and often talked about them.

'You could be anything you wanted to be if you set your mind to it, sweetheart.'

I don't think her grandmother could really believe that Maria would be able to go to university and have the sort of life we knew she was capable of having. I think Babs was trying to be kind and protect her from disappointment when she told Maria not to worry if she didn't do well at school, because '*I* didn't go to university and *I* have a nice life.' But it was frustrating to know that the one person Maria might have listened to wasn't using her influence to encourage her to fulfil her obvious potential.

One day, Maria's new social worker, Luke, told me that Babs had complained to him that I'd refused to buy some school equipment that Maria's teacher asked her to get. Alarm bells rang in my head and I feared that Babs was causing trouble for some reason, though I couldn't think why she would do this. In the light of what Maria had been going through, this seemed very petty indeed. However, we'd learned over the years that Babs didn't normally set out to deliberately cause trouble – it was usually just a case of her inadvertently creating problems by not supporting Jonathan and me in decisions we made that we felt were in Maria's best interests.

Trying my hardest not to sound indignant and without mentioning Luke, I later asked Babs what school equipment she was talking about, because Maria hadn't asked me to buy anything recently, and I certainly hadn't refused.

'I'm sorry, Angela, I don't know what you mean,' Babs said.

Although she was well-practised in the art of sounding innocent when perhaps she wasn't entirely blame-free, Babs did seem to be genuinely bemused on this occasion.

I explained as tactfully as possible that Luke had told me what she'd said to him.

'Oh, that man!' she scoffed. 'He's caused nothing but trouble ever since he took over Maria's case. *Of course* I didn't complain about you. I did buy Maria some stuff for school recently, but it was nothing worth mentioning to anybody. I don't know what is going on here.'

Babs explained that she'd met Maria in town straight after school one day and bought her some pens and pencils that the teacher had asked her to get hold of for an art project.

'I bought them for her then and there, because I *wanted* to,' Babs said, sounding exasperated. 'Maria didn't say anything about having asked you first. Anyway, she can't have asked you, because I met her on the day the teacher asked her to get the equipment. She hadn't even been home yet.'

'Well, what on earth *is* going on?' I asked, scratching my head.

'I don't know. That Luke is nothing but a troublemaker. Honestly, Angela, you've always bought Maria everything she's needed, and far more. Oh, it makes me feel quite upset to think that man told you that!'

As unlikely as it had first seemed, it did appear that it was Luke who had made a mistake and created trouble unnecessarily, not Babs. Unfortunately, the social worker's attitude could be brusque, almost to the point of being deliberately confrontational, and Jonathan and I hadn't really taken to him the first time we'd spoken to him.

Luke wasn't what you would call a 'people person' at all, which was quite a disadvantage to him, because social workers need to get along with all kinds of people. Jonathan and I told ourselves it was just his manner that was unfortunate, not Luke as a person, and we tried to be open-minded about how the miscommunication had come about.

'Perhaps he's got too much work on,' I said to Jonathan.

'There's no *perhaps* about it,' Jonathan sighed. 'Every social worker we've ever come across has too much work. Maybe he's just not coping with it as well as others.'

It never occurred to us that Luke might be deliberately causing trouble, but unfortunately this was not an isolated incident and, as improbable as it seemed, we did start to wonder if Luke was actively trying to break the placement down.

Not long after the pen and pencil mix-up, Luke arranged to have a meeting with us at our house at eleven o'clock one morning. Jonathan had been working in the garden since quite early, and he was just finishing weeding one of the flower borders at 10.50 a.m. when Luke arrived and said, quite rudely, 'Had you forgotten about our meeting this morning? Did you not realise I was coming?'

Jonathan is very even-tempered and tends to take everything in his stride. So while someone less tolerant than he is might have responded equally rudely, he simply said, 'No, Luke, I didn't forget you were coming. I just thought I'd use the last ten minutes I expected to have before you arrived to finish weeding this border. But you go on in. Barbara's manning the shop and Angela's in the house, ready and waiting for you. I'll be right behind you.'

'Well, *you* should be waiting for me too,' Luke said, in a tone of voice Jonathan described to me afterwards as one he himself wouldn't even use to speak to a naughty child.

Once the meeting started, on the dot of eleven, Luke told us

Maria had complained about us 'always going on at her' and not allowing her to have any freedom. Like many fifteen-year-olds, Maria considered we were 'going on at her' when we asked her to do almost anything, so we just accepted that. Her second complaint certainly wasn't true, however. We gave Maria as much freedom as she wanted within safe and reasonable parameters. She was allowed to see her friends, go to the youth club, visit her grandparents, shop in town and go bowling, ice-skating and to the local cinema at weekends. We always made sure we knew where she was and we set times for her to be home and were strict about sticking to them. We also had rules about getting homework done before going out, but we certainly did *not* restrict Maria's freedom.

I told Luke all of this and said I felt the criticism was completely unjustified.

'Well, her grandmother said the same thing about you,' Luke replied tersely, before moving on to the next point he wanted to discuss.

Jonathan and I felt confused after Luke left. We couldn't imagine Maria would complain about having no freedom; how could she? It also seemed unlikely Babs would have been complaining about us behind our backs. And if Luke believed Maria and Babs and felt it was an issue, why had he moved swiftly on? None of this seemed to make sense – unless, of course, it was Luke who was being the troublemaker here.

Although we wouldn't normally ask Maria about anything she'd discussed with her social worker in private, Jonathan and I were so bemused we did talk to her about what Luke had said to us.

'Why would I feel like that?' she said, pulling the 'what-are-you-on-about-now?' face she had perfected in her teenage years. 'I see friends whenever I want to, and I'm often round at Nan's house. I might not always want to do my homework, but it's my teachers who are to blame for that more than you are!' She grinned at us then, and we knew she was telling the truth. I also raised the issue with Babs and I could tell she had nothing to hide either.

'What did I tell you? That man is a liability. Call himself a social worker? More like a social disaster!'

I felt we'd got to the bottom of the Luke situation, and there were no hard feelings between Maria and us, or indeed Babs. But very disappointingly, over the next few weeks, Maria's attitude towards Jonathan and me began to deteriorate. The grin we'd seen on her face was nowhere to be seen, and she started moping around the house and having angry outbursts for no apparent reason. It was heartbreaking to see, as I had felt that since her overdose she'd been making steady progress, and that everything was moving in the right direction. She was still having ongoing CAMHS appointments, and I thought these seemed to be helping.

Now, however, Maria suddenly became extremely sullen and angry with us for no apparent reason. We couldn't understand what was going on at first, until, when she was in a temper with us about something one day, she shouted, 'Yeah well, why don't you complain to Luke about that too? You can add it to the list.'

She stormed out of the room and slammed the door before we had a chance to ask her what she meant. Unfortunately, we found out shortly afterwards that Luke had told her a lot of negative things he claimed we had said about her, all of which were totally untrue.

It was a very difficult period. The things Luke was saying were putting the placement at risk and damaging the relationships we had with Maria, which was not just frustrating, but also devastating.

We loved Maria. We'd known her since she was seven and she'd been living with us for more than six years by now. We wanted nothing but the best for her, so why was this man being so disruptive when it was his job to do the opposite, and to help make placements run as smoothly as possible?

38

'Why does life have to be so hard?'

Jonathan and I eventually heard that Luke had some serious problems at home, and fortunately our support social worker, who was now a very clued-up woman called Cath, began to realise that Luke's attitude towards Jonathan and me was at best unhelpful, and at worst thoroughly destabilising.

One day, when we felt we had no choice but to do so, Jonathan and I took the bull by the horns and said, at one of the regular placement meetings we had with Social Services, that Luke was causing a rift between Maria and us, and creating trouble for us with her grandparents.

'What's happening is making Maria very unhappy,' I said. 'That's the most important thing. None of this is her fault, or ours. It isn't surprising if Maria thinks we're saying negative things about her. I'm afraid Luke has made things very difficult, and Maria is unhappy, which is unacceptable.' Luke was not at the meeting and I certainly did not enjoy speaking about him like this, but I felt it was long overdue and very necessary to do so.

Maria had started to say she didn't want to live with us any more, and that her mum wanted her to move out. Christine had continued to drift in and out of Maria's life without playing any positive, active role whatsoever. It seemed that when there was trouble in Maria's life, Christine's presence was greater, and it didn't surprise me that her name was being mentioned now that there was a contentious issue to discuss.

Our support worker did try to speak to Maria on the phone after that meeting, but because Maria saw Cath's role as being to support *us*, she decided she didn't want anything more to do with her and apparently ended up telling her, 'Go fuck yourself'.

By now Maria was having really bad temper tantrums every day, and was shouting and swearing at Jonathan and me, refusing to go to school and saying she hated everyone.

It was heartbreaking seeing Maria like that, after she'd been so much happier and making such good progress at school.

'We can't continue like this, with Maria so unhappy,' I told our support social worker when I phoned her the next day.

'I can see that,' Cath said. She then let me know that it turned out Christine had also been told things by Luke that were untrue. This was what prompted Christine to ask for Maria to be moved to a new foster home, and it was also behind Maria's statement that she didn't want to live with us any more.

'Clearly this is destabilising for the placement and is not in Maria's best interests,' Cath said. 'She is coming up for sixteen now and doing her exams. Leave it with me.'

Not very long after this Luke was taken off the case. We found out later that he left his job completely and decided to retrain in a totally different field, which I was relieved to hear. I didn't want any other families to suffer the disruption he'd caused us. To this day I have no idea what the problems were at home that caused him to behave the way he did, and I sincerely hope he is doing well now in a job he is more suited to.

Luke was replaced by a new social worker who managed to calm everything down. Within a surprisingly short space of time, Maria had decided that she did like living with us after all and that she didn't want to leave. Her temper improved, although I can't say she seemed particularly happy. She was moody a lot of the time and spent hours alone in her room. Still, things were a lot better – at least for a while.

Once she was back on a relatively even keel, Maria started doing well in most of her subjects at school again, except maths. She had always hated maths, and as her GCSEs approached she was really struggling to keep up, so we decided to arrange for her to have some extra maths tuition at home.

It was one of the teachers at her school who recommended the maths tutor we found. He was already working with children so had undergone the relevant police and criminal record checks. However, at that time, the accreditation was very specific and you had to have a new CRB check for every new job. So, before the tutor could come to the house to teach Maria, he had to go through the whole process again, which fortunately he was willing to do.

By the time this process had been completed, Maria was in a more positive mood, and she told us that she had decided she *would* like to go to university. She said that she understood that to do so she was going to need a GSCE in maths, and so she was going to work hard. So, although Maria didn't enjoy the extra lessons and continued to find maths difficult, she was quite good about doing them and she did put a lot of effort into the extra tuition sessions.

She was also working hard at school generally, but it wasn't all plain sailing. If something annoyed or upset her at school she would come home in a foul temper, stomp through the shop, grunt – at best – if anyone spoke to her, then go into the house and straight upstairs.

When she was in a really bad mood, she would play music in her bedroom so loudly that the walls of the house would, quite literally, vibrate. Fortunately, there are separate electrical circuits on every floor of the house, so when it happened during the evening, if there were no other children in their bedrooms at the time, we could just flick a switch and turn the power off on the floor that Maria's bedroom was on, while leaving us able to carry on as normal downstairs. The first time Jonathan did it, we could hear her effing and blinding for a few seconds before Maria came thudding down the stairs and burst into the living room, where we were sitting watching the early news on TV.

She had obviously thought that the power must have failed throughout the whole house, and the sight of the lit screen stopped her in her tracks for a moment. Then she marched across the room, stood between us and the television, put her hands on her hips and demanded to know, 'Why has *my* electric gone off?'

'Because your music's too loud,' Jonathan told her, equitably. 'I'll be happy to turn it back on if you turn the volume down to a more reasonable level.'

We hadn't yet taught Maria how to change a plug and she had no idea where the fuse box was – or, quite possibly, that fuses existed at all. This meant that she didn't have much choice other than to do as Jonathan asked and reduce the volume to at least a few notches below ear splitting.

It wasn't a complete solution to the problem, of course, and the fuse got pulled on several occasions after that, but she gradually learned her lesson.

Although she was often very cheerful and chatty, Maria didn't really talk to us about what had happened at school to upset her on the occasions when she came home in a bad temper. Generally, we didn't ask. If she wanted to talk, she knew we were very willing to stop what we were doing, give her our full attention and listen. Sometimes she would come downstairs and sit beside me on the sofa, or offer to help with something in the kitchen and one day, when I sensed she was in the mood to chat, I said to her, 'You don't seem to be very happy. Is everything OK?'

'Yes, it's just hard doing all this revision,' she said. 'Why does life have to be so hard?'

'Well, it's worth putting the hard work in. You'll see, when you get the rewards.'

'Sometimes I don't know if it's worth bothering. I could just be like the rest of them.'

'What do you mean?'

'Most of my family. Live on benefits. Have an easy life. Like my nan said, she's all right, isn't she? And *she* never got any exams.'

I raised an eyebrow. 'You're a clever girl and I know that isn't what you want. I know you want to do your best and go to university.'

'You're right; I don't want to live on benefits. Tempting though!'

'How is it tempting? You want to live life to the full, Maria! I know you do! Honestly, think about how satisfying it will be to do well at school, go to university and do a job of your choice, one you will enjoy. Imagine how proud you would be? I know I'll be very proud of you.'

'Yes, I suppose,' she said dreamily. 'Mum and him, they lived a kind of half life, when you think of it.'

I let this hang in the air. I knew Maria was talking about Gerry when she said 'him' and I let her have a moment, to see if she would add anything.

'Spooky, Gerry was,' she said thoughtfully. 'I think "half life" is a good way of saying it. It was like living with . . . ghosts. He scared me. And I never knew whether they'd be there for me or not, and when they were they were . . . well, they were not quite there at all.'

I felt goosebumps prickle my arms. It was a damning indictment of her family and upbringing, but unfortunately, from what I had learned and seen for myself over the years, it was frighteningly accurate.

39

'Maybe it's for the best'

'Angela! Guess what? Maria said excitedly one day. 'Mum's moving again and she wants me to go with her.'

I was taken aback but not entirely shocked, because I'd learned that Maria's moods could change like the wind, especially if her mum was pulling strings in the background.

It seemed Christine and her baby were going to go and live hundreds of miles away, with a man Christine had met online and apparently scarcely knew.

'Mum says I can go with them, as soon as she's settled in her new home, which will be great, because I really want to get to know my little sister better.'

My heart sank. This did not sound like a good plan, especially with Maria's GCSEs looming. I was also saddened to hear Maria say she wanted to get to know her sister 'better'. The truth was, she had never met her, and had only seen one photograph Babs had at her house.

As Maria was still on a full care order she wouldn't be able to live with her mother without the agreement of Social Services, and possibly also the court. I had to talk to the social workers about this offer from Christine. She'd been checked by Social Services and they obviously thought she was capable of looking after her baby, and safe to do so, and for that reason I reasoned they might also agree for Christine to care for Maria again, despite what had gone on in the past.

Though I didn't want Maria to be upset, ultimately I was relieved when Social Services refused to let her go. I felt it was the right decision. Maria needed to at least do her exams, and I didn't want her to be subjected to any unnecessary upheaval if things didn't work out as planned with Christine.

Jonathan also felt very sad when I told him about Maria's initial reaction to her mother's offer.

'It's upsetting, isn't it, how Maria still wants to be with her mum, despite everything?'

'Yes,' I said. 'But there's no accounting for the strength of the bond between mother and child, and how forgiving children generally are.'

Jonathan gave me a hug. Even though I have dearly loved the foster children we have cared for and I know many of them have loved me, I have never considered myself a 'substitute mum' in any way. I don't even call myself a foster mother, in fact. I'm a foster carer, and over the years I have fully accepted and embraced the role, even though at times I have felt as I did now with Maria: completely crushed by the fall-out from that bond.

Social Services did agree to allow Maria to visit her mother and little sister, and in the next school holidays she and Babs excitedly took a train to Christine's, where they also met her new partner, Ben. Social Services paid for everything.

'My little sister is gorgeous and Ben's really nice,' Maria told us when she came back. 'Almost completely the opposite of my stepdad in every way. He doesn't shout and he laughs about things that are funny, not when someone hurts themselves.'

Maria told us she would like to go and live with them after her exams, when she was sixteen. Social Services would have to check out the situation, of course, but ultimately if Christine's new set-up was deemed suitable for Maria, then of course we would have to let her go with a smile on our faces and optimism in our hearts – what else could we do?

One of the things you wish for as a foster carer is that the parents of the children you look after will somehow manage to turn their own lives around so that their children can go home and live with them again in better circumstances. The paradox is that when you become attached to a child – which you very often do, even when they live with you for a relatively short period of time – the parents' gain is, in effect, your loss, and it can sometimes be a wrench emotionally.

Social Services began the checks they would have to make before Maria was allowed to move back with her family, but unfortunately, before the process was even completed, I heard from a social worker that Christine had voluntarily handed over the care of her youngest child to Social Services. Maria was very upset when she found out about it. She locked herself in her room for a while, and then she told me, 'Before you ask, I don't want to talk about it.'

'OK, but if you change your mind . . .'

'I won't. I was stupid to think it would all work out in the first place.'

Babs was typically nonchalant about the situation.

'I told you – she loses interest when they become toddlers,' she said with a sigh, although, at the time, we didn't really know why it had happened.

Despite the fact Christine had put her baby into care, Social Services still had a legal obligation to facilitate contact between Maria and her mother, and Maria went again to visit her mum, with Babs. During this visit Christine suggested that Maria could still go and live with her, even though her sister was in care. Maria was interested in this possibility – her loyalty to her mother seemingly knew no bounds – and as a result Social Services continued their checks into whether or not they would allow this to happen.

They also paid for Christine to visit Maria, including paying for her to stay in a hotel in our town. Maria met her mum at Babs's house, so we didn't actually have anything to do with Christine on this occasion.

'I told Social Services I could stay with you next time so they didn't have to worry about putting me up in a hotel,' Christine apparently told Babs. According to Babs, Christine said this as if she were making some generous gesture towards Social Services, which didn't surprise me. In our experience, it was not uncommon for parents to feel incredibly entitled to have Social Services pay for their travel and accommodation to see their own children. We've fostered some children whose parents refused to see them at all unless Social Services paid the entire cost of their journey, whether it was just a few miles or halfway across the country. But at least Christine came.

While all this was going on, Jonathan and I were both very happy that Maria was staying with us at least for the time being, and she told us she was determined to do well in her exams, whatever happened. Unfortunately, Maria's commitment to studying could be erratic, and she sometimes refused to follow the school's rules.

For example, we didn't know Maria had stopped wearing her uniform until we received a letter from the school and discovered that, after leaving our house appropriately dressed in the mornings, she was calling in at her grandparents' house en route to school to change into trainers and the baggy trousers she favoured at the time. Then, at the end of the school day, she would simply reverse the process and arrive home wearing her uniform again.

When I raised the subject with Babs she seemed uncomfortable for a moment, then looked me straight in the eye and said, 'Maria *does* come here in the mornings, to have a cup of tea before she goes to school. And I let her change into her trainers because she doesn't like her school shoes. They're too small for her and they hurt her toes.'

Making sure that all the children we foster have shoes that fit them perfectly is something we've always been very vigilant about. So, although it was quite possible that Maria had used sore toes as an excuse to her grandmother, I knew it wasn't true.

'I wonder why she hasn't said anything to us about the shoes hurting her toes,' I said. 'They're definitely the right size. I can understand that Maria might not like them. But she has to wear them to school because they're part of the uniform. Trainers aren't allowed.'

'Oh, I see.' Her grandmother nodded, as if to imply that she hadn't realised there was a school uniform at all. 'In that case, I'll make sure she wears them in future.'

Babs really did sound as though she meant what she was

saying. But, even so, I was only mildly surprised when we received another letter from the school a couple of days later and I realised that nothing had changed.

Sometimes, ignoring what we'd said and going behind our backs to elicit the support of her grandmother backfired on Maria quite badly.

'I'm going to get one of those home hair-dyeing kits and put dark streaks in my hair,' she told me one day.

'I'm not sure that putting streaks in is as easy as it might sound,' I said, looking at her mousey-blonde hair. 'It's not as simple as changing the colour overall. But, in any case, your school won't allow it. They have a strict policy on hair dyeing.'

'That's just stupid.' Maria was already flouncing out of the room as she said it, leaving Jonathan and me to count slowly to five as we waited for the sound of her bedroom door slamming.

A couple of days later, Maria went to her grandparents' house after school, where she used a cap with holes in it and a bottle of black hair dye to create a look that would have shocked even the most open-minded zebra! It wasn't funny at the time though. It was exasperating to know that Maria's grandmother had once again allowed her to do something she must have known we – or the school – wouldn't sanction, and it was very sad to see how devastated Maria was when she realised what she'd done.

The one silver lining was the fact that Maria hadn't managed to pull many sections of the hair closest to her scalp through the holes in the cap. A haircut – by a professional hairdresser – dealt with the worst of the streaks. Fortunately, we had a very good relationship with Maria's school, having fostered quite a few children over the years who had gone there. So, after writing an apologetic letter explaining what had happened, it was just a case of waiting for the rest of Maria's streaky hair to grow out.

After that incident, we asked Maria's grandmother yet again, and very politely, if she could check with us before allowing Maria to do anything significant, such as changing her appearance in any way. And yet again Babs told us, earnestly, that she understood what we were saying and that the next time Maria asked to do anything we might reasonably be expected to have an opinion about, she would definitely say no, at least until she'd spoken to us.

Babs didn't ever say no to Maria, of course. She continued to let her do exactly what she wanted to do, however negative the impact might be on Maria herself. For instance, Maria was still overweight, but Babs let her eat whatever junk she wanted. We knew this because Maria made no secret of it, telling us about all the different types of fizzy drinks, biscuits and crisps her grandmother kept in her kitchen. It was so frustrating, when all Jonathan and I were trying to do was guide Maria in the right direction so that she would be healthy, happy in herself and able to make good decisions about her life as an adult.

We told ourselves time and time again that, with a great deal of determination and persistence, it *is* possible to help children turn their lives around – some children, at least – and we didn't give up, despite the way Babs carried on.

There were times when Maria seemed to be learning to make good decisions herself that would enable her to have the life she deserved, and that we knew she had the potential to achieve. And there were times when she didn't seem to have the mental or physical energy to choose – let alone follow – any specific path at all.

Despite putting her second daughter into care, Christine seemed to settle into her new life on the other side of the country with her new partner. However, besides her occasional visits to stay with Babs and visit Maria, and some irregular phone calls, she and Maria had little contact.

Social Services ultimately decided that Maria should stay living with us until she was at least sixteen, when her case would be looked at again. By the time we heard this news Maria seemed to be resigned to that outcome, and was not upset or even disappointed.

'Oh well, we knew that, didn't we?' Maria shrugged. 'Maybe it's for the best.'

Touchingly, she had knitted a hat for her little sister, with my mum's help, and she told me, 'I've already wrapped it up ready to post. I'll do that tomorrow.'

40

'Maria's got something she needs to tell you'

Maria did well in her GCSEs – good enough to do A levels and hopefully go on to university. She told her mum the news over the phone but Christine only managed a muttered, 'Well done,' and that was even after Maria told her, 'I could actually be the first person in the family to go to university!'

Not long after Maria got her results, Jonathan and I were sitting in the garden on a Sunday afternoon, trying to summon up the energy to tackle the jobs that needed to be done out there, when she came and sat on the wall beside us.

'They say that the sun shines on the righteous and it appears to be true,' Maria said. Then she gave a melodramatic sigh of satisfaction and tilted her head up towards the sky for a moment before adding, 'Although I suppose, to be fair, it would be shining on you too, if you weren't sitting under that umbrella.'

'You are quite right to be proud of your achievements!' I told her, smiling.

'Thank you,' she beamed. 'I'm proud of myself.'

After we chatted about something and nothing for a few minutes, Maria suddenly said, 'I've been thinking about stuff, and what I really want to do is stay on at school and do A levels. But the thing is . . .' She took a deep breath. 'I'd really like to stay on at *this* school, and stay with you. But maybe you wouldn't want me for two more years? Maybe Social Services will make me move?'

'Of course we'd want you!' Jonathan and I chorused. It was something we'd already discussed, and we had no hesitation in saying this.

Jonathan nodded as I told Maria, 'We'd absolutely love you to stay, and we will say as much to Social Services. I think it would be lovely if you could do your A levels here, with all your friends. I'm sure Social Services will be OK with it. I'll phone them tomorrow. But let's not get our hopes up until they've officially agreed—'

'I know, I know,' Maria interjected. 'Don't put all your chickens in one basket. No, that's not it. Oh yes! Don't count your eggs before they've hatched. No, that's not it either.' I knew that she was joking to cover her embarrassment, which, on this occasion, was clearly due to the fact that she was pleased.

Social Services did agree to Maria staying on at the same school and continuing to live with us, and her grandparents were delighted when they heard the news. I think Babs had been dreading the thought of Maria moving so far away to live with her mother and the mother's partner, who Christine had actually married by now. Babs was very fond of Maria and she would have missed her terribly. But I think she was worried, too, about how Maria and her mother would get on if they were actually living together. She also had concerns about the marriage.

'Anyway, Angela,' Babs gossiped over a cup of tea one day,

ANGELA HART

'you never know with Christine, her marriage could be over just as soon as it's begun!'

I thought it was a bit unkind of Babs to talk about her daughter's life like that, but in actual fact Babs's prediction turned out to be true. Christine's marriage was brief, and not long after she and her new husband had split up, she announced that she was going to live abroad.

By this time, Maria was the one who made the majority of calls to her mum, as Christine very rarely made the effort. One evening, when Jonathan and I were watching the news on TV, Maria came storming into the living room, slumped down on the sofa beside me and said, 'Right, that's it. I'm not phoning her *any* more. I don't deserve to be treated like this. What have I ever done to her? Well, I've had enough now. That's the last phone call I'm ever going to make to her. Nan has been more like a mum to me than *she's* been anyway. What's that thing you used to say, Angela? Oh yes: "If you can't say anything nice, it's best not to say anything at all." Well, my mum should definitely stop talking, to me at least.'

'Gosh, what is it she said that's upset you?' I asked, choosing my words carefully so that I didn't give the impression I agreed with what she'd said about her mother's negative influence – even though I did.

'It's everything,' she answered. 'She just doesn't ever say anything nice or encouraging, like you and Jonathan do. So, that's it. Enough. I don't want to talk to her any more. It's like I've said before. She's not altogether with it. There's something missing. She's a ghost, I tell you. And he was a freak too, that weirdo Gerry!'

'You might feel differently about it in the morning,' Jonathan said. 'Don't be too hasty, Maria.'

She didn't tell us what her mum had said that so upset her, but from that day Maria vowed never to speak to her mother again.

Sadly, things didn't run as smoothly for Maria during the next couple of years as we'd hoped. In fact, when she returned to school after the long summer holiday to start her AS courses, she hardly did any work at all. We knew she wasn't doing much coursework at home, but if we ever questioned her about it she stormed off to her grandparents' house. Eventually, the inevitable happened and we were called in for a meeting at the school, where Maria's teacher told us that they weren't prepared to keep her on.

'There is absolutely no point in her being here,' her teacher said. 'She could do really well and go to almost any university she chooses. But she isn't even trying. She hasn't done her coursework, she isn't handing in essays, and it's obvious every day in the classroom that she hasn't done any of the reading she's supposed to have done.'

'We knew she wasn't doing enough work,' Jonathan said. 'But we hadn't realised it was quite as bad as that. Can you just give us a chance to talk to her, though, before you make a decision?'

It took some persuading, but eventually the teacher agreed, and when Maria came home that night, we all sat down at the kitchen table and had a long talk.

'You've proved to everyone, including yourself, how well you can do in exams if you put your mind to it,' I told her. 'The whole reason for staying on at school was so that you can go to university. Don't throw it all away now, for heaven's sake.'

'You're right,' she said at last, after an initial sulk. 'It's only a couple of years – less than that.'

So, once again, she got back on track, at least enough for the school to agree to let her stay on, and she ended up just scraping through her AS exams. I think the fact that she didn't do better knocked her confidence a bit, although considering how little revision she did, she was lucky to pass at all.

Then, unfortunately, not long after she started her A level courses, she got a boyfriend – her fears about being gay having long since been forgotten, once her crush on her female classmate was over.

I say 'unfortunately' about the boyfriend because he didn't do anything to encourage Maria to do the work she needed to do. Quite the reverse, in fact. He was in the same year as her at school, but doing different subjects, and although he wasn't a bad lad, he used to encourage her to skive off. This went on for months on end. Apparently, they'd register at school in the morning, then leave again and go to Maria's grandparents' house to pick up the stash of alcohol they kept there, which they'd drink somewhere out of sight.

We didn't know anything about what was happening and thought she was safely at school, but it was the same old story. We'd had several discussions with her grandmother about how important it was for us all to encourage Maria to do the work she had to do to be able to pass her exams and achieve her ambition of going to university. Every time we'd talked about it,

Babs had nodded and agreed with us, while all the time knowing what was really going on.

Then, one Friday afternoon, when Maria arrived home from school, she marched through the shop, scowling at me without replying when I said hello and slamming the door into the house behind her. She was in her final term of A levels by now, so I knew she was under a lot of pressure, but I sensed this was more than just day-to-day schoolwork stress.

There was only one customer in the shop when Maria stomped through it, and her tone was empathetic as she said, 'Teenagers, who'd have them? I'm so glad mine have all grown up and left home. I sometimes used to wonder if they were a different species. But thank goodness it's just a phase and they eventually grow out of it, although I do remember it felt at the time as though it would never end.'

'Something must have upset her in school today,' I said to Jonathan after the customer had gone. 'Shall I go and see what's wrong?'

'Let's leave her till we close,' he replied. 'It will give her time to calm down, and there's nothing we can do anyway.'

I was just agreeing with him when the door from the street opened again and a good friend of Maria's called Sammy came into the shop.

'Is Maria OK?' she asked, looking genuinely concerned. 'I walked back from school with her and tried to talk to her all the way. But she's in a mood about something, and wouldn't answer me at all. I think it may have something to do with her boyfriend. But, then again, I might be wrong. Is she in the house? Can I go and see her?'

'Of course you can,' I told her. 'Just go on through. She's

probably gone to her room. It might be a good idea if you knock on the bedroom door before you go in, just to avoid any chance of upsetting her even more.'

It was about fifteen minutes later when Sammy reappeared in the shop and said, 'Maria's got something she needs to tell you. It's not good news, but I've been sworn to secrecy because she wants to tell you herself. I'll call in tomorrow morning though, if that's OK, to see if she's calmed down.'

'Yes, that's fine, Sammy,' Jonathan said. 'We'll see you tomorrow.'

Then, when Sammy had gone, he looked at me and said the two words I had been thinking myself: 'Now what?'

All kinds of possibilities collided in my head. *Has she been in trouble with the police? Is she pregnant?*

After collecting all the plants and displays from outside, we closed the shop at the usual time. It takes a while to carry all the plants and flowers out and arrange them every morning, then bring them in again in the evening, but it's worth it because they make a great display outside our parade of shops. Bringing them in seemed to take forever on that day though, because I was so anxious to know what Maria's 'not good news' could be.

Friday night is always takeaway night in our house, when we have either a Chinese or an Indian meal, or, occasionally, chips. It's a tradition everyone enjoys, although Maria would really have preferred to go to the McDonald's drive thru and order a large meal with extra-large Coca-Cola, which remained her drink of choice whenever we ate out or had a takeaway. Sadly she was still overweight, and she had still never made any effort to get herself in better shape.

When I went into the house, Maria was sitting in the kitchen with an angry expression on her face.

'Is everything OK? Sammy said you have something to tell us.'

'Um . . . well . . . I don't know how to say this.' Maria swallowed hard. 'Me and a couple of friends got called in to see the head teacher this afternoon. He said he'd had reports about us drinking down by the river and that I was drunk in school – which I *wasn't*. I *was* caught smoking again at lunchtime, though.'

I knew she smoked – we'd had words about it many times – but I thought she'd given up, as that is what she had told me. Worst of all, Maria made it sound as though being wrongly accused of being drunk in school was the only bit of what she was telling me that really mattered. 'Anyway, the head teacher said we're not "good ambassadors for the school".' She mimicked his voice as she said it, then paused and took a deep breath before adding, 'So he's decided to expel us.'

'What?' I was disappointed with Maria for acting so foolishly, but I was shocked by what she was telling me. 'What about your exams? You've only got two months before you're due to take them. Surely he can let you stay on till then. Did you offer to apologise?'

'Yes, of course I did,' she shouted. 'I even said I'd give a talk to the younger students to encourage them not to be as stupid as me. *See*, I knew eventually the truth would come out. Now try telling me I'm not thick and stupid.'

'Maria, you know what I think about you calling yourself stupid,' I told her. 'You are *not* stupid. How many times do you need to be told that? You just make daft choices sometimes. But that's something we all do. Nobody's perfect and we all have to learn by our mistakes. Anyway, I thought you'd given up smoking. And when did you start drinking?'

'I didn't want to be the only one *not* drinking.' She looked embarrassed as she said it. 'But I wasn't drunk, even though they said I was. I didn't like the taste anyway. I can't see why people drink. It's just a waste of money. And I *have* given up smoking. Well, sort of. I only had a few left in the packet and when I was feeling stressed today, I decided I'd finish the packet and give up starting from tomorrow.'

It was the same story she'd told me on many occasions, with minor variations, about the cigarettes, and every time I hoped that, this time, it would be true. Her grandmother used to get on to her about it too, often telling her to 'stop using the coffin nails' – why she never said the same to Stanley, who still smoked like a chimney, I never understood.

'Well, I guess there's nothing we can do about it now,' I said. 'I'll call the school on Monday morning and make an appointment with the head teacher, to see if I can talk him around, again!'

I walked over to the phone as I spoke and absent-mindedly picked up the menus for the local takeaways that we keep beside it. Jonathan and I had been looking forward to a treat, but it didn't seem appropriate to get a takeaway now. I put them down with a sigh. In fact, I felt a bit nauseous and didn't feel like eating anything at all.

41

'Anything is possible . . .'

We had a peaceful weekend, considering the circumstances. Maria spent Saturday evening at her grandparents' house, after pleading with me, 'Will you tell Nan, *please*? She'll be really disappointed with me and it'll sound better coming from you.'

I wasn't sure Maria was right about how disappointed her grandmother was going to be, and when I agreed to tell her what had happened, she responded, 'That's a shame. But never mind, Maria. You can always get a job like I did when I left school, and I didn't even have any qualifications. So don't you worry about it. Ooh, in fact, someone told me just the other day that they're looking for staff at the new burger bar in town. We could go there this afternoon if you like and find out what you have to do.'

'Err . . . no thanks.' Maria looked puzzled for a moment before adding, more emphatically, 'I'm not working *there* for my full-time job! I'm still going to do my exams – I hope. We *are* going into school on Monday, aren't we, Angela?'

'Yes, hopefully,' I said, 'but there's no guarantee that I'll be able to talk the head teacher around this time.'

*

On the Monday morning, before I had time to phone the school, we received a call asking us to go in for a meeting, without Maria.

'Maria has been caught several times smoking on school premises,' the head teacher said when Jonathan and I went into his office. 'She isn't doing her work. She's very insolent when anyone tries to discuss these issues with her and, to top it off, it's now been reported to me that she came in drunk after drinking down by the river. I'm sure you can see that that sort of behaviour is unacceptable. I have to think of the other students, to whom she is setting a very poor example. I'm afraid we've come to the point when enough is finally enough.'

'But she's done almost all her coursework,' I said. 'Couldn't she stay on just these last few weeks until study leave or until she takes the exams? We'll talk to her and . . .'

'I'm sorry.' The head teacher shrugged as if to indicate that the decision had already been made and the matter was now out of his hands.

We have fostered a lot of children who've gone to that school and we've always had good relationships with all the teachers and other staff there. We knew they'd made allowances for Maria on several occasions and that they'd been more tolerant with her than most other schools would have been. But she'd finally pushed them too far and, this time, no amount of pleading would make the head teacher change his mind.

'She can come back into school to sit her exams,' he said. 'Other than that, she'll have to get notes from her friends doing the same subjects and revise at home.'

'I couldn't bear it if she let it all fall apart now,' I told Jonathan as we were driving home after the meeting. 'It's so frustrating, knowing how well she *could* do if she put her mind to it.'

'I know,' he said. 'And what a difference it would make, to her self-esteem and to her entire life, if she passed her exams and went to university.'

'It's your life, Maria,' I told her when we got the chance to talk to her on her own later that evening. 'You're nearly eighteen now, and I can't tell you what to do even if I wanted to. But you really *can* do this, you know? You've told me you want to be an English teacher and it's a goal you're perfectly capable of achieving. You do know that, don't you?'

'I suppose so.' She put her elbows on the table and rested her chin on her hands. 'It's just that . . . Oh, I don't know. Maybe other stuff just gets in the way.'

Maria arranged with a couple of her friends to collect up the coursework copies and drop them off at the shop on their way home from school. Thankfully, this was a system that worked well, and there was only one occasion when they forgot to do it.

'Why don't you draw up a work schedule?' Jonathan suggested one evening as we sat down to eat our meal. 'It doesn't have to be anything too demanding. There's no point doing something you aren't likely to stick to.'

So, it was agreed that Maria would get up at 9 a.m. every weekday, work for at least five hours – with a break for lunch – and then do whatever she wanted to do for the rest of the day. And she did stick to it, most of the time.

When she wasn't catching up on her work or revising for her exams, she went to her grandparents' house or out with her boyfriend, or stayed at home reading and listening to music in her room – which she now played a few notches below ear-splitting level without having to be asked.

In June, she went back to school to sit her exams, and then got a part-time job working in a local supermarket. She had broken up with her boyfriend by then, but it wasn't until later that she told us why. 'He was trying to persuade me to smoke cannabis,' she said. 'And he was cheating on me too, which I only found out about when one of my friends saw them together.'

Jonathan and I had a two-week holiday in a log cabin that summer, taking with us another child who was with us for a short respite stay at the time. Maria had just turned eighteen and decided she was 'too old to go on holiday with you' and chose not to come with us. Fortunately, she was able to stay with her grandparents. So Jonathan and I had a nice break while Barbara and her friend ran the shop.

By the time we got back from Devon, Maria was getting anxious about her exam results. She had revised for the exams, although maybe not as much as she could have done, but she was convinced that she had failed them all. The results were going to be available at school on a Thursday morning towards the end of August, and as soon as we sat down to eat our meal the night before, she told us, 'I'm going in to collect my results as early as I can tomorrow.'

'Do you want me to come with you?' I asked.

'No! I'm a big girl now. I can go on my own. Well, actually, I'm not going on my own. I'm meeting Sammy and we're going in together. Then we're going out afterwards to celebrate or commiserate. Sammy will definitely be celebrating, and I'm just keeping my fingers crossed. I'll call you when I get them, just to put you out of your misery wondering how "bad" I've done.'

'There's nothing like positive thinking, I always say.' Jonathan smiled at Maria, then added, 'I have full confidence in you, Maria. Good luck.'

The next morning, Maria was up, washed and dressed by 8.30, in time to meet Sammy so they could walk to school together. On her way out, she helped us to display the flowers outside the shop – which was a first!

'What do they call it?' she asked, grinning, when we were clearly surprised by her offer of help. 'Oh yes, displacement activity. Doing this takes my mind off the results. So maybe don't hold your breath waiting for the next time.'

Sammy arrived on the dot of nine o'clock, just as we were opening the shop, and the two girls left together, chatting nineteen to the dozen. After they'd gone, the morning seemed to drag by. We knew the results were being given out at 10.30 and Maria had promised she would phone us as soon as she'd opened the envelope. But 10.30 came and went, then 11.30. So in the end I texted her and when she didn't reply, I phoned. My call went straight to voicemail and I was regaled by the sound of her singing:

> *Twinkle, twinkle little star,*
> *Bet you're wondering where I am.*
> *Well, put your mouth up to the phone,*
> *And leave me a message for when I get home.*

347

> *And if you can make your message rhyme,*
> *I'll call you back in half the time.*

It was a craze that was going round at the time. All her friends were using these funny voicemail messages, some of which lasted far longer than the one Maria had chosen, so that by the time they finished and you heard the beep, there was no space left for you to say anything.

After that, there was nothing else we could do but be patient and wait for Maria to call.

I had gone into the house to prepare lunch and was peeling some carrots when my mobile phone finally rang. Dropping the peeler on to the work surface, I ran my hands under the tap and then dried them quickly before snatching up my phone and saying, 'Hello, Maria?'

'Has she rung you?' It was Babs.

'Oh, no. I've not heard a thing. Have you?'

'Yes. She rang me just after 10.30. She's passed, but . . .'

My heart was thudding as I asked, 'But what?'

'She hasn't got the grades she needed to go to the university that was her first choice. She's at the school now. They're helping students with their university applications. She said she'd be home at about 3.30.'

'Thanks for letting me know. Did Maria ask you to call us?'

'No. I just thought I would because she was in a bit of a tizzy and I thought she might forget.'

As soon as Babs had rung off, I went back into the shop to tell Jonathan what had happened, and for the rest of the afternoon we tried to keep our minds occupied by thinking about other things.

*

It turned out that although Maria was a bit disappointed not to have got the grades she'd hoped for, she was offered a place at the university that had been her second choice.

'If you haven't made any other plans, let's have a celebration meal on Saturday evening,' Jonathan suggested, when she finally got home and told us the good news.

So that's what we did. We invited Maria's grandparents, her brother Colin and my mum, and as soon as we'd all sat down at the dining table, Maria's grandfather Stanley raised his glass of Coca-Cola – which Babs had brought with her – and said, 'I propose a toast to Maria. Congratulations!'

'To Jonathan and Angela,' Maria answered, smiling as she lifted her own glass and clinked it against his. 'For making me believe it was possible.' Then she laughed and added, 'And for not giving up on me – however horrible I was and however much they might have wanted to!'

'You weren't *ever* horrible, Maria,' I said. 'Although you did test us to the limit when you kept trying to run off when you were younger! Do you remember that?'

'Yes I do!' she laughed. 'And all I can say is, thank God you caught me!' Then she gave us a big, meaningful smile.

The university Maria went to was an hour away by train. Although she could have travelled there every day, she chose to go into the halls of residence, which was something she later regretted because she didn't like the way everything in the first year seemed to revolve around alcohol. It was an irony that she was the first to recognise, having been expelled from school for drinking.

Fortunately, she was also given supportive lodgings near our home, as Tom and Dillon had when they went to college. This meant she was able to come back every Thursday evening and work in a local shop over the weekend, to help offset what would otherwise be a very large debt by the time she left university.

Maria gradually got used to university life and really enjoyed being the first person in her family ever to embark on a university degree. We saw her most weekends when she came home, and it was a joy to see her growing into a thoughtful and kind young woman.

One weekend, Maria invited Jonathan and I to visit her at university, as she knew we were heading in her direction for a weekend away. We'd dropped her off when she first moved in, but it would be nice to see her room and meet some of her friends and neighbours now she'd settled in.

When we arrived on the campus, Maria was there to greet us, smiling and waving and eagerly waiting to show us around. She gave us a great tour and took us to the student cafe, where she insisted on buying a big pot of tea for us to share.

'Here's to you two,' she said, raising her cup. 'The best foster carers in the world!'

It was a lovely gesture and such a wonderful thing for her to say, and I will never forget how touched I felt in that moment. Jonathan was the same, and we gave each other a knowing look, each of us thinking how worthwhile our efforts were with Maria and all the other children we fostered.

I was very pleased to see Maria had lost weight and she told us she was doing some exercise classes once or twice a week to slim down further. Her bedroom was neat and tidy and Jonathan made a joke about this, asking how it was possible, as Maria had never been very tidy when she lived with us.

'You already know the answer to that,' she said with an enigmatic smile on her face.

We both looked quizzical and waited for her to continue.

'Anything is possible, when you put your mind to it,' she said proudly. 'You taught me that. And I've never forgotten something else you used to say to me, when I was younger.'

Again Jonathan and I stayed quiet and waited for Maria to carry on.

'It's worth putting the hard work in. You'll see, when you get the rewards.'

Epilogue

Maria is in her early thirties now, works as a teacher and is a very proud mum to two young boys. She keeps in touch with Jonathan and me regularly, never forgetting our birthdays and always making the effort to come to the reunions we hold from time to time, to which we invite all the foster children we have stayed in touch with over the years. At a recent reunion – a garden party at our home – it was wonderful to see Maria interacting with her children, especially when the youngest had a tantrum because he kept losing in a game of hoopla.

'You can do it,' Maria encouraged. 'Don't give up. Keep trying, and the more you practise the better you'll get.'

'Can't!' he snapped. 'I'm rubbish. Everyone's better than me!'

'That is not true at all,' Maria said firmly but kindly. 'You are a very clever little boy and you can do it! Come on, I'll help you.'

I can't tell you how rewarding it was to witness that scene, and I was taken back to that day on Maria's university campus, when she reminded Jonathan and me that we used to tell her, 'It's worth putting the hard work in. You'll see, when you get the rewards.'

Maria never talks to us about her past, although over the years I have found out some more details about her childhood. Babs, inevitably, was the person who filled in some of the blanks. She is no longer with us, but before Babs passed away I spent many hours chatting to her, usually around my kitchen table, as she continued to visit for many years after Maria went to university. Some of the information Babs shared came from Colin, who occasionally witnessed Maria's mistreatment first-hand, and other details came from things Maria told her grandparents. Apparently, she used to talk to Stanley quite a lot, which surprised me at first, until Babs quipped one day, 'I think Maria liked talking to Stanley because he didn't answer back and kept looking at the telly!' I imagine Stanley's indifference made him the ideal person for Maria to unload on.

Gerry was a worse bully that I feared. At mealtimes, he sometimes decided Maria was not allowed to use a knife and fork like everybody else, and she had to eat with her hands or sometimes lick food off the plate. Then Gerry told her she was 'disgusting' and he made her move around the house on all fours, 'like a dog'. Apparently, her mother decided to change the rule, so that Maria could walk but was not allowed on the carpet.

As for the physical abuse, it seems it was a miracle Maria did not suffer more broken bones or injuries to her body. She was thrown down the stairs on many occasions, made to balance on one leg on top of the garden shed and was hit with Gerry's snooker cue and Christine's heated curling tongs. On top of this there was a sustained campaign to 'spook' Maria by playing mind games and creepy tricks on her, such as playing the soundtrack of horror movies from a hidden tape recorder.

When she was really small, the boys and Gerry also managed to convince Maria that 'ghosts' her mother had connected to on the 'other side' were living under the floorboards. For years she believed that not only could Gerry see her every move, even when he was miles away, but that her mum's 'ghosts' might be watching her too, and that they would talk to her mum about what she was doing and saying.

Christine still lives abroad, and to my knowledge Maria never spoke to her from the day she vowed not to, after the angry phone call at our house. Stanley passed away a few years before Babs and, other than Maria, Colin was the only member of the family I recognised who went to Babs's funeral. We never did find out what the historic issue was that prevented Maria from living with her grandparents, although on one occasion Colin made a reference to the fact Stanley had once 'served time,' when he was a young man. We can only assume his criminal record meant it was impossible for Social Services to allow Maria to stay with her grandparents, although from everything Jonathan and I saw over the years, it appeared to us that Maria would have been better off there than with her mother.

I'm happy to say that Colin seems to have settled into a good life, and is also the father of two young children who get on well with Maria's boys.

Tom and Dillon, incidentally, are also doing well. It was Tom, not Dillon, who turned out to be the entrepreneur, and he runs his own online business. Dillon, meanwhile, put his artistic skills to good use and works for a graphic design company. Neither have married but both have steady girlfriends and have bought their own homes. They both came to one of the reunions, and I have a very precious photograph of them from that day. They are standing either side of Maria, all three of them smiling broadly.

Other stories from foster mum Angela Hart . . .

The Girl Who Just Wanted to be Loved

A damaged little girl and a foster carer who wouldn't give up

The first time we ever saw Keeley was in a Pizza Hut. She was having lunch with her social worker.

'Unfortunately Keeley's current placement is breaking down,' our support social worker, Sandy, had explained. 'We'd like to move her as soon as possible.'

Sandy began by explaining that Keeley was eight years old and had stayed with four sets of carers and been in full-time care with two different families.

'Why have the placements not worked out?' I asked.

'Both foster carers tell similar stories. Keeley's bad behaviour got worse instead of better as time went on. That's why we're keen for you to take her on, Angela. I'm sure you'll do a brilliant job.'

Eight-year-old Keeley looks like the sweetest little girl you could wish to meet, but demons from the past make her behaviour far from angelic. She takes foster carer Angela on a rocky and very demanding emotional ride as she fights daily battles against her deep-rooted psychological problems. Can the love and specialist care Angela and husband Jonathan provide help Keeley triumph against the odds?

Available now in paperback and ebook.

Terrified

The heartbreaking true story of a girl nobody loved and the woman who saved her

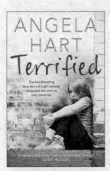

Vicky stared through the windscreen, her eyeballs glazed like marbles. She was sitting completely rigid in her seat, frozen with fear.

I took a deep breath and then asked Vicky, as gently as possible, if she was all right. 'I'm here, right beside you, Vicky. Can you hear me? I'm here and I can help you. Take a deep breath, love. That's what I've just done. Just breathe and try to calm yourself down. You're with me, Angela, and you're safe.'

Vicky seemed all self-assurance and swagger when she came to live with Angela and Jonathan as a temporary foster placement. As Vicky's mask of bravado began to slip, she was overtaken with episodes of complete terror. Will the trust and love Angela and her husband Jonathan provide enable Vicky to finally overcome her shocking past?

Available now in paperback and ebook.

The Girl with No Bedroom Door

ANGELA
HART

The Girl
With No
Bedroom
Door

'I hope Angela Hart inspires many others to foster'
TOREY HAYDEN

A true short story

Available now in ebook

Fourteen-year-old Louise has been sleeping rough after running away from her previous foster home. Unloved and unwashed, she arrives at foster carer Angela Hart's door stripped of all self-esteem. Can Angela's love and care help Louise blossom into a confident and happy young woman?

extracts reading groups
competitions books new
discounts extracts extracts discounts
competitions
books new extracts events
events books reading groups
extracts books discounts
new titles reading groups
interviews new
events extracts extracts events books
discounts
new books events interviews new books extracts
events new events
discounts extracts discounts

www.panmacmillan.com

extracts events reading groups
competitions books extracts new books